Truth and Probability

Essays in Honour of
Hugues Leblanc

Volume 1
We Will Show Them! Essays in Honour of Dov Gabbay, Volumes 1 and 2
S. Artemov, H. Barringer, A. S. d'Avila Garcez, L. Lamb and J. Woods, eds

Volume 2
Truth and Probability. Essays in Honour of Hugues Leblanc
B. Brown and F. Lepage, eds

"Tributes" Series Editor
D. M. Gabbay   dov.gabbay@kcl.ac.uk

Truth and Probability

Essays in Honour of Hugues Leblanc

edited by

Bryson Brown
and
François Lepage

© Individual author and College Publications 2005. All rights reserved.

ISBN 1-904987-19-2
Published by College Publications
Scientific Directors: Dov Gabbay, Vincent F. Hendricks and John Symons
Managing Director: Jane Spurr
Department of Computer Science
King's College London
Strand, London WC2R 2LS, UK

http://www.collegepublications.co.uk

Cover design by Richard Fraser, www.avalonarts.co.uk
Printed by Lightning Source, Milton Keynes, UK

All rights reserved. No part of this publication may be reproduced, stored in a retrieval system or transmitted, in any form, or by any means, electronic, mechanical, photocopying, recording or otherwise, without prior permission, in writing, from the publisher.

CONTENTS

Truth and Probability: Essays in Honour of Hugues Leblanc   vii
Bryson Brown and François Lepage

Part I: Truth and Consequence

The Preservation of Truth   1
Ray Jennings and Darko Sarenac

Ontology and the Theory of Meaning   17
Kirk Ludwig and Ernest Lepore

Tarksi's Grelling and the T-Strategy   29
Greg Ray

The Semantics of Denial   49
Edwin D. Mares

Truth Translations of Relevant Logics   59
Robert K. Meyer, Yoko Motohama and Viviana Bono

Part II: Probability and Induction

The Reference Class Problem is Your Problem Too!   87
Alan Hájek

A Formal Model of Epistemic Coherence   111
Charles B. Cross

How do the Harper and Levi Identities Constrain Belief Change?   123
Oliver Schulte

Higher Order Probability Theory and Defeasible Reasoning   137
Charles G. Morgan

Real Logic is Nonmonotonic   175
Henry E. Kyburg, Jr

Part III: Formal Metaphysics

Branching Histories Approach to Indeterminism and Free Will   197
Nuel Belnap

Truth and Probability: Essays in Honour of Hugues Leblanc
BRYSON BROWN AND FRANÇOIS LEPAGE

Hugues Leblanc was one of 24 philosophers, logicians and mathematicians who met in Montréal, in November of 1970, to found the Society for Exact Philosophy (SEP). The society's aim, then and now, is to explore and promote the use of tools from the exact sciences in philosophical inquiry. Hugues' contributions to this project are wide-ranging and influential. A distinguished logician, Hugues made fundamental contributions to free logics, truth-value (substitutional) semantics, probabilistic semantics for classical and intuitionist logic, and a wide range of approaches to natural deduction. His work on the substitutional theory of quantifiers reduces the semantics of the first order predicate calculus to a verificational semantics, contributing to the development of a far more ontologically economical alternative to model theory. He also published substantial work on confirmation and on statistical and inductive reasoning.

Leblanc's greatest contributions concern the relation between logic and probability, specifically the probabilistic interpretation of logic, classical as well as intuitionist. Two questions particularly worried him. The first concerns the logical relation between probabilistic judgments: What constraints should one impose on belief functions so that the relations between probabilities of statements of the calculus correspond to fundamental intuitions about rationality? The second question, which he pursued throughout his intellectual career, was the role of probability in the foundations of logic.

Almost all of Hugues Leblanc's work is extremely technical, demanding mastery of the logico-mathematical instruments that have become, over the course of the last century, the everyday tools of philosophers of science and logicians. But in his work, technique is never a blind and autonomous engine: Philosophical motivation is his constant guide. What interested him most was detecting the flaw, the philosophical defect in an almost universally accepted theory. For him, formal tools were not ends in themselves, but instruments for constructing a *philosophically* finer and more adequate theory.

Educated at the Université de Montréal and Harvard, Leblanc received his PhD in 1948, under the direction of W.V.O. Quine. He took a position in philosophy at Bryn Mawr College, where he worked until 1967. From then until his retirement in 1992, Leblanc was a member of the philosophy department at Temple University. After his retirement, he returned to Montréal, where he was appointed adjunct professor at the University of Québec at Montréal.

A helpful and sociable colleague, Leblanc often engaged in collaborative projects, co-authoring many papers and encouraging and supporting the work of younger logicians. One of us (Brown) met him in 1992, at the meetings of the Canadian Philosophical Association, where he was presenting work on probabilistic semantics with one of his later collaborators, P. Roeper. His gentle manners and enthusiasm were striking; his response to comments on his paper was engaged and inquisitive, and he suggested that the two of them might work together on a project in the area — a suggestion Brown regrets not taking up.

This volume collects papers presented at and deriving from the June 2001 meetings of the SEP at the Université de Montréal. The meeting was dedicated to Hughes Leblanc who died after a long illness on September 10th, 1999. The papers were selected to reflect recent work on some of the topics Hugues contributed to over the years, as well as the range of colleagues who have known Hugues and learned from his work. From Nuel Belnap, also a founding member of the SEP, to the younger members of the group, including Charles Cross, Ed Mares, and Alan Hájek, the volume presents a rich sample of contemporary work in exact philosophy, and of ongoing work on some of the projects that interested Hugues during his long and influential career.

Introductory Remarks
Part I: Truth and Consequence

The role of truth in formal logic begins with the standard account of validity as guaranteed truth-preservation. If a proper consequence relation must aim exclusively at meeting this standard, then formal models of consequence relations must *ipso facto* (though perhaps only implicitly) provide formal constraints on our understanding of truth conditions. Nevertheless, the question of just how much philosophical hay can be made from this point remains open; the range of formal consequence relations may leave too much open to significantly illuminate us about the nature of truth. Moreover, some have questioned the assumption that formal consequence relations should be bound by this casual, everyday understanding of validity. This section of the book is a bit of a Cook's tour, including a number of interesting contemporary points of view on questions about the relations between truth, consequence, and other logical issues including the paradoxes, denial, and relevance logics.

The Preservation of Truth

Jennings and Sarenac's exploration of the nature of truth and its preservation in consequence relations begins with a declaration of sympathy for Pilate and his much-maligned question, 'What is truth?' Our ordinary understanding of truth, they claim, though perfectly functional in everyday conversation, leaves us with no philosophical insight into this question. Worse, it leaves us with an understanding of truth that plays no active role in our understanding of language or in the practice of science. Of course, in logic the appeal to truth, and especially to *logical* truth, has had a long run. But the focus has shifted to concern with satisfaction and validity, to consequence relations, and to more formal standards: characteristically, a "sound" turnstile must be such that, whenever all the functions to the left produce the value 1, some function on the right must do the same. That we still call $\{0,1\}$ the set of *truth values* is philosophically innocent so long as we have (and pretend to have) no useful account of truth beyond this use of $\{0,1\}$.

This polemic serves to introduce the dramatis personae of Jennings and Sarenac's paper, the *aletheist* and the *preservationist* approaches to logical theory. While the aletheist wants the $\vdash$ (or $\rightarrow$) of their logical system to preserve truth, the preservationist is interested in versions of $\vdash$ or $\rightarrow$ that preserve "whatever suitable, mathematically well-defined properties interest us in the proposed domains of application." [Jennings and Sarenac, section 3] Suitable properties should not be (in general) preserved in supersets; but beyond this little need or should be presupposed about them. The potential gains here are clearest where premise sets are inconsistent: at this point, preservation of truth loses all traction, while a variety of mathematically definable properties worth preserving remains. The aletheist who believes that inference from inconsistent premise sets is constrained must reinvent her notion of truth and allow inconsistent premises all to be simultaneously true while some conclusions remain false. But the preservationist will happily invoke the preservation of other properties to constrain inference, without feeling the metaphysical urge to identify such properties as forms of *truth*.

Jennings and Sarenac argue that, while we have a good grasp of the truth-conditional effects of certain words, including "not" and "and", we lack a deeper and more general understanding of truth. Our grasp of these words is founded in the bright daylight of their ordinary conversational use, not in deeper or darker waters: When we suppose a sentence to be true, we infer that the negated sentence will be false; when we suppose the sentence to be false, we infer the negated sentence to be true. And we infer that a conjunction will be true on the supposition, and only on the supposition, that both conjoined sentences are true. These judgments are not written in stone, and the search for counterexamples may even prove fruitful. But it seems wise to explore preservationist alternatives as well.

The subsequent explorations reveal interesting hints of deeper waters, focusing on an elegant treatment of multi-criterial (in fact, denumerable) models of truth. The central notion here is a *Cantor propositional model*: a pair $\langle U, V \rangle$ where U is a non-empty set of *states*, and V is a function assigning to each state/atom pair an infinite sequence of 1s and 0s, each 1 representing a criterion passed, and each 0 a criterion not passed. This starting point leaves many options in the theory of truth open, including what should count as passing the overall test, i.e. as being *true*. There are many possible answers, ranging from requiring all tests be passed (here truth behaves like $S5$ necessity) to requiring merely that at least one be passed (here truth behaves like $S5$ possibility). More interesting options can be easily characterized in terms of the list of test indices at which the sentence passes the test — for example, passing all the tests at or above a certain index, and passing a countable infinity of tests. In the latter case, the result is a *Meyer* system, i.e. one for which modus ponens preserves validity but does not preserve truth; further, $\wedge$-intro fails as well. But the theorems are classical; explosion is avoided (and paraconsistency achieved) by restricting multi-premise rules to cases where "pigeon-holing" forces the premises to hold all together at some infinite set of indices.

Further connections to modal logics emerge, along with doubts about whether non-alethic modal logics should be thought of as weak theories of *necessity*, or as weak theories of *truth*. The moral is that by opening the door to such readings, we open the door to a range of formal semantics (potential *analyzed* theories of truth) that can be said to include both semantics suitable for capturing certain ideas about truth, and semantics that are too weak to do so. At this level of abstraction, we may be able to learn something about our understanding of truth. But for now at least, Pilate's question remains open. On the authors' view this is not an impediment to formal logic: we are free to explore any and all, without fear of somehow missing our way, since there is no settled notion of truth sufficiently clear to make a single view right from the start.

Ontology and the Theory of Meaning

Ludwig and Lepore question the value of meanings (considered as entities that serve as the semantic values of linguistic symbols) to our understanding of language. The authors acknowledge that the combinatory approach, building meanings of formulae out of the meanings of their component symbols, is quite helpful. But they question whether the basic components employed in this construction matter at all; since a well-behaved combinatory system for assigning meanings to the sentences of a language can be given that clearly conveys no understanding at all.

The combinatory system Ludwig and Lepore consider aims to produce, for each sentence s in the object language, a meaning assignment of the form

$$[M]s \text{ means } p.$$

The result assigns meanings of subject-predicate sentences as a function of the meanings of subject term and the predicate in a familiar way: A function assigned as the meaning of the predicate takes the item assigned as the meaning of the subject as its argument, and the resulting value is the meaning of the subject-predicate sentence. Then sentential connectives and quantifiers are brought in, again in familiar ways.

The trouble arises when Ludwig and Lepore construct a parallel theory that does the same job without creating any illusion of *understanding*. An answer to the question, "What does s mean?" still emerges from the theory, in which functions and arguments of functions determine values for complex expressions. Instead, the authors suggest, talk of meaning should be understood in terms of translation. The work done by the original theory presented is done by producing a systematic way of translating sentences into sentences we understand. On this view, "'A' means B" gets read, roughly, as 'A' can be translated by 'B', where 'B' is assumed to be understood: "The meaning drops out as irrelevant: the work is done, and can only be done, by matching terms already understood with terms they translate." [Ludwig and Lepore, Section 1. Introduction] Ludwig and Lepore's later proposal for "means" takes it to be "a predicate relating an expression and another expression, which, however, we require someone to understand in order to understand the sentence".[Ludwig and Lepore, Section 3. The Inutility of Meanings]. This account echoes Wilfrid Sellars' view of what sentences of the form:

$$\text{``}A\text{''} \text{ (in } L\text{) means that-}P.$$

tell us; Sellars, too, holds that the key point is to see that such uses combine translation with the (presupposed) understanding of 'P'.

Speaking of the "meanings" of individual words, and of understanding words as "grasping" their meanings is clearly not helpful — talk like this will never produce an understanding that isn't there to begin with. Nevertheless, Ludwig and Lepore argue that the rule-governed combination of the meanings of simple symbols to produce meanings for complex expressions does do some real work. But the real work that it does is to produce understood translations for sentences; what is "combined", (i.e. meanings as entities) makes no difference. To illustrate this point, they substitute a systematic set of rules for translation from (very simple, regimented) French into English. The result tells us what we want to know, on the assumption that we already understand English. Building this assumption explicitly into a new, translational theory of "meaning" allows for the phrase 'x is ambitious' in:

$T2$. Means('x est ambitieux', x is ambitious)

to be treated both as mentioned (reading means as it is *translated*) and used. That is, in $T2$ its familiar use in English is invoked as paralleling — in systematic but as yet unspecified ways — the use of "x est ambitieux" in French.

On this view quantification over "meanings" can be dispensed with as unproductive. The combinatorial analysis of one language in terms of an understood language allows for systematic translation into the understood language, and hence understanding. The result, the authors claim, is that the truth theory that results from such a systematic treatment of translation *shows*, without stating, "how truth conditions for sentences are built up compositionally out of extensional properties of their component expressions and their mode of combination". [Ludwig and Lepore, Section 4: General Methodological Conclusions]

Tarski's Grelling and the T-strategy

Greg Ray presents Tarski's use of the liar, and goes on to develop an account of why Tarski professed to prefer the Grelling paradox for the purpose. Ray argues that the result of replacing the liar with the Grelling paradox is an improvement, but argues further that deployment of a modified liar can achieve the same improvement. This leads to a serious problem for Tarski, viz, a tension between "Tarski's T-*strategy of truth definition*... and the fact that (as Tarski held) not all T-sentences are true". (Ray, introduction, p. 29). The problem is that for Tarski, an adequate truth definition should entail the T-sentences, but we know a priori that not all T-sentences are true. Ray proposes a solution of this problem based on an account of the conceptual status of T-sentences.

Tarski's exact indefinability thesis appears in his (1944); Ray formulates it thus:

For exactly specified language L, truth for L is indefinable in any exactly specified language M in which i) a liar argument for

L is formulable, ii) the identity premise of that liar argument is an assertible sentence, and iii) the normal laws of logic hold. (Ray, section 1, p. 30).

A liar argument for language L, expressed in some metalanguage M, has two premises, the T-sentence premise:

1. 'The sentence with feature F is not true in L' is true in L iff the sentence with feature F is not true in L.

and the identity premise:

2. 'The sentence with feature F is not true in L' is identical to the sentence with feature F.

The conclusion follows straightforwardly,

3. 'The sentence with feature F is not true in L' is true iff 'The sentence with feature F is not true in L' is not true in L.

The exactness of L imposes some important constraints here; an exactly specified language is "an interpreted language with distinguished primitive vocabulary and grammar, a set of axioms, and both rules of inference and definition." (Ray, Section 1, p. 31) If M and L are both exactly specified, and M provides an adequate truth definition for L, and M can formulate the T-sentence premise for a liar argument, then the T-sentence premise is provable from its definition(s) and the axioms of M. (Ray, Section 1, p. 31). Further, a sentence D defining a predicate p in an exactly specified language M is formally correct only if, for every consistent and assertible set of sentences A in M not including D, $A + D$ is consistent. On Ray's account assertibility applies to the axioms of M, to (well) confirmed empirical sentences of M, and is closed under M's rules of inference — thus a formally correct definition sentence D could be inconsistent with some consistent set of sentences of M by imposing constraints on predicates other than p involved in D, but not inconsistent with those that we regard as correctly assertable. Some such condition on formal correctness is needed for Tarski's argument to work; but the details don't matter much here, since the sentences we will need to have in A are premises like the identity premise above.

With this apparatus in place, Ray presents a straightforward argument for Tarski's exact indefinability thesis. Suppose we can formulate, in M, the sentences necessary for a liar argument and in which the identity premise of the liar argument is assertible, and M allows us to use the normal laws of logic. Then an adequate truth definition for L in M will allow us to formulate a liar argument, leading to an inconsistency. So an adequate truth definition for L in M must be formally incorrect.

The conditions required to obtain this result are the formulability of the liar argument in M and the assertibility of the identity premise. Tarski hoped to strengthen his thesis by applying the Grelling paradox to avoid the need for an empirical premise (the assertibility of the identity premise) in the argument. Without this modification, applying the thesis to a given language would require that we somehow *recognize* the identity of the F sentence with the sentence, 'The F sentence is not true in L'.

The result, if the stronger version of the thesis goes through, would be that the exact indefinability thesis is a "purely conceptual thesis", (Ray, Section 3, p. 35) that we can establish a priori, rather than an a posteriori conclusion we can draw only after examining a language to see whether, for some feature of sentences F, the identity premise turns out to be true. More importantly, though, Ray believes that if Tarski's strengthening of his thesis succeeds, there is a serious problem for the T-strategy for defining truth.

Ray's concern about the Grelling version of the indefinability thesis is that it, too, requires an empirical premise — and one that seems to be *un*assertable, to boot: The Grelling thesis requires a definition of "self-applicability". But its conclusion seems to show that this definition cannot be formally correct. Still, given that definition, it seems to be mere grammatical knowledge that allows us to see that a particular sentence, substituted into a particular context, is identical with a given quoted sentence. But the gains here seem less than impressive. After all, some versions of the liar are similarly grounded in nothing more than our ability to recognize the same string of symbols occurring all over again.

We are also led to the conclusion that we can know a priori that there is at least one untrue T-sentence for L in M. This leads to a serious problem for Tarski's attitude towards Convention T; if we know a priori that at least one T-sentence is false, then Convention T seems indefensible — surely we cannot require a satisfactory definition of truth to prove a sentence known a priori to be false! How can the demands of Convention T be an important conceptual constraint if we know a priori that it implies at least one false sentence?

Ray's response to this puzzle is to recur to the intuitions that link disquotation and truth. To account for the credibility of Convention T despite its necessarily having a false instance, he introduces a notion he calls *simple conceptual warrant*, (Ray, Section 7, p. 44) which is meant to capture the fact that some sentences can be known a priori to be true *if* certain semantic conditions regarding predicates and referring terms occurring in them are met. While Ray does not think that T sentences have simple conceptual warrant, they have a similar status that he labels *subtle concep-*

tual warrant (Ray, Section 7, p. 45). This sort of warrant is only slightly more conditional than simple conceptual warrant, adding to simple conceptual warrant's semantic conditions the further demand that the person who grasps such a sentence's conditional truth must recognize and understand a certain sentence as the referent of a term in the sentence.

Knowing that some such sentences are false, of course, only goes to show that sometimes the semantic conditions these forms of warrant suppose cannot always be met. And the semantic conditions themselves reflect a kind of ideal contact between a language's conceptual structure and the items we use the language to describe. So from Ray's point of view, what Tarski's result shows is that these ideals cannot be met for all the concepts and referring terms of a sufficiently expressive language.

The Semantics of Denial

Ed Mares examines the notion of denial, beginning with an important opening point: the standard Fregean argument for rejecting denial as a primitive in our account of attitudes towards sentences (or propositions) doesn't apply to many "deviant" logics, because, for these logics, the denial of a sentence simply isn't equivalent to the assertion of a negation. The key semantic question for Mares is, what are the success conditions for denials? Mares points out that straightforward attempts to employ denial against the strengthened liar paradox fail when denial predicates are introduced into the object language, but argues that a subtler treatment of denial, modeled on Barwise and Etchemendy's treatment of truth predicates, avoids the denial liar.

The opening point is straightforward: In the presence of either truth value gaps or truth value gluts, denial ceases to be equivalent to asserting a negation. In particular, intuitionists who reject some instances of excluded middle cannot express this rejection by asserting their negation, since that negation is an intuitionist contradiction.

The initial example Mares aims to explore is *partially defined predicates*, i.e. predicates that apply to some cases and whose negations apply to some other cases, but such that these two lists of cases do not exhaust all the possible cases. Tappenden has proposed treating the truth predicate as partially defined; this, coupled with treating denial as a primitive speech act, rather than defining it as the assertion of a negation, promises to save Kripke's theory of truth from the strengthened liar paradox.

But "denial liars" are waiting in the wings to undermine hopes for a general resolution of paradox; Mares considers three examples, the simple, normative and semantic denial liars, which declare (respectively), "I deny this sentence", "I should deny this sentence", and "This sentence is accurately denied".

Mares' response to the first two invokes two ways of escaping paradox. The first, directed against the normative denial liar, is to tolerate some level of "doxastic hypocrisy", that is, a failure, for ideal doxastic agents, of the inference from "X believes X should accept (reject) Φ" to "X should accept (reject) Φ". The second (which also applies to the simple denial liar) is to give up on the completeness of acceptance/rejection for ideal agents, so that when such an agent finds she cannot accept a statement, she need not respond by rejecting it. Mares' suggestion here is that surrendering "pragmatic completeness" (Mares, Section 4, p. 54) is less costly than surrendering pragmatic consistency.

The semantic denial liar requires a more complex treatment. The first step towards this treatment is to consider a time-indexed semantics. Partial interpretations of predicates provide, for each n-ary predicate, world, time triple, $\langle P, w, t \rangle$, a function mapping the triple into a pair of sets of n-tuples of individuals. The idea, of course, is that one such set provides the n-tuples of which the predicate is correctly asserted in w at t, and the other provides the n-tuples of which the predicate is correctly denied in w at t. Mares assumes consistency, requiring that these sets of n-tuples be disjoint, while recognizing that the apparatus could easily allow for paraconsistent treatments. A "language slice" is picked out by an interpretation based on this semantic apparatus at some time index.

A denial negation is defined as a Boolean complementation connective, i.e. a connective forming a sentence that is correctly assertable for the complement of the cases in which the original sentence is correctly assertable, and correctly deniable when the original sentence is correctly assertable. So denial negation forces a kind of completeness on the initial partial interpretation of the predicates, in a way that parallels the use of "not true" in the strong liar. Needless to say, a connective like that leads to trouble — and the way out of that trouble also suggests an escape from the strong liar.

The first point about denial negation that Mares makes is that, in the presence of his **Principle 1 (Persistence)** (Mares, p. 55), it trivializes the temporal picture of language he is applying, since the two together demand that at a given world every time slice makes all the same sentences true. Given a choice between the two, Mares is inclined to retain persistence and reject denial negation.

We can still bring denial into the object language, so long as we reject denial completeness, i.e. the principle that for every world w and every sentence A either A is correctly denied at t in w, or A is true at t in w. Rejecting this principle is what allows us to escape the semantic denial liar.

Mares closes by linking his proposal to Barwise and Etchemendy's view of truth in their (1987), and applying his account of denial to block a criticism of their view. Gupta (1989) objects to Barwise and Etchemendy by pointing out that their account of truth violates the supervenience of truth, viz. that all that's required for 'It is true that A' to be true is that A be true. Mares suggests his account avoids this objection by its explicit rejection of denial completeness.

Truth Translations of Relevant Basic Logics

Finally, R.K. Meyer, Yoko Motohama and Viviana Bono provide a rich account of how the relevant logics **B+** and **CB** (the conservative Boolean extension of **B+**) can be captured within a class of first order models satisfying a theory, **CBMODEL**. **CBMODEL** uses the familiar ternary accessibility relation together with a set of predicates, one corresponding to each propositional variable, and a set of individual variables. The predicates are used as the base of a recursive construction producing complex predicates corresponding to all the formulae of **B+**. The main theorem demonstrates that, for each theorem of **CB**, of the form $A \to C$, there is a corresponding theorem of **CBMODEL**, of the form $\forall w([A]w \supset [C]w)$, where $[A]$ and $[C]$ are the predicates corresponding to the formulae A and C respectively. Thus provability in **CB** is shown equivalent to first order validity. The authors argue that this classical reduction of relevant logics provides us with the minimal relevant logic, analogous to the minimal normal modal logic **K**; from this point of view, **R** and **E**, the relevant logics first developed by Anderson and Belnap, resemble less general modal systems like **S5**, whose semantics require the imposition of special conditions on the frame.

Along the way, the authors briefly consider the additional semantic postulates required to produce the more familiar systems of relevant logic, and reflect on what these postulates amount to. For example, **R+** (the positive fragment of **R**) requires adding ternary reflexivity, much as **S4** requires binary reflexivity:

Ternary Reflexivity Postulate. $Rwww$ (TRP)

But (as Pierce noted some time ago) relational products of ternary relations include relations of arbitrarily high 'arity', and provide more than one way to define such higher-order relations. Defining a 4-ary relation thus:

$$Rxyzw = df \exists a (Rxya \wedge Razw)$$

We must add to TRP the further constraint,

Pasch Postulate. $Rwxyz \Rightarrow Rwyxz$ (PP)

To get **R+**.

These constraints have reflections in the λ-calculus and in combinatory logic; TRP is linked to the duplicating combinator $\lambda x.xx$ (Curry's Δ or **WI** or **SII**), while PP is a permutating maneuver related to Curry's **C**($\lambda wxy.wyx$). Connections like these arise for other relevant logics as well, linking formulas with types, once Curry's types are extended to cover conjunctions and not just pure $\rightarrow$ formulas.

The authors are heterodox on the question of how logic relates to truths; since logic aims primarily to codify 'right reason,' it is chiefly concerned to capture the right consequence relation(s) linking the sentences of other languages. But logic is formulated as a "deductive discipline, with its own axioms and rules of inference", so the presentation of logic as a collection of truths is also important. So, while the focus here is on the relational formulations, the logics explored also appear in assertional guise.

However, it's worth noting that things may not always work out so tidily. The relational formulation's simple correspondence with the assertional formulation depends on thinking of the relation in question as holding between formulas rather than sets of formulas. Since there are alternative ways to type-raise such a consequence relation to a parallel relation between sets of formulas, a single assertional logic will turn out, in general, to correspond to a number of distinct relational logics. Further, embedding the consequence relation in the object language in the form of the connective '$\rightarrow$' requires that we make sense of nested implications — something that does not arise naturally on the relational side.

Five themes are taken as the groundwork for these semantics: The semantics is based on worlds (i.e. indices at which sentences receive truth values); logical entailment is captured by *truth-preservation* over (some range of) worlds; extensional particles receive values depending only on values of the components they operate on, while intensional particles invoke values assigned at other worlds, and there is no "*universally preferred* relevant logic" (Meyer et al., section IV).

The apparatus begins with *positive model structures*, defined as triples of the form $\mathbf{K} = \langle 0, K, R \rangle$, where K is a set, $0 \in K$, and R is a ternary relation on K. A binary relation on $K, \subseteq$, is defined:

$$d \subseteq \cdot a \subseteq b =_{df} R0ab$$

with the postulates, for $a, b, c, x \in K$:

$p1 \cdot \subseteq$ is reflexive and transitive
$p2 \cdot a \subseteq x$ and $Rxbc \Rightarrow Rabc$
$p3 \cdot b \subseteq x$ and $Raxc \Rightarrow Rabc$
$p4 \cdot x \subseteq c$ and $Rabx \Rightarrow Rabc$

With familiar definitions of truth conditions and a hereditary condition on ⊆, along with a definition of positive validity as validity in all positive model structures, we arrive at soundness and completeness for **B+**.

A classical Boolean negation can be conservatively added to **B+**, producing the system **CB**. The key to proving this claim turns on a further postulate,

$$p0 \cdot a \subseteq b \text{ iff } a = b$$

With $p0$ in place, $p1$–4 come for free. But **B+** is still complete for the resulting model structures, $b + ms$. And with this strong condition on R in place, Boolean negation can be added without causing difficulties for the hereditary condition on ⊆.

Finally, the authors note the implied convergence of the study of propositional relevant logics with certain classical first-order theories. Whether the translation itself represents progress is in some doubt; the first-order theories in question are far more complex than the simple relevant logics they translate. But along the way, the position of **B+** at the base of the relevant logics has become clearer, as well as links between relevant logics (especially in their relational formulations) with the type theories of combinatory logic and the lambda calculus. Further work, they hope, will contribute new insights into these systems and their relations.

Part II: Probability and Induction

The Reference Class Problem is Your Problem Too

Alan Hájek argues that the standard interpretations of probability theory all suffer from some variant of the reference class problem. And the cost of avoiding it is to offer no account of probability at all. Some solution to this problem is needed if we are to make probability (as Butler remarked), "the very guide of life". The key to Hájek's response is to reject one-place probabilities in favour of conditional probabilities as the primitive notion of probability: "The ubiquity of the reference class problem only drives home the essential relativity of probability assignments" (Hájek, Introduction, p. 86).

The problem originates with Venn's observation, that "This variety of classes to which the individual may be referred owing to his possession of a multiplicity of attributes, has an important bearing on the process of inference..." [Venn, 1876: 196, cited in Hájek, Section 1, p. 86]. The resulting problem is obvious for frequentists — to determine the probability of an individual having some property, we must decide what *class* of cases (among all the classes that the individual case belongs to) is the *right* one, i.e. the one for which the frequency of the property in question gives the probability. But Hájek claims that other interpretations of probability — classical, logical, subjectivist and propensity — also suffer from "something akin to the reference class problem" (Hájek, Section 1, p. 86).

The problem can be formulated a little more generally. Suppose that what we want is a probability for some proposition E. While we can easily assign certain conditional probabilities of the form $P(E$ given $A)$, we cannot use these to arrive at a probability for E tout court without having unconditional probabilities for the As. If we think there is a well-defined probability for E, then we have a metaphysical problem: What determines this probability? And if we think that we should be able to assign such a probability to E, then we also have an epistemic problem: How shall we decide the unconditional probability of a proposition, given some conditional probabilities?

Hájek's thesis is that all the standard interpretations of probability either suffer from a version of the reference class problem, or fail to provide a sufficiently strong account of what probability is to justify guiding our choices according to its precepts. As we've already noted, in the case of frequentism, the problem is straightforward. Frequentism defines probability as relative frequency — but the appeal to relative frequency invokes membership in some class of cases, and the question, "Which class", arises immediately. The details vary for different forms of frequentism; for Reichenbach, not only what hypothetical sequence of events is considered, but its ordering, too, can affect the probability an event is assigned. Von Mises' use of *collectives* resolves some of these difficulties, but the principal problem remains, and von Mises responds to it by rejecting single case probabilities as "nonsense". By contrast, Reichenbach proposes that we select the "narrowest class for which reliable statistics can be compiled". But this is not a general solution, when we lack a clear standard of reliability and many equally narrow classes may be available.

Classical interpretations turn on counting (or measuring) possible outcomes; equipossible outcomes for a single experiment replace the frequentist's appeal to the outcomes of a number of similar experiments. But the close parallel between these ensures that a similar reference class problem will arise for the classicist, even when symmetry considerations have been used to restrict what should count as equipossible outcomes: choosing different symmetries will lead the same proposition to be assigned receive different probabilities. So classical probabilities must also be relativised.

Logical theories of probability encounter relativisation at three stages, first with respect to the language in which the event is described, second with respect to the total evidence, and third, with respect to the choice of Carnap's λ (and possibly other parameters determining how assigned probabilities will change in response to evidence).

Propensity theories, Hájek argues, either turn out to be similarly relativised, or amount to "dormative virtue" theories, that leave probability and its role in rational choice entirely mysterious. Frequency-based propensity theories inherit the relativisation worries we have already encountered for frequency theories. And symmetry-based propensity theories are relative for the same reasons that classical theories are. For example, Mellor's principle of connectivity holds (in an echo of classical theorists' appeal to indifference) that the propensities of outcomes are the same unless their causes differ. This principle leads to relativisation with respect to how we divide up the outcomes. And less structured appeals to dispositions, tendencies, possibilities-with-degrees, etc., leave us with no understanding of the nature and significance of these "probabilities" (including why they should obey the axioms of probability theory).

Finally, subjectivist theories can be uninformative in much the same way (radical subjectivism allows as "rational" probability assignments that would be, not only eccentric, but positively suicidal as guides to action). But where they invoke expert assignments or expert functions (which may be based on frequencies, symmetries, objective chances, or the opinions of selected human experts) to constrain your subjective probability assignment, we encounter relativisation both with respect to disagreeing expert assignments or functions, and with respect to any relativisation that arises for the expert assignments and functions themselves.

Hájek's response is to suggest that we take the hint, and put conditional probabilities first. The standard "ratio" definition of conditional probabilities in terms of simple probabilities fails when we consider 0-probability antecedents — but not all such conditional probabilities are intuitively ill-defined. Moreover, if we allow (as most do) for vague probabilities, the vagueness of some probabilities should not affect all the conditional probabilities we can formulate involving them — but avoiding this will require some adjustment to the ratio definition. Finally, even in some cases where the terms of the ratio definition don't receive determinate values, we can still assign reasonable conditional probabilities. Better, Hájek suggests, to accept that "it's conditional probabilities all the way down" (Hájek, Section 3.3, p. 105).

One important question remains unanswered here: If conditional probability is "the guide to life", as Hájek asserts, then we need to know how to use it, i.e. which of all the many conditional probabilities should we use to evaluate risks and make decisions? If we accept, as Hájek's arguments suggest, that probabilities are always relative and conditional, then we need to make a choice before we can apply our conditional probabilities to the business of life. But perhaps, like the application of theories more generally, this is a matter of pragmatic commitment, not further information about probabilities.

A Formal Model of Epistemic Coherence

The principal idea underlying Cross's paper is his account of *non-monotonic* inconsistency, a counterpart of logical inconsistency in the context of non-monotonic reasoning. The model of coherence Cross proposes treats it as a multi-dimensional measure, turning on many distinct virtues that a belief set should have, but here Cross focuses on freedom from "unexplained anomalies".

The intuitive idea is that a set is epistemically coherent if and only if the conclusions it somehow non-monotonically supports are consistent. But care is required to make this intuitive notion work. A set as whole surely only supports a consistent set of conclusions; if it provides evidence both for and against some claim, then we must (as Hume argued) *weigh* the evidence on both sides. If proper subsets are appealed to in determining what conclusions the set supports, detatchment must be restricted. Non-monotonic reasoning must allow for conflicts between conclusions we can draw from subsets even for sets that are not intuitively incoherent. So we need to distinguish cases where the evidence has merely shifted from cases in which the evidence, as it stands, is somehow in conflict.

Cross's approach treats anomalies as inconsistencies that arise when different subsets of the belief set are closed under a non-monotonic consequence relation. Cross defines a "point of unresolved conflict for a set X" as a statement p such that p is non-monotonically supported by at least one subset of X, $\neg p$ is non-monotonically supported by at least one subset of X, and either X non-monotonically supports neither p nor $\neg p$, or X non-monotonically supports both. In this situation, the conflict between p and $\neg p$ is unresolved in X because X doesn't decide between them (Cross, Definition 5, p. 127).

An interesting historical example of such a conflict is the late-nineteenth century debate about the age of the earth. Calculations of the age of the earth and sun by William Thompson (later Lord Kelvin), based on thermodynamic models, first appeared in the early 1860s. Though some, including T.H. Huxley, expressed doubts about Kelvin's methods (and sharp differences about the impact of such limits on geology as it was then being done), in fairly short order most geologists had chosen to limit their estimates of the age of the earth to Kevin's preferred figure, on the order of 100 million years. (Kelvin's figure also appears in Mark Twain's *Letters From the Earth*.) Darwin, in later editions of the *Origin*, gave increasing emphasis to Lamarkian mechanisms in an effort to reduce the time required for evolution. In the 1890's further calculations reduced the time allowed by Kelvin-type models. The response from the geological community was a stiffening of resistance. 100 million years might be sufficient, but many regarded Kelvin's new figures of 10 to 40 million as far too brief to fit the geological observations. This example fits Cross's account very nicely — the physical evidence, at least as read by Kelvin and his allies, clearly pointed to thermodynamic limits on the age of the earth and the sun. The geological evidence, at least as read by a substantial majority of geologists, pointed to greater ages than Kelvin would allow. And the evidence as a whole might be claimed to support both views,[1] or neither.

From this starting point, Cross explores how various constraints on the non-monotonic consequence relation produce constraints on this notion of non-monotonic inconsistency before applying it to the notion of epistemic coherence. The key concept in Cross's account of epistemic coherence is that of *anomalies*:

> p is an anomaly relative to a set statements X iff there exist q and Y such that $X \vdash q$ and $p \in X_q^-$ and $Y \subseteq X_q^-$ and $X_q^- \not\hspace{-2pt}\mid\hspace{-2pt}\sim q$ and $X_q^- \not\hspace{-2pt}\mid\hspace{-2pt}\sim \neg q$ but $Y \mid\hspace{-2pt}\sim q$ and $\{p\} \mid\hspace{-2pt}\sim \neg q$ (Cross, Definition 8, p. 132).

Where X_q^- is the set X *contracted on* q. An anomaly is not necessarily a point of unresolved conflict — X may resolve the conflict in favour of q, and may not include p. But X contracted on q supports p (non-monotonically, of course), so p is locally supported in X. As a result, we can say that the status of p produces a kind of evidential tension in X. Moreover, X_q^- has a point of unresolved conflict, so the existence of an anomaly implies the existence of unresolved conflict in a *contraction* of the commitment set.

This leads to a straightforward proposal for a definition of epistemic coherence:

> A set X of sentences is coherent iff (i) no sentence is an anomaly for X, (ii) $X \not\hspace{-2pt}\mid\hspace{-2pt}\sim$ and (iii) $X = C(X)$.

Coherence is thus defined as absence of anomalies and non-monotonic inconsistencies, together with closure under the non-monotonic consequence relation (which is taken to be necessary to coherence because maximizing coherence is the driving force behind ampliative reasoning).

However, this is a very demanding requirement, unlikely to be met by any rich system of sentences. The requirement that *no* subsystems of a

---

[1] See M. Bryson Brown, Science in Conflict (PhD. dissertation, University of Pittsburgh, 1985), for a substantial discussion of this case.

coherent system support (non-monotonically) conflicting conclusions is too much to ask. It's all too easy, given a large collection of claims to sort through, to find carefully selected bodies of evidence that intuitively support conflicting conclusions. Conspiracy theories and the legal profession thrive on the careful selection of evidence — but their ability to "make a case" in this way does not demonstrate any incoherence in the larger system of statements their "evidence" is selected from. The existence of what are, from the wider point of view, evidentially *misleading* subsets of a set of statements is more or less inevitable. Consider for example a simple case involving repeated measurements of a distance. We will often be able to select subsets of the measurements that "support" incompatible judgments about the distance in question.

Perhaps a more modest requirement would result from developing a *measure* of coherence to replace this definition; Cross proposes a straightforward measure based on his definition of coherence, ordering sets of statements according to whether they contain more or fewer anomalies, more or fewer points of unresolved conflict, and more or fewer of the statements in their (identical) closures under non-monotonic consequence. The result is, as it should be, a partial ordering.

But this measure of coherence does not help to resolve the difficulty just noted, since it builds on the definitions already employed. It seems to us that what we need is a way to recognize that some sets of sentences include anomalies, in Cross's sense, while *resolving* them, i.e. the actual evidential bearing of these sets is not in tension despite containing subsets that support inconsistent conclusions.

Nevertheless, Cross's careful development of the notion of non-monotonic inconsistency and its relation to an interesting definition of coherence is a step forward. If it can be enriched with a distinction between those conflicts of evidence that persist and those that are resolved by the set in which they occur, we may well learn some very interesting lessons about epistemic coherence.

How do the Harper and Levi Identities Constrain Belief Change?

The naive picture of inference as modeled on the logical consequence relation is clearly an outright mistake; identifying consequences of our commitments is just as often a reason to alter our commitments as it is a reason to believe any newly identified consequences. A more tenable view of the contribution of the consequence relation to epistemic rationality treats it as a closure condition on commitments. Models of belief change such as those proposed by Gardenfors have focused on the contribution of the logical consequence relation to constraints on rational belief change, proposing models of revision (the changes consequent on adding new information to our commitments) and contraction (the changes consequent on removing some information from our commitments). In "How do the Harper and Levi Identities constrain Belief Change", Oliver Schulte explores the symmetries linking revision and contraction, symmetries that seem to be required by the fundamental dual symmetries of assertion and denial that characterize the underlying classical consequence relation.

Quine's (1951) suggestion that rationality requires *minimal* belief change has inspired efforts to characterize just what minimal belief change requires. Schulte explores how identities linking revision with contraction are related to other constraints on belief change. Isaac Levi first proposed a definition of revision in terms of contraction that turns on a two-stage process: to obtain the revision of T that adds to T the information that p, first contract T on $\neg p$, and then add p to the resulting set. Formally,

$$T * p = T \dotdiv \neg p \cup \{p\}$$

"Mild" assumptions about logical consequence lead to the result that this identity will hold so long as revision is logically weaker than the set theoretic union, i.e. so long as

$$T \cup \{p\} \vDash T * p.$$

This principle is $K * 3$ in the AGM postulates; Schulte maintains that it is a fundamental postulate for minimal belief change. It is closely linked to the constraint Schulte calls *Pareto-minimality*, where $T * p$ is Pareto-minimal iff any other change to T retracting fewer beliefs must have more added to meet basic conditions for revision on p, and any change to T adding fewer beliefs must have more retracted to meet the conditions. It is also supported by the Ramsey test, which applies Ramsey's view of conditionals to translate rules for belief revision into conditionals, and which renders $K * 3$ as $(p > q) \to (p \to q)$, where '>' is our conditional connective and '$\to$' is the material conditional.

Harper proposed the Harper Identity in (1975); this principle requires

$$q \in T \dotdiv p \Rightarrow q \in T \text{ and } q \in T * \neg p$$

The Harper identity suggests a way of extracting a contraction function from a given revision function: Simply set $T \dotdiv p =_{df} T \cap (T * \neg p)$.

The consequence relation involved here is defined on a standard propositional language. Oddly, though an entailment relation holding between sets is specified, this entailment is not the usual set-set consequence relation. $\Gamma \vdash \Gamma'$ holds iff $\Gamma' \subseteq Cn(\Gamma)$, where $Cn(\Gamma)$ is the closure of Γ under the usual set-formula consequence relation. At the very least the dual, left/right symmetries between assertion and denial would be more obvious here if the set-set entailment relation were the familiar one based on a sentential consequence relation: $\Gamma \vdash \Delta$ holds iff some element in $C(\Gamma, \wedge), \gamma$, and some element of $C(\Delta, \vee), \delta$, are such that $\gamma \vdash \delta$.

Theories are defined in the usual way as sets of sentences closed under $\vdash$. The basic conditions for belief revision and belief contraction functions are quite asymmetrical:

DEFINITION 4. *A belief revision function is a function* $* : T \times L \rightarrow T$ *such that for all formulas p, it is the case that* $T * p \vdash p$.

DEFINITION 5. *A belief contraction function* $\div$ *is a function* $\div : T \times L \rightarrow T$ *such that for all theories T and for all formulas p, it is the case that* $T \vdash T \div p$.

The asymmetry here is striking — T is preserved from right to left by subtraction, but p is preserved from left to right by revision. These definitions make perfect sense from an intuitive point of view. But there is also something more symmetrical in the air here. Just as our aim in contraction is to preserve as much of T as possible while removing any commitment to p, our aim with revision is to alter T as little as possible in order to be *free* to add p to the result. In both cases T is being both modified, and, subject to the specific change to be achieved by the modification, modified as little as possible. The difference between contraction and revision is the difference between making *room* for a certain kind of commitment without making the commitment, and making a commitment, while *also* (of course) making the necessary room for it. This makes the first condition above pretty easy to understand. Whatever we do to T when we revise on p, p is meant to end up as part of our commitments when we're done. The second is harder to follow: Whatever we do when we contract on p, we are to wind up not committed to p. But the condition given requires something weaker, viz. just that whatever we end up with after a contraction is to be entailed by what we started with. This is compatible with $\div$ being the identity function, which is clearly not the intent of contraction. Intuitively, we might want $T \div p \not\vdash p$ as the key condition. But $\div$ needs to be defined for all sentences in the language, so this condition is trouble — no operation can satisfy it for tautologies. Definition 5 above is more general, imposing an important, if slightly subtler constraint: contraction should not expand our commitments. This condition allows $\div$ to be defined for all sentences. (In particular, it seems likely that "contraction" on a tautology will leave us with the same set we started with.)

Given these very general characterizations of revision and contraction functions, Schulte presents necessary and sufficient conditions for satisfying the Levi and Harper identities, and for making the Levi Identity invert the Harper Identity. Schulte stipulates that ∗ satisfies (or is generated by) the Levi Identity if there is a contraction function ∸ such that applying the Levi Identity to ∸ produces ∗.

> Let ∸ be a belief contraction function with associated belief revision function ∗. Then for all theories T and for all formulas p, it is the case that $T + p \vdash T * p$. (Schulte, Lemma 8)

> Let ∗ be a belief revision function that respects double negation (i.e. such that, $\forall T, T * p = T * \neg\neg p$). Then the Levi Identity inverts the Harper identity applied to ∗ ⇔ for all theories T and formulas p, it is the case that $T + p \vdash T * p$. (Schulte, Proposition 9)

> If a consequence relation Cn satisfies disjunctive syllogism ($\Gamma \vdash p \to q, \Gamma \vdash \neg p \to q / \Gamma \vdash q$), a ∸ that respects double negation can be generated by the Harper Identity iff for all theories T and for all formulas p, $T \dotdiv p + p = T + p$. (Schulte, Corollary 10)

The first result shows that a belief revision function that satisfies the Levi Identity must respect Gardenfors' $K * 3$. The second shows that, *when the belief revision function treats formulas and their double negations identically*, the two identities are inverses iff $K * 3$ holds. $T \dotdiv p + p = T + p$ is called the *recovery principle*, because it tells us that the result of eliminating any commitment to p and then adding p to our commitments is the same as that of merely adding p to our commitments, i.e. that we can *recover* from a contraction simply by adding the contracted sentence back in. So Schulte's Corollary 10 shows that, *in a certain kind of environment*, the Harper Identity is equivalent to the recovery principle.

We would be very interested to see how this idiom of revision and contraction would appear when set in a context that gave more balanced emphasis to commitments to the *denial* of certain sentences. The work that Schulte is exploring and extending here is focused exclusively on assertive commitments — hence its assymetrical treatment of the consequence relation. In a classical context, where commitment to a denial is equivalent to commitment to the assertion of a negation, this may be harmless. But when we seek, as Schulte does here, to explore a wider range of cases and characterize relations between various principles as generally as possible, a more balanced view of the relation between assertion and denial grounded in a set-set picture of the consequence relation could be illuminating.

Higher Order Probability Theory and Defeasible Reasoning

Morgan's paper presents an account of "ordinary reasoning", where we are inclined to tentatively draw conclusions from our information, despite the fact that these conclusions are not guaranteed true given that our information is. Morgan's view of such reasoning is grounded in his conviction, argued for elsewhere, that "non-monotonic consequence relation" is an oxymoron. Any such consequence relation, he maintains, must violate "canons of rationality" grounded in relative frequency considerations. Nevertheless, defeasible reasoning is something we clearly do (and must do). Morgan's proposal is not to introduce a new consequence relation, but instead to add defeasible inference rules, such as a rule telling us that we may infer, from "Tweety is a bird" that "Tweety flies." Defeasibility arises in two ways, on the simple account Morgan explores here. If a non-defeasible rule produces a conflicting result, then the defeasible inference rule doesn't apply to the affected cases. And if a defeating *condition* holds, then the defeasible rule again fails to apply. If Tweety is a penguin, and we know that no penguins fly, then a non-defeasible (monotonic) rule tells us that Tweety doesn't fly, and the defeasible inference rule leading from "A is a bird" to "A flies" is blocked for Tweety. If Tweety is injured, and we know that (depending on the details of the case) injured birds may well be unable to fly, then our defeasible inference rule is again blocked, though this time without our having decided whether Tweety can fly or not.

Morgan's approach to characterizing these rules involves three sorts of conditionals: The basic, monotonic '$\rightarrow$', standing for the familiar material conditional, the non-monotonic conditional, '$\Rightarrow$', which expresses defeasible inference rules, and the undercutting conditional, '$\rightsquigarrow$', where '$X \rightsquigarrow Y$' is read 'If X, then it might not be the case that Y'. (Of course the 'might' here must be stronger than the 'might' that characterizes the possible failure of any defeasible inference.)

Within a defeasible theory (which is a pair $\langle K, R \rangle$, where K is a set of literals representing our background knowledge and R is the set of monotonic and non-monotonic rules), a distinction is maintained between sentences that follow monotonically from the background information and those sentences that follow, but only non-monotonically. In effect, the non-monotonic consequences are treated *modally*; they themselves are not consequences of the theory — instead, their combination with a monadic operator E (read "evidently"), is taken to be a "consequence" of $\langle K, R \rangle$. The monotonic consequences of $\langle K, R \rangle$ are also said to be evident. The result is that ' "Evidently P" holds if there is some rule with consequent p, each of whose antecedents is evidently the case, but there is no rule whose consequent is $\sim p$, all of whose antecedents are evidently the case'. (Morgan, Section 2,

p. 138).

Morgan's main aim is to explore the links between probability and defeasible reasoning. The most obvious way to connect the two is to claim that when $A \Rightarrow B$ is a non-monotonic rule in some $\langle K, R \rangle$, the probability of something being B conditional on its being A is high. But this seems to fail outright. Defeasible reasoning is transitive, but high conditional probability is not. Morgan's response to this difficulty is to say that accepting an inductive pattern of reasoning such as the transitivity of non-monotonic consequence does not require that it always be a correct pattern of reasoning — all we should require is that it is "generally legitimate". The motto is, "Defeasible logic is inductive reasoning about reasoning". (Morgan, Section 3, p. 140)

This leads to an examination of *higher order* probabilities, explored by means of statistical models that combine categorical tables (providing exhaustive descriptions of the items in the model in terms of their properties) with numbers for each such "kind" of item. Morgan proposes to determine the higher order probability $Ph(X, K \cup R)$, by sampling the space of models. The rules in R correspond to statistical properties of the model; if they are not satisfied in a given model, we ignore that model. If they are, we increment tot♯ by 1, and then consider the area of the selected R model in which all the literals in K hold, and determine the "value" of X in that area. For X unquantified, the value of X is the proportion of K that is X; for X quantified, the value of X is 1 if it holds of the K area and 0 otherwise. We then increment suc♯ by the value of X in K. Once we have a large sample of such R models, we set $Ph(X, K \cup R) = $ suc♯/tot♯. Some technical issues arise; in particular, the conjunction principle fails, but this are not hard to resolve and doesn't make much difference to the results either.

The upshot is that transitivity works well by this measure, even though it clearly fails in some instances (some particular models of R). A range of inferences involving transitivity are tested in this way, and some interesting anomalies are discussed. Morgan concludes that the links between defeasible reasoning and higher-order probability warrant further research; he also makes the methodological point that using his sampling approach to explore "inductive reasoning about inductive reasoning" is computationally tractable, and suggests that concentrating on orderings rather than measures might produce more "reasonable" results.

Real Logic is Nonmonotonic

Kyburg's paper is, in part, a reply to Morgan's argument for the monotonicity of logical consequence; his aim is to explain how a well-motivated notion of logical consequence could be non-monotonic. Kyburg's strategy is to identify the features of Morgan's account of consequence relations that give rise to his proof of monotonicity, and identify some alternatives that would block the proof.

Kyburg identifies five issues to address here. First, the nature and aim of logic itself; second, Morgan's argument, third, the potential (and limitations) of probability as a "possible non-monotonic representation of reality". (Kyburg, Section 1, p. 175), fourth, an account of what a non-monotonic logic that avoids Morgan's objections ought to look like, and, finally, the relation between this proposal and Morgan's defense of monotonicity.

Argument is the central notion in Kyburg's account of logic; the role of logic in argument is as a court of last resort. To persuade someone of something by means of an argument, one must present premises that this someone accepts, and reason from them in a way that she accepts. Logic provides us with a set of rules that, once agreed to, can underwrite, and (where necessary) be explicitly invoked, step-by-step, to show that, given the premises, a particular argument really "gets" its conclusion. As Kyburg emphasizes, in the case of deductive argument, soundness (i.e. that the truth of conclusions reached in accord with the logic's demands be guaranteed by that of the premises) is essential to a system of logic; completeness, on the other hand, is only desirable. Monotonicity, defined straightforwardly: $A \subseteq B \supset (\forall \alpha)(A \vdash \alpha \supset B \vdash \alpha)$ (Kyburg, Section 2.1, p. 177) clearly applies to any logic that is sound in this sense, so the question becomes, can we give an account of inductive argument that is grounded in a non-monotonic consequence relation?

Inductive arguments are clearly non-monotonic; a set of premises that inductively supports some conclusion can easily be extended in ways that leave that conclusion unsupported. Kyburg considers two ways in which this situation can arise — in the first, we consider, step by step, the evidence available to us. As more and more evidence is considered, we may find ourselves accepting a given conclusion, rejecting it, accepting again, and so on. In the second, while we suppose that at any given time all the available evidence has been considered, as time goes on more and more evidence becomes available. Kyburg suggests that if we consider the inductive conclusions that are *legitimate* for us to be those supported by the totality of the available evidence, rather than just the evidence we have taken into account, we needn't worry about capturing the first sort of reversal in our logic; such reversals will represent mistakes, not changes in the conclusions the logic should allow us to draw.

What would a logic that plays the role of "court of last resort" in relation to inductive arguments look like? The key question for Kyburg is, "Is there something akin to validity that is our goal in the case of inductive arguments?" (Kyburg, Section 2.2, p. 178). The fact that people present arguments for inductive conclusions is prima facie evidence that there is such a notion. But some have argued that "inductive arguments" are always enthymemes for deductive arguments. Of course it's easy to produce candidate "presuppositions" for deductive counterparts to inductive arguments — the most direct way is just to add a conditional with the conjoined premises as antecedent and the desired conclusion as consequent. When this is too crude, we can easily hedge to make things subtler. One reason for rejecting the existence of an inductive logic is the absence of a widely accepted one. But Morgan has argued directly that there cannot be such a logic — if this argument succeeds, the issue is closed. However, before considering Morgan's argument, Kyburg turns to a discussion of probability.

Probability can be incorporated into the object language, or part of the metalanguage; either way, there is a straightforward kind of monotonicity that applies to probability functions. $A \subseteq B \to P(A) \leqslant P(B)$, where A and B are sets of 'possibilities' (subsets of the sample space). This monotonicity applies to conditional probabilities as well, but only to the sets in "first position": $A \subseteq B \to P(A,C) \leqslant P(B,C)$, but $A \subseteq B \not\to P(C,A) \leqslant P(C,B)$: Conditioning on a narrower set of possibilities can either raise or lower a conditional probability.

Kyburg begins with a metalinguistic approach, applying probability to sentences, sets of sentences, and pairs of these. When we reason deductively about such probabilities, of course, the results are monotonic. If we place constraints on a system of probability values, and deduce further constraints from these, those further constraints remain deducible as we add further information about the probabilities to our premises. When we "conditionalize" on new evidence, we haven't changed our probability function so much as changed our minds about what probabilities we are prepared to act on, and again, nothing non-monotonic is going on. (See Hájek's earlier paper, pp. 85–108, for a related view emphasizing the centrality of conditional probabilities.)

But rules of inference based on some measure of "desirability" could still be non-monotonic. The question is, could a system of such rules constitute a *logic*?

Morgan's proof turns on three principles governing what Morgan calls *belief structures*, defined as relations on 2^L:

Reflexivity: $\Gamma \mathbf{LE} \Gamma$
Transitivity: If $\Gamma \mathbf{LE} \Gamma'$ and $\Gamma' \mathbf{LE} \Gamma''$ then $\Gamma \mathbf{LE} \Gamma''$
The subset principle: If $\Gamma \subset \Delta$, then $\Delta \mathbf{LE} \Gamma$.

LE is to be read "no more confirmed than"; a logic L, for Morgan, is a set of such belief structures: $\mathbf{L} = \{\mathbf{LE}_1,,\ldots,\mathbf{LE}_n\}$. This makes logic less a canon of argument, and more a criterion of rational belief or commitment; in a given belief structure, to be committed to a set of sentences Γ is to be committed to all the sets Γ' such that $\Gamma \mathbf{LE} \Gamma'$.

Kyburg challenges both transitivity and the subset principle; but to see how this challenge creates room for a non-monotonic logic, we need to think first about how these belief structures constrain logical consequence. Morgan's proposal here is quite liberal:

> Soundness: If $\Gamma \vdash_b A$, then $\Gamma \mathbf{LE}\{A\}$ for all (most) rational belief structures $\mathbf{LE} \in \mathbf{L}$.
>
> Completeness: If $\Gamma \mathbf{LE}\{A\}$ for all (most) rational belief structures $\mathbf{LE} \in \mathbf{L}$, then $\Gamma \vdash_b A$.

The job of the **LE**s, then, is to stand in for different views of the *comparative* rationality of commitment to various belief sets. When we think of this socially, we can imagine many different standards being proposed, and these "soundness" and "completeness" criteria would ensure that the consequence relation respects "majority opinion" on what commitments follow from what other commitments.

If such a loose, opinion-based standard for logic still gives rise to monotonicity, one might well despair of non-monotonicity. And monotonicity follows easily here. Suppose that $\Gamma \vdash_b A$. Then by soundness we have that most belief systems are such that $\Gamma \mathbf{LE}\{A\}$. If $\Delta \supseteq \Gamma$ it follows by the subset principle that for all belief systems, $\Delta \mathbf{LE} \Gamma$, and then by transitivity we get that for most belief systems $\Delta \mathbf{LE}\{A\}$. And then completeness requires that $\Delta \vdash_b A$.

But Kyburg has already questioned both transitivity and the subset principle. And if we say instead that they hold only for most belief structures, then the argument for monotonicity fails.

For first order logic, monotonicity is a straightforward consequence of soundness and completeness. Soundness tells us that any conclusion we can derive from some premises holds in every model of those premises. It follows that any such conclusion will hold in every model of any superset of the premises. And so, by completeness, it will be derivable from any such superset. But soundness is the key here — it limits us to conclusions that are already implicit in the premises we have accepted. Inductive reasoning (and therefore any inductive consequence relation, if there are such) will have to reach beyond what is already said in our premises.

Further, deductive consequence relations are not inference rules. When we recognize that a sentence follows deductively from premises we have accepted, we may respond by adding the sentence to our commitments, *or* by rejecting some of our premises (or, to complete the list, by weakening our consequence relation). So the deductive consequence relation functions more like a closure condition on cognitive commitments. That is, commitment to a set of sentences includes, implicitly, commitment to their consequences (and nothing more). But real rules of inference will aim to tell us how our commitments should change, not what our commitments implicitly include or fail to include. What we are seeking here is a procedure we can use to *extend* our commitments. Such a procedure must be *unsound*, producing conclusions not already implicit in the commitments it starts with.

Next, Kyburg sketches an account of such a procedure. Given background knowledge Γ, S a statement that Γ provides inductive support for, $m(\Gamma, S)$ a set of models determined by Γ and S, and ε a contextually determined level of risk-tolerance, the acceptance rule he proposes is:

Accept(S, Γ, ε) if and only if S is true in a fraction of at least $1 - \varepsilon$ of the models in $m(\Gamma, S)$. (See p. 186.)

It is important to note here that $m(\Gamma, S)$ is a *superset* of the models of Γ. In addition to the models of Γ, it also includes models 'brought to our attention' by our consideration of S.

To accept a sentence on these grounds is *not* to add it to Γ. If we were to add S to Γ, and then consider a further sentence (say, $\neg S$) for acceptance, the rule would have us consider a set of models $m(\Gamma \cup \{S\}, \neg S)$. And the fraction of such models in which $\neg S$ is true will be 0. Adding accepted sentences directly to our evidence leaves us with no way back;[2] once a sentence is accepted we are stuck with it. So monotonicity is inevitable if accepting S means adding S to Γ.

Thus Kyburg keeps what is accepted separate from the evidential grounds on which we have accepted it. In the previous paper, Morgan keeps sentences supported by some evidence separate from the evidence itself by combining them with the monadic operator 'E' (for 'it is evident that') and adding *that* new sentence to our commitments. But Kyburg's proposal is a little bit different. Kyburg distinguishes between two sets of statements: The evidential certainties, Γ_e (corresponding to Γ above) and the practical certainties Γ_p (these can be thought of as sentences so probable, on the evidence, that given the stakes we are playing for, it is rational to employ them as premises in all of our practical reasonings).

What is acceptable as evidence is included in what is practically acceptable: As Morgan would put it, $\Gamma_p \mathbf{LE} \Gamma_e$. But the selection of the set of models $m(\Gamma, S)$ depends both on Γ and S. Extending Γ can move us to a

---

[2]See Sellars, 'Induction as Vindication', *Philosophy of Science*, 31:3, p. 219, 1964.

new set of models, $m(\Gamma', S)$ in which the fraction of models where S holds is too low for Accept$(\Gamma', S, \varepsilon)$ to hold.

Important questions remain. How to arrive at $m(\Gamma, S)$, whether Γ must be treated as an incorrigible foundation, or can be itself uncertain and revisable, and what are the logical closure conditions on Γ_p? (In the light of the lottery paradox, closure under conjunction in particular seems dubious.) Kyburg discusses these briefly, but in the conclusion Kyburg focuses on how presupposition-based approaches to inductive argument relate to the framework he has proposed.

Morgan has suggested that inductive reasoning involves the selection of a 'presupposed' subset of the models of our evidence; inductive conclusions are sentences that hold in all these presupposed models. But Morgan repudiates any search for a 'logic' governing how we select these presupposed sets of models, proposing instead that this process is a matter of human psychology. Other presupposition-based accounts convert inductive arguments into deductive ones by adding further premises to our evidence. But Kyburg emphasizes the normative aspect of logic, and opposes this shift from concern with standards of correct reasoning to a merely descriptive account of how we argue inductively. And he sees no need (as his model of induction makes clear) to convert inductive arguments into deductively valid ones. Finally, Kyburg argues that justifying such presuppositions leads us right back to the central problem, viz., how shall we go about *extending* our commitments, beyond what we take to be our evidence? Trying to settle the problem of induction by appeal to presuppositions seems to trap us in Hume's familiar circle.

Kyburg prefers the non-monotonic route, focusing on sets of models picked out by Γ and by our consideration of S, and considering the fraction of such models in which S holds. 'This', he declares, 'is what "real logic" comes to: deduction leaves us right where we started' (Kyburg, Section 7, p. 192). Logic, from this point of view, is about inference, after all — and the deductive systems we have generally *called* logic fail by this standard. Morgan's argument shows that a nonomontonic logic providing a closure condition on rationally accepted sets of sentences will not do — nonmonotonic conclusions must be kept separate from our evidence base. Kyburg describes how such a system can ground statistical reasoning by allowing us to combine, in the "stash" of nonmonotonic conclusions, both a justified claim to the (probable) representativeness of a sample, and a justified claim about the proportion of individuals sampled, that have a given property.[3] He concludes with a brief critical review of the presuppositions approach,

---

[3] See P. Maher "The Hole in the Ground of Induction", *Australasian Journal of Philosophy*, 74, 3 423–432.

and a strong appeal for a genuinely non-monotonic logic to underwrite non-monotonic argument.

Part III: Formal Metaphysics
1 Branching Histories Approach to Indeterminism and Free Will

Contemporary metaphysics has been strongly influenced by the development of formal methods in logic. Broadly, these methods allow us to construct formal structures that can then be proposed as rigourous models of various metaphysical ideas. Perhaps the most familiar and widely discussed example of metaphysics conducted by these means has been the radical realism about possible worlds developed and articulately defended by the late David Lewis. In this paper, Nuel Belnap presents a very different formal model of branching time that includes just one world. The model aims to provide an account of the role of (real) possibilities in the world, and of a necessary condition for a libertarian account of freedom. The main aim is to give our humanistic intuitions about these matters a form that reconciles them with our best current physical understanding of the universe, including both relativity theory and the peculiar non-locality of quantum mechanics (what Belnap calls 'funny business') — here Belnap, like Wilfrid Sellars, aims at a synoptic image that will combine aspects of both the scientific and the manifest images of us-in-the-world.

There are several basic intuitions that motivate these efforts. The first, and perhaps the most important, is the need for a notion of objective (as opposed to linguistic or epistemic) possibility, possibility *based in reality*, as Belnap (citing Xu 1997) puts it. Belnap's proposal is to invoke branching histories to ground objective possibility in real features of the world. For Belnap, objective possibility is required for objective probability, for action, doing, responsibility and agency, and for causality. From this point of view, the deterministic tradition in modern philosophy (motivated by the brilliant success of classical mechanics, and including figures like Laplace, Hume, and Kant) collapses the distinctions between possibility, actuality and necessity; we need to find a clear and distinct way to restore them.

The concepts needed here begin with the world and its possibilities, events, histories, consistency, branching and causality. Possibilities are grounded in this world, not in different worlds. Branching histories aim to account for how real possibilities can arise, exist, and eventuate or fail to eventuate, all within a single, consistent world. The need for branching arises because events that are possible individually may not be possible collectively, i.e. they may not be *jointly consistent*, as Belnap puts it. A history is a maximal consistent collection of events; but at any given time in a history there exists more than one possible future history.

The key concept, of course, is branching. The model of (objective) possibility that Belnap proposes involves a single world with branching, rather than (as in Lewis' account) multiple worlds that are indistinguishable up to a certain point in time. On this view, the period leading up to a branch point is literally identical for two possible histories that separate at that point — and the two histories are completely distinct thereafter, no matter how similar. The only connection between such histories lies in their shared past. A somewhat more sophisticated view of branching is needed when we consider space-time, rather than time alone. But every possible event, in the sense of objective possibility Belnap presents here, is connected to every other possible event by literally sharing a past, however remote.

A "prior choice" principle then underwrites a notion of causation (in the sense of "objective, originating cause"):

> *When we are looking for a token-level cause of some outcome, we may always look to the past. (Belnap, Section 2.2, p. 215)*

The upshot is pretty common-sensical — suspiciously so, to someone who believes that our scientific understanding of the world radically alters many common sense notions, including space, time and causation. Despite the symmetry of the two time directions in fundamental physics (mutatis mutandis, as CPT symmetry requires), in Belnap's metaphysics the past and future directions in time are radically asymmetrical, because branches always and only overlap in the past; the future is open to different possibilities, while the past is 'fixed in stone' (Belnap, Section 2.3, p. 215)

The application of these ideas to action and agency, and the exposition of an 'unpretentious' form of free will, is a central concern for Belnap. The first notion required here is an agentive modality, 'sees to it that': whenever someone is an agent, there is some sentence X such that that someone sees to it that X. To refrain from an action can be treated by iterating this modality. To refrain from going out is to see to it that one does not see to it that one goes out. Of course to do this is not to see to it that one does not go out — someone who refrains from going out may end up out nonetheless, but not by virtue of having seen to it.

(Some might be worried at this point. After all, Belnap's aim is *not* to expound a linguistic notion of possibility, and the role of sentences in this modality raises questions about the language in use here, especially whether it is really adequate to represent the choice that was made by the agent. But the definition below makes 'seeing to it' secondary to choices. By means of a choice, a particular branch (and everything that all branches along that branch agree on while disagreeing with all other branches emerging from that choice point) is brought about, and thus a wide range of sentences (in the various languages we could use to describe these histories) are *seen to*.

Choice is something that occurs at branch points, i.e. (just) prior to any differences between the possible history(ies) chosen and those not chosen: 'choice must come prior to any outcome that is settled by the choice' (Belnap, p. 217) This allows a definition:

> To see to it that X is to make some prior choice that guarantees that X.

Because choices constitute branch points, they can only occur where other possibilities (other choices) are 'available'. Further, no choice can be made before its time — it cannot occur until the branch point is reached. So 'pre-commitment' strategies don't make future choices — they *eliminate* them.

The 'sees to it that' formula is the central notion in Belnap's account of free will. On this account, free will requires a particular agent, a particular outcome, and a particular branch point. The account is kept 'unpretentious' by focusing on these particulars, rather than considering the world as a whole or on the conditions and times surrounding the branch point. At the branch point, the choice is made; prior to it and afterwards, things can remain as deterministic as some imagine them to be.

Of course, this approach is unpretentious in another, more worrisome way. The fact that in this model, some branch points are said to be choices, doesn't help us to distinguish the choice type of branch points from those that are not choices. And answering this question seems to involve a dilemma: Suppose there is something about the agent's character or decision process leading up to the branch point that *explains* why one branch rather than the other was taken. Then it seems the branching had already occurred, and we are driven either to some sort of regress or into some form of compatibilism. But suppose that there is nothing about the agent's character or decision process that explains this. Then it seems that choice has been *reduced* to chance. The metaphysical worries Belnap hopes to avoid by focusing on particular agents, outcomes and branch points seem to creep in again when we ask this question. Perhaps to be truly unpretentious we will have to just refuse to ask. But then the account seems at best incomplete, and at worst it just equates choices with a chance or possibility somehow *associated* with an agent. See the distinction between choices and 'metaphorical' choices Belnap draws (see p. 211), while making his second point about locality, and the discussion of two histories (one including a cat on a mat some afternoon, the other including the same cat in a tree all that afternoon) and the 'choice point' at which the first is ruled in and the second ruled out.

The last topic Belnap addresses is *modestly local* branching in a relativistic space-time. In such a space-time events are not always strictly ordered with respect to time. Some events are past with respect to a given event, some are future, and some are 'space-like' related to the event (though some of these will be past and future with respect to each other). Two events are consistent if and only if they share a history, i.e. if and only if at least one event lies in their common future. Conversely, two events are inconsistent if and only if no event lies in their common future, i.e. there is no point in any of the branches of space-time as a whole at which *both* are part of the past. Choices are also to be treated locally, and the choice points that made actual contingent events inevitable are to be sought in the local causal past of these events. Belnap says it is tempting to suppose that space-like related events are independent of each other. But experimental confirmation of the Bell inequality shows us that this principle is violated. And there is nothing in the theory of histories and branching presented here that conflicts with this strange result of quantum entanglement.

Closing Comments

Exact philosophers' use of formal tools in philosophical inquiry continues to expand vigorously in many different directions. As these essays make clear, fundamental questions tend to remain open — the natures (if there are any) of truth and probability, the problem of induction — these, one suspects, we will always have with us. But the development of new tools that we can use to address them, and the exploration of how these tools relate to each other, are healthy, progressive enterprises — ultimately, they are clarifying ones. One great pleasure of doing philosophy with formal tools is that we can often decide important questions about what a given application of such tools implies: when the results illuminate the questions that guided their construction in the first place, we can make truly fundamental discoveries. Sometimes, of course, what we discover is that our tools cannot do what we have asked of them. Then we must either return to the drawing board, or learn to question the questions that brought us to this impasse. But in either case we have learned something worthwhile. Formal tools have long been part of the standard equipment of working scientists — now, working philosophers are beginning to catch up.

Part I

Truth and Consequence

The Preservation of Truth
R. E. JENNINGS AND DARKO SARENAC

ABSTRACT. On the classical account of validity, an argument is invalid iff there is a model in which its premisses are true but its conclusion false. A rigid adherence to this account has led some paraconsistentists, the so-called *dialetheists*, to account for the invalidity of *ex falso quodlibet* (efq) by recourse to models that satisfy classically inconsistent sets of sentences on non-classical interpretations of negation or conjunction or both. Preservationists have generally countered that the problems with *ex falso quodlibet* are application-specific and would be better solved by requiring an inference relation to preserve mathematically well-defined semantic measures of sentence-ensembles.

It is undeniable that formal manipulations such as those of the dialetheists will yield efq-free sublogics of classical logic. It is however deniable that their model theory confirms any metaphysical claim about the tolerances of truth or the meaning of negation. In fact it is arguable that folk-truth need play no very serious role in the formal sciences where designated values will do, or in the physical sciences where confirmation is all that can be had. No one has yet given a theory of truth capable of playing an active rather than token role in formal semantics.

This paper reintroduces an essentially Leibnizian conception of truth as the satisfaction of countably infinite sets of standards, and explores the consequences for truth-based semantics of inference of the standards of truth that are adopted. The account is realized in models that assign to atoms valuations registering, for each standard, whether the atom satisfies it or does not. It is shown that semantically licensed proof-theoretic behavior of propositional connectives depends upon the properties of adopted standards of truth, even when (a) compositionally classical truth-conditions for connectives are retained, and (b) inference is required only to preserve truth.

1 Truth in animadvertising

'What is truth? said jesting Pilate, and would not stay for an answer', wrote Francis Bacon, and did not go on to give one. His implicit assumption, that only a jokester could claim to be at a loss about truth must be a fundamental of theology. Certainly the idea of truth is a hot property for the religionist and a source of warmth for the religious. But in religion this is only what we should expect, for no greater detail can be hoped for in matters of religious doctrines. Since we cannot expect to learn of them, say, what they mean, or what their detailed physical significance is, or how in detail they come about, there can be little more to be said of specifically theological claims than that they are true. At any rate, for the purposes of religion, an assurance that they are true seems to be sufficient.

But even among the secular humourists of philosophy there is a kind of confidence that there is nothing much worth knowing about truth beyond our intuitive understanding. Questions such as 'Are any value-judgements true?' remain contentious. Not that there has been no progress on these scores. Reflective religious adherents realize that they must take on faith that their favourite doctrines mean anything at all. And secular intellectuals have reluctantly accepted that they don't really know what their talk of truth is about. If Bacon thought Pilate must be joking because he thought the answer was obvious, Mill at least characterizes Pilate's question as 'scornful', on the grounds that the inquiry into truth is 'difficult and noble'([10], 98) So, as compared with Bacon's response, Mill's is the more sympathetic to our own doubts on the matter. Whatever one might be inclined to say on the point of nobility, that the nature of truth is difficult can safely be placed beyond dispute.

But we go further than Mill in our exoneration of Pilate. It is merely tiresome of anyone to speak of having come into the world to bear witness to the truth, or to claim to be heard by people who are of the truth. Especially *in gallicantu*, but surely at any time of the day, such talk would set anyone's teeth on edge who had given the matter any thought. So Pilate represents, to the theological outsider at any rate, not so much an icy douche as a refreshing eddy. Truth is no more our bath water than it was Pilate's, and, with all due respect to Jeez and Bacon and all who, like Rupert Brooke, find benison in hot water, we do not know whose bath water it has been.

Now of course at a conversational level we know how the language of *truth* is to be used. So, to disarm the obvious rejoinder we do want to say clearly here no more than what we take to be true, and we want to be neither dishonest nor mistaken. But this can only be to say that we are engaged in the usual way in trying to say something, and we want what we say to satisfy the usual standards for such attempts. That much we can say without a studied theoretical understanding of what it is for something to be true, or of what those propositional somethings are to which truth is to be attributed. We have only what our early upbringing has given us: some command of the language, and some standards of intellectual deportment. It would be delicious to have more, but philosophy has given us no instruction. There were the usual desultory lectures about coherence and correspondence, but neither of these was defined, and we quickly passed on to other topics, those two analyses having been found unsatisfactory and interest having been exhausted.

We need not dwell on the fact that for the physical sciences, truth plays no very serious role. Suffice it to say that although like us, scientists have never had a studied account of what truth is, science has rubbed along, even had the odd success, without one. Certainly scientists want themselves to be understood, particularly by ultimate sources of research funds, as searching for the truth. Who does not? After all, it's true. But if truth plays any more substantial role than that, it is evidently a role for which no deep understanding of its nature is required.

2 Truth in Logic

Now the language of *truth* has always had an honourable place in the culture of logical theorizing. The pursuit of logical truths was traditionally its chief end. But as a part of the subject matter of logic, it was always doomed to give way to the hierarchical language of satisfaction and validity. And in the characterization of the status of metatheorems, or of deep assumptions such as that of the axiom of choice, it does no logically essential work. The label *logically true* has spent its later career seconded to general philosophy as a label for banalities, from which work it seems mercifully to be passing into early retirement.

Again, the notion that a system of inference is sound if its provability relation preserves truth, accounts historically for much of the philosophical interest in such systems, even for philosophers for whom, as for Mill, truth remains nobly problematic. And perhaps for applications where truth has useful conversational traction, that traditional notion of soundness should persist as a desideratum of strategic inferential planning. But the success of a system of logic in such applications does not depend upon a philosophically recognizable doctrine of truth. Its inference relation need only satisfy the condition that for any input for which every function on the left of the turnstile outputs a 1, some function on the right of the turnstile should also output a 1. *Truth-preservation* provides a *reading* of that requirement, but it is only a reading and not an interpretation. It cannot be an interpretation without some independent understanding of what truth is.

To be sure, even logicians distrustful of *truth* or disdainful of metaphysics might yet refer to the set *2* as the set of *truth-values*. After all, the semantic role of the model depends upon its mathematical properties, not upon our conversation about them. But there are also logicians for whom the language of truth is not merely convenient habit or noble end, but a source of uberous conceptual nourishment. And, it hardly needs saying, dreamily steeping in the bath water, one is naturally susceptible to the insidious charms of the rubber ducks, particularly that of truth-preservation. This then is the difference between the bath party and the rest: for the former the goals of logical theory are defined by their philosophically charged reading of the designated value *1*; for the rest, the reading in itself holds no irresistible charm, while the intellectual history of the mathematics is insufficient to dissuade them from wanting to explore alternatives to it.

3   The Preservationist Intervention

That, wisecracks aside, is a pretty fair account of the difference between what have been called the *aletheist* and the *preservationist* approaches to logical theory. The working hypothesis of the former is that the only legitimate semantic aim of any system of logic is that its ⊢ (alternatively its →) should preserve truth; that of the latter that systems of logic should be designed whose ⊢'s and →'s preserve whatever suitable, mathematically well-defined properties interest us in the proposed domains of application. What makes a property suitable must not be circumscribed too closely, but one obvious requirement is that the property, like classical satisfiability, must be *naturally non-monotonic*, that is non-monotonic along set-inclusion; for a property that was *preserved* under the operation of forming supersets would not permit the distinction between inferrability and non-inferrability. Now it is evident that the differences between the two approaches must emerge most dramatically in applications that from time to time encounter inconsistent sets of premises, since, on the face of it, the preservation of truth can place no constraint at all upon inference from premises that cannot be true, nor could the preservation of *any* property that, like truth, was incompatible with inconsistency. Since there are suitable properties that are not incompatible with inconsistency, the preservationist's intuition that inference from inconsistent ensembles can be constrained is at least mathematically well-founded. By contrast, for the aletheist, the corresponding intuition must inevitably require what classicists would regard as a radical model-theoretic adjustment, one that will permit all of an inconsistent ensemble of sentences to be simultaneously satisfied. Since the aletheist is philosophically committed to an alethic reading of satisfaction, their notion of truth must acquiesce in the adjustment. If only truth-preservation constrains inference, then if our intuitions about inferrability tell us that inference from inconsistent ensembles is constrained, then those intuitions about constrainedness must be made to inform our intuitions about the extension of truth, certainly our intuitions about the conditions under which the sentences of the formal language are satisfied, particularly conjunctions and negations. In short, the account of the conditions of what makes a negation or a conjunction true must be modified in such a way as to permit $\alpha \wedge \neg \alpha$ to be true if we are to reject the inference from $\alpha \wedge \neg \alpha$ to arbitrary β.

Now even if we have no very well worked out theoretical account of truth, we can nevertheless have a pretty clear idea of the truth-conditions of *and* and *not*. The reason is that our account of those truth-conditions is grounded in our ordinary conversational understanding of truth. Thus, for example, for the ordinary run of sentences, and in our ordinary way of speaking, a sentence is true if and only if its negation is not. The aletheist must, therefore, send out for some new intuitions based on counterexamples to the old. We do not here wish to argue that none will be forthcoming, only that we not waste the meantime by ignoring alternative avenues of research. The suggestion that some special as yet unformulated sentences of a known physical theory, or those of some abstruse and as yet unformulated physical theory, might not obey that principle is hardly an argument for the elaboration, just on spec., of a highly particular class of models based upon an equally highly particular amendment of our ordinary conceptions. Whence, it might be asked, come the highly particular intuitions as to what should and what should not be theorems? Shall they be decided upon, like the doctrines of the merged churches of St. Asaph and St. Osaph, by a majority vote of the common shareholders, or perhaps by a survey of the ASL?

The model-theoretic recipe (schematically)

$$(\emptyset) \models^{\mathfrak{M}}_x \alpha \wedge \beta(\neg \alpha) \Leftrightarrow \gamma$$

presents only two points of adjustment. We can adjust γ or we can adjust $\models^{\mathfrak{M}}_x$. In a manner of speaking, both sorts of adjustment have been studied. Some have added structural features to the universe of the model, to which γ then makes essential reference, for example the familiar star-semantics for negation.

$$\models^{\mathfrak{M}}_x \neg \alpha \Leftrightarrow \not\models^{\mathfrak{M}}_{x*} \alpha$$

Critics of such strategies complain that although such strategies non-trivially realize sentences of the form $\alpha \wedge \neg \alpha$, they thereby make $\neg(\wedge)$ a mere homonym of the classical negator (conjunctor).

Others have added preservational features to $\models$, requiring it to preserve more than truth. That is, they specify certain properties ϕ of a set Σ (perhaps the value of some coherence-measure $\mu(\Sigma)$ for Σ) and require that if $\Sigma \models \alpha$, then $\mu(\Sigma) \leq \mu(\Sigma \cup \alpha)$. See, for example, [16], [9], and [1]. But since the properties that they propose the $\models$ should preserve are undefined or constant for $\emptyset$, the strategy has no systemically distinct expression for the case of valid wffs. And again, these strategies agree with propositional logic on inferences from singletons. Accordingly they must distinguish between the pair $\{p, \neg p\}$ and $\{p \wedge \neg p\}$. It follows that they can find expression only in implicational systems in which conjunction is non-classical.

Could there be a specifically preservationist approach to implication? Certainly the various variable-sharing requirements of relevant logics could be considered preservationist in spirit. In some vague but comforting way it might be taken to reflect the intuition that an implication requires that the consequent be about some feature of the world of which the antecedent is about some subfeature or vice versa. Implication then is required to preserve a kind of aboutness. The analytical implication of W.T. Parry [11] would be an early example.

A separate preservationist strategy first proposed in [7] and then more fully and systematically explored in [15] and [12] takes a different tack. It focuses upon the character of truth and its preservation. Properties have properties and properties of properties have properties. Whatever sort of property truth is, it presumably has properties and its properties have properties. In [7] truth-values of atoms are taken to be either fixed or unfixed, those of molecular wffs as fixed if no change in the truth-value of an atom will change its truth-value, unfixed else. This yields a 4-valued semantics that distinguishes paradoxes from non-paradoxical contradictions. The implication is required to preserve both truth and fixity. In the other work cited, this idea is extended to an infinite hierarchy by a generalization of Jaśkowski's Γ function (for an account of which *vide* [4].)

Here we consider a third, deeper but related alternative, one that, as we shall see, is not new except perhaps in this interpretation. We adjust $\vDash_x^m$, not by adding preservational restrictions to $\vDash$, or preservational requirements on $\rightarrow$ but by genetically so altering $\vDash$ that even for atomic wffs it is non-primitive: that is, it does more than distinguish 1 from 0. To put the matter another way, we take the usual account to embody what could be called an *unanalysed* truth-theory, and consider the prospects for an *analysed* truth-theory. We propose no particular analysis of truth, indeed profess no reason to suppose that there is any single such analysis that will do for all sentences from those about unanalysed medium-sized objects to those about quantum phenomena.

4 Taking truth seriously

No preservationist has yet proposed a system of inference the $\vdash$ of which did not preserve unanalysed truth. On any preservationist scheme ever proposed, if every wff of Σ is assigned a designated value and $\Sigma \vdash \alpha$, then α

receives a designated value. Our reservation is as to whether that requirement, that way stated, is sufficiently rich to capture any metaphysically satisfying conception of the preservation of truth. Even a eulogist at a funeral would find more to say than that. So presumably more will be required for a resurrection. Does it not behove us to work up an account of truth that will take us beyond the featureless conversational notion and the bare mathematical recognition that whatever else they are, truth and falsity are distinct items? Sentences are composite objects: if they are to be true, then which parts they have in which order must play some role in determining whether they are true or false. So even for the simple sentences of ordinary life, truth must consist in some composition of features. And in the case of physical-theoretical sentences, to which in working life we never apply the language of truth without reservation, the case must be even more difficult to make out: a sentence's lease in a theory has at best an indefinite term; it runs from observation to observation, and can be terminated without notice whenever a more desirable tenant appears, or whenever what it pleases the landlord to call *the edifice* is renovated. We could not find out which of its empirical sentences were genuinely true at any finite stage in the history of a physical theory.

4.1 Leibnizian truth and Meyer logics

Leibniz supposed that all truth was analytic truth: but that the truth of those sentences called logically true is discoverable by finite analysis, while that of those thought of as empirically true requires an infinite analysis of which only God is capable. We make no such adventurous claim here. We suppose only that the notion of truth is infinitely rich, and that in consequence the truth-conditions of sentences have infinitely many bits to them. No one need disagree with this: the usual representation can be recovered by supposing that the infinitely many bits are indistinguishable. So we might have called our account 'leibnizian', not 'Leibnizian', naming it not after Gottfried Wilhelm Freiherr von Leibniz, but after Kleine Buchstaben von Leibniz, the one for whom the leibnizian truth-condition for necessity is named.[1] It will be evident in the sequel that such models might more descriptively be called Cantor models[2], as atoms find their values in the space of denumerable binary sequences.

DEFINITION 1 (Cantor Models). A Cantor propositional model is a pair $\langle U, V \rangle$ where U (the *universe* of the model) is a non-empty set, and V is a *hyper-assignment*, that is, a function from $U \times$ At (At is the set of

---

[1] Michal Arciszewski, reminded us of this historical echo.
[2] The label was suggested by a remark of Oliver Schulte's.

atomic wffs) to 2^N. That is, V assigns to each state/atom pair, x, i a function $V_{(x,i)} : N \to \{0, 1\}$.

Intuitively, the hyper-assignment tells us, for each atom p_i and each object x, which subset of a countably infinite set of tests the atom would pass at that object. The atom p_i would pass test j at x if $V_{(x,i)}(j) = 1$; p_i would not pass test j else. The conditional tense reflects the notion that no actual sequence of experimental tests is envisaged, merely that in order for an atom to be true, it must meet a set of conditions.

Of course this does not yet give us a truth-theory, except perhaps for sentences of the metalanguage asserting that an object-language sentence satisfies a condition, and thus would pass a test. But bear in mind that tests would be passed at objects, the natures of which have not been given. The most we can say of them is that for the language in question, an object in U is expected to provide at most the resources for a countably infinite set of hypothetical tests. So if the leibnizian approach seems to find after all an application for unanalysed truth, it is one that we understand only schematically. And we need make no assumption (though here we do so for simplicity's sake) that the objects do provide such resources. Nothing we have said so far settles the question as to what would count for an atom to pass a test, nor what for a non-atomic wff. Nor does anything we have said so far dictate the relationship between not passing a test, and failing it, or between the failure of p_i and the success of $\neg p_i$. Leibnizian truth-theory may be atomically gappy, though, again, the connection between atomic and molecular gappiness is so far unspecified.

As we have mentioned, we assume, for the sake of simplicity, that the pass/fail conditions for propositional wffs mimics the standard unanalysed truth-conditions. So $V_{(x,i)}$ is extended to a hyper-valuation for Φ (the set of propositional wffs) by:

$$V_{(x,i)}(\neg \alpha) = 1 - V_{(x,i)}(\alpha)$$
$$V_{(x,i)}(\alpha \to \beta) = Max(1 - V_{(x,i)}(\alpha), V_{(x,i)}(\beta))$$

The truth-theoretic question is this: how many and which tests must a wff pass in order to count as true?

In the simplest cases,

$$\models_x^{\mathfrak{M}} \alpha \text{ if } \forall i \in N, V_{(x,i)}(\alpha) = 1;$$
$$\not\models_x^{\mathfrak{M}} \alpha \text{ else.}$$

Evidently on such a truth-theory, truth can be represented as S5 necessity: gappy but not paraconsistent. For some $\{\alpha, \neg\alpha\}$ pairs, neither will pass all of the tests at x, but for no such pairs will both pass every test. On the other hand, at the other extreme, if the truth-theory is such as to give

$$\models_x^{\mathfrak{M}} \alpha \text{ if } \exists i \in N : V_{(x,i)}(\alpha) = 1;$$
$$\not\models_x^{\mathfrak{M}} \alpha \text{ else.}$$

then truth can be represented as $S5$ possibility: paraconsistent but not gappy. For some $\{\alpha, \neg\alpha\}$ pairs, both wffs will pass sufficiently many of the tests at x, but for no such pairs will neither pass sufficiently many. This modal logical connection is also a Jaśkowski connection [5]. Although $\{\alpha, \neg\alpha\}$ is an inconsistent set the closure of which is trivial, in $S5$, $\{\Diamond\alpha, \Diamond\neg\alpha\}$ is classically consistent. Thus a codification of the closure conditions on a set of $S5$ possibilities codifies a paraconsistent inference relation. Evidently such an inference relation does not admit $\wedge$-introduction, the $\Diamond$ of $S5$ being non-aggregative. In this respect, Jaśkowski's approach to paraconsistency is akin to that of some of the preservationist proposals. Apart from the major differences of detail, the larger scale difference between the two approaches is that for Jaśkowski, the non-aggregativity of the $S5$ $\Diamond$ and the consequent exclusion of $\wedge$-introduction are precisely the appeal, whereas for the preservationists, it is typically some preservational requirement that defeats $\wedge$-introduction; it is by no means a grand strategy of the approach. For Jaśkowski it is itself a strategy; for the preservationists it is the consequence of a preservational requirement.

We have said by now enough to reveal that this territory is not completely unfamiliar historically, and other historically canvassed cases will have come to mind.

DEFINITION 2 (truth-profiles). $[\![\,\alpha\,]\!]_x^{\mathfrak{M}}$ (the profile of α at x in $\mathfrak{M}$) is $i \in \mathbf{N} | V_{(x,i)}(\alpha) = 1$.

Then the truth-theories we have considered can be given as:

$$[1] \models_x^{\mathfrak{M}} \alpha \Leftrightarrow [\![\,\alpha\,]\!]_x^{\mathfrak{M}} = \mathbf{N};$$

and

$$[2] \models_x^{\mathfrak{M}} \alpha \Leftrightarrow [\![\,\alpha\,]\!]_x^{\mathfrak{M}} \neq \emptyset.$$

but a truth-theory could plausibly be labelled *intuitionistic* (again lower-case) if it adopted as its standard:

$$[3] \models_x^{\mathfrak{M}} \alpha \Leftrightarrow [\![\,\alpha\,]\!]_x^{\mathfrak{M}} \text{ is convex and cofinite}$$

since by this standard, α is true iff α is such that it would pass some test or other and thereafter pass every test. And, one might be tempted to say, so on. Leibnizian truth looks like leibnizian necessity, and the generalizations look like the generalizations of leibnizian necessity with necessity masquerading as truth, and truth masquerading as the passing of tests. We will say more later both about the air of familiarity and the persistent whiff of modality. For the moment we come to rest with a simple truth-conditional profile that does not on its face look like a disguised form of any independently known necessity. It is a particular instance of what might be called a *practical truth-theory*, one that recognizes the imperfection, perhaps the imperfectability, of working theoretical languages. It treats a sentence of a theoretical language as true, as it were, *for practical purposes*, if it satisfies sufficiently many sufficiently important conditions. We consider here an idealized and simplified form of such a truth-theory in which all that truth demands is a sufficient accumulation of satisfied conditions, more particularly, in this case,

$$[4] \models_{x}^{\mathfrak{M}} \alpha \Leftrightarrow [\![\alpha]\!]_{x}^{\mathfrak{M}} \text{ is infinite.}$$

Observe first of all that on such a truth-theory the set of valid formulae, that is, the set of wffs true at every point in every model, is the set of classical tautologies. Thus this sort of truth is systemically classical, and therefore, for example, all instances of $p \to (\neg p \to q)$ are valid and *modus ponens* preserves validity. Nevertheless, the associated entailment is paraconsistent, since, as a moment's reflection reveals, *modus ponens*, like other non-trivially multi-premiss rules, does not in general preserve this kind of analysed truth. Neither, for example, does the system admit unrestricted $\wedge$-introduction. Now a system, one for which *mp* preserves validity, but not truth, is called a *Meyer system*.[3] So we can call the logic for the truth-theory [4] MPL, for Meyerized PL.

A word or two *de modo ponendo*. Corresponding to the preservation of validity is the proof-theoretic principle that MPL-provable implications preserve MPL-provability. That is, the condition [mp]

$$\frac{\alpha, \alpha \to \beta}{\beta}$$

is a closure condition on the set of theorems. But corresponding to the semantic feature that that condition is not a closure condition on the set of truths, is the proof-theoretic restriction that *mp* cannot be invoked unrestrictedly in MPL proofs. As a closure condition on MPL-theorems, the

---

[3] So called for Bob Meyer, who professes not to like *modus ponens*.

condition [mp] is the condition that provable implication preserves provability. But observe that valid implication preserves truth as well as validity, and correspondingly, a weakened form of *mp*, one citing $\alpha \to \beta$ as the last line of a proof from $\emptyset$ can justify a line of an MPL-proof. Furthermore, semantically, true implication preserves the truth of validities. So if $\vDash \alpha$ and $\vDash_x^{\mathfrak{M}} \alpha \to \beta$, then $\vDash_x^{\mathfrak{M}} \beta$, and correspondingly, weakened *mp* can justify β as a line, if the α line input ends a proof of α from $\emptyset$. But a set of tests that alternately favoured $\alpha \wedge \neg \beta$ and $\neg \alpha \wedge \neg \beta$, would make α true, and would make $\alpha \to \beta$ true, but would not make β true.

A similar fate meets other multiple-premiss rules in MPL. The truth-theory is importantly holistic: pigeon-holistic. It admits all and only such multiple-premiss rules as are forced by pigeon-hole arguments. The upshot is that MPL takes us as near as damn to inferential explosions, but always denies us the final inferential ingredient.

The lesson is this: with a reformed truth-theory, even propositional logic is paraconsistent. On this simple diagnosis of classical propositional logic, the fault lies not in the interpretation of the connectives, but in the place of the interpretation within a theory of truth.

THEOREM 3 (The fundamental theorem for MPL). *Every PL-consistent wff is true in a Cantor model.*

Proof. Let α be a PL-consistent wff. Let $E = \{\beta_1, \ldots, \beta_i, \ldots\}$ be an enumeration of the set Φ of wffs, and Σ_0 be the maximal consistent extension of α along E. Now let $\gamma_1, \ldots, \gamma_i, \ldots$ be the natural ordering, induced by E, of the set $\{\alpha \wedge \beta \mid \beta \in \Phi \& \{\alpha, \beta\} \nvdash \bot\}$. Let Σ_i be the maximal consistent extension of γ_i along E.

Let $\mathfrak{M} = \langle \{\Sigma_i\}, V \rangle$, where V, the hyper-assignment, constantly assigns to each Σ_i, p_j pair, the function $V_{\{i,j\}}$, defined by

$$\forall i, j, V_{\{i,j\}} = 1 \text{ if } p_j \in \Sigma_i;$$
$$= 0 \text{ else.}$$

Evidently, $\forall \beta \in \Phi, \forall_{i=0}^{\infty} \Sigma_i \vDash_{\Sigma_i}^{\mathfrak{M}} \beta \iff [\![\beta]\!]_x^{\mathfrak{M}}$ is infinite. In particular, $\forall_{i=0}^{\infty} \Sigma_i \vDash_{\Sigma_i}^{\mathfrak{M}} \alpha$. ∎

4.2 The modal logical connexion

The truth-theory of [4] alone among those so far cited has no obviously modal inspiration. However, that truth-theory is equivalent to one according to which the natural order of the set of conditions on truth is taken to be an ordering of importance and given alethic significance, as in

$$[5]\ \models_{\overline{x}}^{\mathfrak{M}} \alpha \Leftrightarrow \forall y \notin [\![\, \alpha \,]\!]_x^{\mathfrak{M}}, \exists z \in [\![\, \alpha \,]\!]_x^{\mathfrak{M}} : y < z.$$

Once again, truth is paraconsistent; validity is not, but multiple premiss rules cannot unrestrictedly be brought to bear inferentially, since they do not preserve truth. In fact the logic corresponding to this truth-theory is MPL.

But [5] once again wears the look, or at least the smell, of modality. In fact it apes the semantic idiom of natural frames:

$$[6]\ \models_{\overline{x}}^{\mathfrak{M}} \Box \alpha \Leftrightarrow \forall y \notin [\![\, \alpha \,]\!]_x^{\mathfrak{M}}, \exists z \in [\![\, \alpha \,]\!]_x^{\mathfrak{M}} : y <_x z$$

the set of validities of which is completely axiomatized by the weak self-dual system that has elsewhere been labelled $SCon$ ('S' for 'Segerberg'; For an account, see [6].)

[N] $\vdash \Box\top$
[RM] $\vdash \alpha \to \beta \Rightarrow \vdash \Box\alpha \to \Box\beta$
[Con] $\vdash \neg\Box\bot$.

Now one reading of [5] has as the requirement for the truth of a sentence that for every test that it fails, there is a more significant one that it passes, as [6] has as the requirement for (deontic) necessity of a sentence that for every state in which it fails to obtain, there is a better one in which it does. It suggests as a reading for $\models_{\overline{x}}^{\mathfrak{M}} \alpha$, that α *ought to be regarded as true*. Lou Goble [2] has independently presented the same modal system in a related semantic idiom that adopts the truth-condition

$$[7]\ \models_{\overline{x}}^{\mathfrak{M}} \Box\alpha \Leftrightarrow \exists y \in [\![\, \alpha \,]\!]_x^{\mathfrak{M}}\ \&\ \forall z, y <_x z \Rightarrow z \in [\![\, \alpha \,]\!]_x^{\mathfrak{M}}.$$

The truth-theory of

$$[8]\ \models_{\overline{x}}^{\mathfrak{M}} \alpha \Leftrightarrow \exists y \in [\![\, \alpha \,]\!]_x^{\mathfrak{M}}\ \&\ \forall z, y <_x z \Rightarrow z \in [\![\, \alpha \,]\!]_x^{\mathfrak{M}}.$$

which is to [7] as [5] is to [6], is apparently stricter than that of [6], in that it requires eventual convexity of $[\![\, \alpha \,]\!]^{\mathfrak{M}}$, nevertheless corresponds also to MPL. The pigeon-hole strictures of the earlier discussion apply here also, save only to the non-convex portion of $[\![\, \alpha \,]\!]^{\mathfrak{M}}$.

Again the logic of $SCon$ is the intersection of the logics of the $KnCon$ systems of weakly aggregative deontic logics. These are the logics which adjoin to $SCon$ instances of the schema

$$[K_n]\ \Box p_1 \wedge \cdots \wedge \Box p_{n+1} \to \Box \tfrac{2}{n+1}(p_1, \ldots, p_{n+1})$$

where $\frac{2}{n+1}(p_1,\ldots,p_{n+1})$ is the disjunction of all pairwise conjunctions of p_i, $p_j (1 \leqslant i \neq j \leqslant n+1)$. The interest of this family of logics is that the system Kn is completely axiomatized by the specification of a paraconsistent closure condition, n-forcing, on necessities.

$$\Sigma \mmodels_n \alpha \Leftrightarrow \forall \pi \in \Pi_n(\Sigma), \exists c \in \pi : c \vdash \alpha.$$

Thus, system *SCon* is therefore completely axiomatizable by the specification that, for every n, the set of necessities is closed under n-forcing, together with the postulate that $\bot$ is not a necessity.

5 The Moral

We understand *necessity* no better than we understand truth. *Necessarily alpha* is therefore a reading for $\Box\alpha$, and not an interpretation of it. In any of the uncountably many modal logics lacking the principle [T] $\Box\alpha \to \alpha$, we do not even have the excuse that that fundamental assumption of alethic necessity is satisfied, but needs must apply other Hellenic modifiers (*deontic, doxastic, stochastic* and so on) to suit the case, but we have nothing but intuition to tell us which principles distinguish the readings, nor which of the principles that a given semantic idiom imposes are principles that are wanted. In general we have no grounds for strong convictions about how the various semantic idiomata should be understood. One should, therefore, feel free to challenge the labels under which these systems are marketed. If systems that include all instances of [T] are to be called systems of (kinds of) necessary truth, why should systems lacking [T] be referred to as weak systems of necessity rather than as weak systems of (kinds of) truth?

Evidently a very strong paraconsistent propositional system is representable in the modal system *SCon*. Evidently, stronger such systems are representable in its *KnCon* extensions, stronger, that is, in admitting mixed and/or-introductions that *SCon* does not allow. And again, evidently, each such paraconsistent system can be thought of as introducing a distinctive theory of analysed truth, not, to be sure, one representable by hyper-assignments to $2^{\mathbf{N}}$, but an analysed truth-theory nevertheless.

Now all these technicalia will be of interest, no doubt, to those who find this sort of thing interesting. But it all prompts some observations both skeptical and hopeful. The skeptical observation is that we understand the notion of necessity no better than we understand the notion of truth. In fact, the Lady Chapel of alethic modal logic harbours all of the theological dustbunnies that blow about the larger shrine. The hopeful observations are, first, that the formal study of modal logic also comprises logics that are not alethic. Secondly, that therefore in studying the formal semantics of a mathematically abstract notion of necessity through the study of frame theory, formalists have been studying at a useful level of abstraction, the mathematical structure of theories of truth.

We can revisit the classic representation theorems in the light of this observation: Gödel's representation of Intuitionistic logic in $S4$ and Goldblatt's representation (in [3]) of orthologic in Brouwersche modal logic can be understood as demonstrations of the mathematical structures of the truth-theories appropriate to the intended domains of application: constructive mathematics on the one hand, and quantum physics on the other. That an atom p_i of intuitionistic logic should require for the representation a translation into $\Box q_i$, that an atom of orthologic should require translation into $\Box \Diamond q_i$ can be interpreted as evidence that the atoms of some languages, perhaps the very languages where the dialetheists hoped for examples of mathematically or physically realized contradictions, are capable of being understood within particular analysed truth-theories.

We can also revisit the Kn systems. There we will now discover paraconsistent implicational logics, where before we found only modal representations of the familiar illative systems of forcing.

Acknowledgements

The research of the second author was supported by Social Sciences and Humanities Research Council, under Grant No. 752-2000-2237. We thank J.F. Pelletier and Oliver Schulte for useful comments.

BIBLIOGRAPHY

[1] Bryson Brown, *Yes, Virginia, there really are paraconsistent logics.* The Journal of Philosophical Logic (1999) 489-500.
[2] Lou Goble, *Multiplex semantics for deontic logic* Nordic Journal of Philosophical Logic (2000)113-134.
[3] R.I. Goldblatt, *Semantic Analysis of Orthologic.* Journal of Philosophical Logic, 1974.
[4] S. Jaśkowski, *Recherches sur le système de la logique intuitioniste.* Congrès International de Philosophique Scientifique, Paris, 1936, 58-61.
[5] S. Jaśkowski, *Propositional calculus for contradictory deductive systems.* Studia Logica (1969) 143-57.
[6] R.E. Jennings, *Natural Frames and Self-dual Logics.* Fundamenta Informaticae 46 (2001) 1-10.
[7] R.E. Jennings and D.K. Johnston, *Paradox-tolerant Logic.* Logique et Analyse, 1983.
[8] R.E. Jennings and P.K. Schotch, *Some remarks on (weakly) weak modal logics.* Notre Dame Journal of formal Logic. 1981, 309-314.
[9] R.E. Jennings and P.K. Schotch, *Preservation of coherence.* Studia Logica, 1984.
[10] John Stuart Mill, A System of Logic. Longmans, Green and Co. Ltd., London, 8th Edition, 1872.
[11] W.T. Parry, *Ein Axiomensystem für eine neue Art von Implikation (analytische Implikation).* Ergebnisse eines mathematischen Kolloquiums, 1933, 5-6.
[12] D. Sarenac and R.E. Jennings *Beyond truth(-preservation)* Proceedings of WCP II. (To appear) 2001
[13] D. Sarenac and R.E. Jennings *Preservatioin, Implication, and Truth* Proceedings of International Conference on AI, Volume II. H.R. Arabnia (Ed.) 2001

[14] D. Sarenac and R.E. Jennings *The Preservation of meta-valuational properties and the meta-valuational properties of truth.* John Woods and Bryson Brown, eds. Logical Cosequence: Rival Approaches, Hermes Science Publishing, Oxford, 2001. 261-274.
[15] D. Sarenac, *A Preservationist Approach to Implication.*, M.A. Thesis Simon Fraser University, Burnaby, British Columbia, Canada, August 2000.
[16] P.K. Schotch and R.E. Jennings *Inference and necessity.* The Journal of Philosophical Logic, 1980, 327-340.

Ontology and the Theory of Meaning

KIRK LUDWIG AND ERNEST LEPORE

> You say: the point isn't the word, but its meaning, and you think of the meaning as a thing of the same kind as the word, though also different from the word. Here the word, there the meaning. The money, and the cow that you buy with it. (But contrast: money, and its use.)   Wittgenstein, 1961

1 Introduction

Ever since Frege it has been a persistent feature of much theorizing in the theory of meaning to introduce entities as finely individuated as equivalence classes of synonymous expressions for the purpose of helping us to understand how we understand the languages we speak. There are been notable skeptics of this tradition, such as Quine [2; 3], and in a different, less extreme fashion, Davidson [1], and also, in a different tradition, as our epigram indicates, Wittgenstein [?, #2383]. Quine urged complete nihilism about not only meanings as entities, but about even the notion of synonymy and analyticity. Davidson has urged all the work of the theory of meaning can be done within a framework that makes no essential appeal to meanings as entities. This paper advances a general argument, inspired by some remarks of Davidson, to show that appeal to meanings as entities in the theory of meaning is neither necessary nor sufficient for carrying out the tasks of the theory of meaning. The crucial point is that appeal to meanings as entities fails utterly to provide us with an understanding of any expression of a language, *except* insofar as we pick it out with an expression we understand which we tacitly recognize to be a translation of the term whose meaning we want to illuminate by the appeal to assigning to it a meaning. The meaning drops out as irrelevant: the work is done, and can only be done, by matching terms already understood with terms they translate. This makes way for seeing a statement of appropriate knowledge about a truth theory doing all the work that needs to be done and that can be done in the theory of meaning, and shows that there is an interesting sense in which Wittgenstein's claim in the *Tractatus Logico-Philosophicus* [4], that the facts about how our language represents the world cannot be stated but can only be shown, is true.

2 The Project

The project of the theory of meaning, broadly construed, is to explain how we understand the languages we speak. Conceived as a philosophical project, we want to abstract away from facts about how any particular set of speakers understand the languages they speak and focus on facts about speakers and languages as such, that is, about what's involved in any conceivable speaker understanding a language. This involves saying both how it is that speakers understand individual words, and how speakers understand complex expressions, ultimately, and centrally, sentences constructed from them.

The introduction of meanings as entities to help us understand individual words seems on the face of it fatuous. We might stretch a point and allow as Russell did that the meaning of a proper name is the individual it refers to, so that we are indeed informed of the meaning of 'Sir Walter Scott' by being informed that it refers to Sir Walter Scott–provided that we can do this in a way that does not simply use the words whose meaning we want to be informed about. We might point, for example, to the individual, saying, "That's him," or identify him as the author of *Waverley*. Let us try to explain our understanding of a noun such as 'author', however, by saying it is the sense or meaning of 'author', and to explain our understanding of the word by saying it consists in "grasping" its meaning, and it is immediately apparent that we are merely playing with words. No one, given these explanations, would be any the wiser about what 'author' means in English or what understanding it comes to.

Meanings, construed as entities, begin to look more useful when we come to try to explain how we understand complex expressions on the basis of our understanding of the simpler expressions that are combined in them and their arrangement. Individual words are meaningful. The meaningful complexes in a language obviously are understood on the basis of their parts and mode of combination. Assign the individual words meanings, i.e., things which we call meanings, and we can then assign to the complex a meaning which we think of as composed in some suitably abstract sense out of the meanings of the words, or at least as a function of them. We have then a structured entity at the level of meaning that corresponds to the structured syntax of the complex expressions. The illusion of understanding is increased when we realize that this makes available to us the apparatus of quantificational theory in giving a systematic account of the meanings of complex expressions on the basis of the meanings of their parts and mode of combination. The sense of understanding is illusory, however, as we will show, because what is essential to this approach can be preserved while leaving us completely in the dark about the language for which we give such a theory. To show this, we first lay down a criterion of adequacy on a meaning theory which is to enable us to understand complex expressions on the basis of understanding their parts and mode of combination:

> [C] A meaning theory M for a language L is adequate only if it enables someone who understands it to understand any potential utterance of a sentence in the language given an understanding of its primitive expressions.

In the next section, we give a sample meaning theory, in a neo-Fregean style, that satisfies [C], for a compositional language with an infinity of non-synonymous sentences. In the section following, we show that what is essential to it, the systematic assignment of meanings as entities to expressions, can be retained *without* satisfying [C], and identify the crucial mechanism at work in satisfying [C]. We then draw some general conclusions about the inutility of meanings in the theory of meaning, where illumination in the theory of meaning is to be sought, and what kinds are available.

3 A Neo-Fregean Meaning Theory

Davidson is famous for having claimed that there are insuperable difficulties in the way of formulating a compositional meaning theory which quantifies over meanings. In fact, it is relatively easy to do so, for a well-understood language, with the resources of classical quantification theory, if the only object is to generate true theorems for each object language sentence of the form [M].

> [M] s means p.

The trouble is not that it cannot be done, but that the meanings we quantify over do no real work. But first we show that it can be done.

The theory we present in the present section treats every meaningful word unit as having assigned to it an entity which is understood to be its meaning. These entities are to be individuated as finely as equivalence classes of synonymous expressions, and thus as finely as Fregean senses. Departing from Frege, we will treat expressions as referring to their meanings. We will suppose also, in contrast to Frege, that the meaning of a proper name is just its referent (though this is inessential). The basic idea is to introduce a rule giving the meaning of a complex expression as a function of the meaning of predicative terms, treated as functional terms, and their argument terms.

Take the simplest case of a subject-predicate sentence. Let us interpret 'means' as 'refers to'. We begin with the following axioms.

A1. Means('Ceasar', *Ceasar*)

A2. Means('x is ambitious', *x is ambitious*)

A3. For any proper name α, for any predicate P, the result of placing α in argument position for P means the value of the meaning of P given the meaning of α as argument.

A4. The value of any sentential function for an argument denoted by a referring term is denoted by the expression that results from placing the referring term in the argument place of the sentential function.

Instantiate A3 to 'Ceasar' and 'is ambitious' to get 1,

1. 'Ceasar is ambitious' means the value of the meaning of 'is ambitious' given the meaning of 'Ceasar' as argument.

The meaning of 'is ambitious' is *is ambitious*, and the meaning of 'Ceasar' is *Ceasar*, by A2 and A1 respectively. The value of the meaning of 'is ambitious' given the meaning of 'Ceasar' as argument is *Ceasar is ambitious*, by A4. So, we can infer 2.

2. 'Ceasar is ambitious' means *Ceasar is ambitious*.

Now, let us add axioms for connectives, which we will treat as having meanings which take us from meanings of sentences or formulas to meanings of sentences or formulas. An axiom for negation and for conjunction will suffice for the purposes of illustration (here 'P', 'Q', and 'S' are variables just as 'x' is above–not schematic letters).

A5. Means('P and Q', *P and Q*)

A6. Means('$\sim S$', $\sim S$)

A7. For any binary connective $\Delta(x, y)$, and any formulae φ, ψ, the result of placing φ and ψ in the places of 'x' and 'y' respectively in $\Delta(x, y)$ means the value of the meaning of Δ given the meaning of φ and of ψ as first and second arguments.

A8. For any unary connective $\Delta(x)$, any formula φ, the result of placing φ in the place of 'x' and in $\Delta(x)$ means the value of Δ given the meaning of φ as argument.

A9. The value of any truth function for a sequence of arguments denoted by a sequence of formulae is denoted by the expression that results from placing the formulae sequentially in the argument places of the truth function.

Instantiate A8 to '∼' and 'Caesar is ambitious' to get, 3.

3. '∼ Ceasar is ambitious' means the value of the meaning of '∼' given the meaning of 'Ceasar is ambitious' as argument.

With A9, this gives us 4,

4. '∼Ceasar is ambitious' means ∼*Ceasar is ambitious*.

Now let's introduce an axiom for a universal quantifier.

A10. Means('For all $x : F$', *For all x: F*)

A11. For any unary quantifier $Q : F$, any formula φ, the result of placing φ in the place of 'F' in $Q : F$ means the value of the meaning of Q given the meaning of φ as argument.

A12. The value of the meaning of any unary quantifier for an argument denoted by a formula is denoted by the expression that results from placing the formula in the argument place of the quantifier.

Instantiate A11 to 'For all $x : F$' and '∼ x is ambitious' to get:

5. 'For all $x :∼ x$ is ambitious' means the value of 'For all $x : F$' given the meaning of '∼ x is ambitious' as argument.

From A12 we get 6.

6. 'For all $x :∼ x$ is ambitious' means *For all x: ∼x is ambitious*.

This clearly generalizes to relational predicates and multiple quantifiers. Every expression is assigned a meaning, and we can produce for any complex expression an assignment of meaning that seems intuitively to give the right result.

The theory can be generalized so that it is given in a language that does not embed the object language. We need to modify A4, A9, and A12 in this case. We indicate the modification to A4 as a guide.

A4'. The value of the meaning of any sentential function for an argument denoted by a referring term is denoted by any expression that results from placing a term that refers to the argument in the argument place of a term that refers to the meaning of the sentential function.

This enables us then to use axioms of the form of A1 and A2 to produce a term in the metalanguage that refers to the meaning of the sentence 'Ceasar is ambitious' in the object language so as to produce a theorem of the form of 2 with a metalanguage sentence on the right hand side even when the metalanguage does not embed the object language. Thus, for example, we might replace A1 and A2 with A1′ and A2′ (understanding 'Means' and other semantic predicates relative to the object language, regimented French in this case).

A1′.   Means('César', *Ceasar*)

A2′.   Means('*x* est ambitieux', *x is ambitious*)

4   The Inutility of Meanings

Thus a meaning theory that works by way, it seems, of assigning meanings to every expression of the language and which exhibits the meanings of complex expressions as a function of the meanings of their parts and mode of combination. It would appear that the appeal to meanings as entities in the theory of meaning has been vindicated.

Would that it were so. But, first, the appeal to meanings is not what does the work. Second, what work is done could be done (almost) as well by a translation theory. Third, a theory that does just as well is easily constructed exploiting exactly the features of the original which was important for its fulfilling its purpose, without, however, any quantification over meanings.

To show that the appeal to meanings is not doing the work, we alter the base clauses of the theory. The base clauses still assign meanings to entities systematically, and still allow us to systematically say what each expression of the language, simple and complex, means, that is to say, what meaning each expression has, when we understand this as what meaning entity is assigned. But it does this in a way that provides no insight into how to understand any expression of the language. The alterations are as follows (note that the metalanguage names 'Brutus', 'Cassius', 'Antony', and 'Portia' are names of *meanings*, not people):

A1*.   Means('Ceasar', *Ceasar*)

A2*.   Means('*x* is ambitious', *Brutus*)

A5*.   Means('*P* and *A*', *Cassius*)

A6*.   Means('∼ *S*', *Antony*)

A10*. Means('For all $x : F$', *Portia*)

Now, with A3, A7, A8, and A11, we can derive 7-9.

7. 'Ceasar is ambitious' means the value of Brutus given Ceasar as argument.

8. '∼ Ceasar is ambitious' means the value of Antony given the value of Brutus given Ceasar as argument.

9. 'For all x :∼ x is ambitious' means the value of Portia given as argument the value of Antony given Brutus as argument.

It is clear that 7-9 do not enable us to understand any of the object language expressions. Yet, one cannot fault them for failing to tell us, as least as well as the original theory, what each expression of the object language means, in the sense of telling us what meaning entity is assigned to it.

What is the crucial difference? In our original theory, we assigned meanings to primitive expressions in our object language by using expressions in the metalanguage which were in the same grammatical category, and which it was tacitly assumed were translations of the object language terms. This is what enabled us to understand the object language primitive expressions. A4, A9, and A12 then told us that certain forms of complex expressions in the metalanguage which we already understand had the same meaning as certain corresponding expressions in the object language, thereby allowing us to match systematically complex object language expressions with complex metalanguage expressions alike in meaning, i.e., synonymous with them. But the key to our being able to come to know what the complex object language expressions meant lay in our already understanding the metalanguage expressions in the sense in which we wished to understand the object language expressions and being given information sufficient to know which metalanguage expression was synonymous with which object language expression. Being told what meanings, construed as entities, each expression is to be assigned, is not sufficient. Being given a way to match an object language expression with an already understood metalanguage expression that we know is synonymous with it was. The assignment of entities to expressions, which was to be the key to a theory of meaning, turns out to have been merely a way of matching object language expression with metalanguage expressions thought of as used (in referring to their own meanings), so that we are given an object language expression and a matched metalanguage expression we understand, in a context which ensures they are synonymous.

That nothing more is involved can be shown by noting that the original theory gives all the information we need to write out a shorter recursive translation theory. To increase interest, let us shift to a regimented fragment of French as the object language. (We use brackets for corner quotes.)

T1. Translates('César', 'Ceasar') [cf. A1]

T2. Translates('x est ambitieux', 'x is ambitious') [cf. A2]

T3. For any P, α, translates($[\alpha P]$, trans(α)_trans(P)). [cf. A3–4]

T5. For any P, Q, translates($[P$ et $Q]$, trans(P)_' and '_trans(Q)])

T6. For any S, translates($[\sim S]$, '$\sim$'_trans(S)) [cf. A7–9]

T7. For any F, translates([Chaque x : F], 'For all x: '_trans(F)]) [cf. A10–12]

In the above, 'translates' is a two place predicate relating an expression to an expression that translates it (we suppress explicit relativization to the two languages here). 'trans(x)' is a function that yields the translation of the object language expression x into the metalanguage, where for all y, trans $(x) = y$ iff translates (x, y). Relative to knowledge of the metalanguage, this provides as much information as our original theory. It might be said that there is still a crucial difference, however, namely, that what the original says is sufficient whereas what the translation theory says is not. But this difference has to do only with the fact that using expressions to refer to their own meanings makes it look as if to understand the meaning statements we must understand the used expressions, so that understanding the theory gives us knowledge of the meanings of the relevant translations into the metalanguage of the object language sentences. However, in effect, the one grip we have on what entity is supposed to be associated with an object language expression is by way of a description we can construct using the metalanguage expression, namely, in the case of, e.g., A2, 'the meaning of "is ambitious"'. Reference to the meaning, whatever it is, is beside the point. We think of the meaning in this way, but we understand the expression we use to pick it out, and that understanding and the assumption of synonymy is what enables us to understand the object language expression.

With a minor modification to our translation theory, we can duplicate this effect of using the metalanguage expression without appeal to meaning entities. For this purpose, we replace 'translates' with 'means'. But we do not interpret 'means' as a predicate relating an expression and a meaning, but as a predicate relating an expression and another expression, which, however, we require someone to understand in order to understand the sentence. We write this, for example, as follows.

'est ambitieux' means *is ambitious*

This is true just in case 'est ambitieux' in its language is translated by 'is ambitious' in the language of the sentence. The requirement that one understand 'is ambitious' to understand the sentence is simply an additional convention governing its use. Thus, we have the effect of using 'is ambitious' in the sentence, though its usual extensional properties are irrelevant to the truth of the containing sentence.

Now we rewrite the translation theory with some additional axioms to provide a meaning theory as follows.

T1. Means('César', Ceasar)

T2. Means('x est ambitieux', x is ambitious)

T3. For any P, α, means($[\alpha P]$, means(α)⌣means(P)).

T5. For any P, Q, means($[P$ et $Q]$, means(P)⌣' and '⌣Q])

T6. For any S, means($[\sim S]$, '$\sim$'⌣means(S))

T7. For any F, means([Chaque $x : F$], 'For all x: '⌣means(F)])

Where 'means' has two arguments it is the relational term, where it has one it is a function yielding as value the metalanguage expression that translates the object language expression which is its argument. We add that the convention for substituting for a variable in the context following means is to substitute the expression which is the value of the variable without quotation marks but in italics (note that in T3–T7 we have descriptions in the second argument place for 'means', and thus quantifiers binding the variable there). This signals the convention that the expression is both mentioned and understood. (Consider the standard use of quotation marks for dialog, where a similar convention seems to hold.) This theory allows us to infer, e.g.,

'Chaque $x :\sim x$ est ambitieux' means *for all $x :\sim x$ is ambitious*

and so on. The features of our original theory which quantified over meanings which enabled it to serve the purposes of helping us to understand object language sentences have been preserved, but without any commitment to meanings.

5 General Methodological Conclusions

The first conclusion we wish to draw from this is that quantification over meanings in the theory of meaning serves no real purpose. The introduction of meanings as entities is not sufficient to enable us to understand object language sentences. The introduction of meanings as entities is not necessary. The illusion that they are helpful is generated by choosing terms that refer to meanings in the metalanguage in a way that matches object language terms with metalanguage terms in the same semantic category which are understood to be translations of the object language terms. The use of them to refer to meanings gets them out of quotation marks so that we have the illusion that in understanding the theory we must understand the terms that refer to the meanings. Thus the theory seems to state something knowledge of which is sufficient for understanding object language terms. But it is not much different from a translation theory together with knowledge of one of the languages. And the crucial elements, matching object language sentences with metalanguage sentences that translate them, but using the sentences in a way that requires understanding them in understanding the theory, can be replicated without the pointless quantification over meanings.

One thing this shows is that to give a compositional meaning theory for a language, it is necessary to have a metalanguage we understand which has the same expressive resources as the object language. A theory that aims to produce from statements about primitives and the complexes we can grammatically form from them what every expression means in a way that ensures that understanding the theory helps us understand the language requires basically that we match object language sentences with metalanguage sentences "in use" in a way that enables us to see that the metalanguage sentences are translations of the object language sentences. There is no way to state what an object language expression means (as opposed to explaining it, which we do when explaining the meaning of an expression to someone who knows no expression with that meaning) without using terms the same in meaning as it, and so understood. The understanding is achieved not by sudden grasp of an abstract object associated with the expression, but by showing what it means by means of an expression the same in meaning as it.

This is how the project of giving a theory of meaning by way of an interpretive truth theory works. We use axioms in the truth theory which employ terms in the metalanguage which are translations of them, or provide relative to contextual parameters the contribution of the expression in use to what is said in using it. The "minimal" proof of a T-sentence then provides a sentence in the metalanguage we can know to be synonymous with the object language sentence. The truth theory uses the metalanguage expressions used to give truth conditions, ensuring that we are, in light of our knowledge about the truth theory, in a position to interpret the object language sentence (perhaps relative to an occasion of use for a context sensitive language). But the use of a truth theory has an additional advantage. For the proof of the T-sentence from assignments of reference and satisfaction conditions to primitive expressions, non-recursive and recursive, exhibits how the expressions in the object language sentence contribute, through their meaning, mirrored in the metalanguage expressions, to the extensional properties of the terms relevant to determining whether the sentence is true or false. We gain genuine insight in this way into the compositional mechanisms of the language, how truth conditions for sentences are built up compositionally out of extensional properties of their component expressions and their mode of combination. Our sample meaning theory above (the one dispensing with meanings), while it matches object with synonymous metalanguage sentences, does not exhibit any information about the systematic contribution of expressions in the object language to conditions under which they are true. It is not clear how else to get this kind of illumination than by way of an interpretive truth theory. The truth theory does not state any of this, of course; it rather shows it. If we are right, there is no other route to the same effect. Thus, as we said at the outset, there is an interesting sense in which, as Wittgenstein maintained in the *Tractatus Logico-Philosophicus*, facts about how our language represents the world cannot be stated but can only be shown.

Further illumination of what it is for words to mean what they do (to use Davidson's phrase), comes not from inventing abstract objects associated with expressions, but by considering what facts are relevant to our different understandings of the different words and expressions we use and how we understand each one in the specific way we do. This observation is not of course a novel one. But there have been two poles of thought in the theory of meaning about where illumination of meaning is to be sought. One has been the appeal to meaning entities; but this we have shown to be sterile. The meanings are superfluous, and what work is done is done by matching sentences with understood sentences understood to be alike in meaning. Further understanding of the sources of meaning must be sought by relating talk about meaning to the things we do with words and to our thoughts and extralinguistic purposes.

BIBLIOGRAPHY

[1] Davidson, D. (1984). Truth and Meaning, *Inquiries into Truth and Interpretation* (pp. 17-36). New York: Clarendon Press.

[2] Quine, W. V. O. (1953). Two Dogmas of Empiricism, *From a Logical Point of View* (2nd ed.). Cambridge: Harvard University Press.
[3] Quine, W. V. O. (1960). *Word & Object*. Cambridge: MIT Press.
[4] Wittgenstein, L. (1961). *Tractatus Logico-Philosophicus*. London: Routledge & Kegan Paul Ltd.

Tarski's Grelling and the T-Strategy

GREG RAY

Tarski's use of the liar paradox is famous, but officially it is the Grelling paradox that has final pride of place in Tarski's argument, not the Liar at all. Tarski explicitly gives argumentation that adverts to the liar argument, but it is an alternative argument—one he only hints at and which adverts to the Grelling—which he says has the advantage. In this paper, we will examine how the Grelling might be used in place of the Liar in Tarski's argument for his *exact indefinability thesis*, and assess in what way the difference might be significant. In brief, the results of this investigation will be as follows. First, the version of the Grelling that Tarski sketches does not serve the purpose, but we can construct a version that does. With it, one can argue for a strengthened version of the exact indefinability thesis just as Tarski alleges. Second, a simple variant of Tarski's Liar would have done just as well. Third, the success in this regard of the Grelling variant of Tarski's argument exacerbates a tension in Tarski and undermines the typical justifications for Convention T. This vexed, but noted, tension in Tarski is between Tarski's T-*strategy* (which underlies Convention T) for the truth definition problem, and the fact that not all T-sentences are true. We can pose this as a problematical question: what is the status of T-sentences such that i) it makes sense to insist that an adequate truth definition should entail them, even though ii) it is knowable apriori that not all of the T-sentences in question are true? The apriority alluded to in the second clause is the fruit of Tarski's success with the Grelling, and raises the stakes on this question accordingly. In the final part of the paper, I will offer a precise characterization of the conceptual status of T-sentences that answers the question and resolves the tension.

1 Tarski's Use of the Liar

It will be important for our purposes to get very clear about Tarski's use of the Liar. The received view about this seems to be that Tarski introduces the paradox, stresses its seriousness and then offers a solution of some kind to it. In fact, this is not a correct depiction of Tarski's involvement with the Liar and will not serve us here. Tarski does not offer a *solution* to the Liar *per se*. He evidently believed that a satisfactory solution of the paradox was extant, and says as much at the outset of his central paper on truth [4, p. 152]. We do not need to dwell on this interpretive matter here, however. All we need agree on is the indisputable fact that Tarski's introduction of a liar argument in both [4] and [5] is explicitly *in the service of establishing the indefinability of truth in certain kinds of languages*. The arguments offered in those two papers are distinct and support different though related indefinability theses. The arguments have in common that they refer to a liar argument. We may formulate the two indefinability theses as follows.

> *Colloquial Indefinability Thesis (1935):* A truth predicate for a colloquial language is indefinable in that colloquial language.
>
> *Exact Indefinability Thesis (1944):* For exactly specified language L, a truth predicate for L is indefinable in any exactly specified language M in which i) a liar argument for L is formulable, ii) the identity premise of that liar argument is an assertible sentence, and iii) the normal laws of logic hold.

In this paper, I shall be concerned only with Tarski's considered view, which is represented by the exact indefinability thesis of (1944).

To understand the exact indefinability thesis and how reference to a liar argument yields an argument for this thesis, there are several notions which need to be spelled out. First, Tarski *refers* in his argument to a liar argument of the following form.

1. 'The sentence with feature F is not true in L' is true in L iff the sentence with feature F is not true in L

2. 'The sentence with feature F is not true in L' is identical to the sentence with feature F.

3. Hence, 'The sentence with feature F is not true in L' is true in L iff 'The sentence with feature F is not true in L' is not true in L.

Where some particular *feature F* is used in the case such as being a sentence occuring on a certain page of a certain book. This feature is carefully chosen so as to vouchsafe the truth of (2). Note, it is an incidental feature of our formulation that the same sorts of words are used in the quote marks as without. All that is important is that the string in quote marks have the same meaning in our target language L as does the sentence used on the right side of the biconditional in (1). We shall refer to the first premise as the *T-sentence premise* of the liar argument, and the second premise as the *identity premise*. If the target language of a liar argument is L and the argument itself is given in a language M, then let us say that it is *a liar argument for L in M*. We note for future reference that the above argument is classically valid, and its conclusion is (classically) deductively inconsistent.

Also, for our purposes, I introduce below minimal principles regarding exactly specified languages, assertible sentences, formally correct definitions, and adequate truth definitions. Throughout our discussion, we will only be concerned with *exactly specified languages*, where an exactly specified language is just an interpreted language with distinguished primitive vocabulary and grammar, a set of axioms, and both rules of inference and definition.

Principle of Adequacy: For exactly specified languages M and L, if there is an adequate truth definition for L in M, and the T-sentence premise for a liar argument for L is formulable in M (or becomes so by dint of the rules of definition), then that T-sentence is derivable from the definition together with the axioms of M.

Condition on Formal Correctness: For any exactly specified language, M, and any sentence, D, and predicate, p, of M: if there is a (possibly empty) set of sentences, S, such that i) term p is not used anywhere in S, ii) S is deductively consistent, iii) S is a subset of the assertible sentences of the language, iv) $S + D$ is deductively inconsistent, then D is not a formally correct definition of predicate p.

My reconstruction of Tarski's indefinability argument will appeal to the above two principles. The Principle of Adequacy is entailed by Tarski's Convention T [4, p. 188]), considered generally. And while Tarski never makes explicit just what formal correctness comes to, something like the above Condition on Formal Correctness is quite necessary for the argument for his exact indefinability thesis.[1] It is, in any event, a condition that no one should object to, provided we mean by *assertible sentences of the language* something reasonably sensible. For our discussion, we will take the assertible sentences of an exactly specified language, M, to be the least

---

[1]Benson Mates [1, p. 201], whose book owes its largest debt to Tarski, takes a formally correct definition to be one that satisfies the now-traditional requirements of eliminability and non-creativity. The condition I have formulated above is a kind of *strict* non-creativity condition. Non-creativity only in Mates' sense is, as far as I can see, not adequate to support Tarski's colloquial or exact indefinability results.

set of sentences that i) includes the axioms of M, ii) includes all empirical sentences of M that are confirmed to some (here unspecified) standard, and iii) is closed under the rules of inference of the language [4, p. 166], [5, pp. 346–7]. Clause (ii) is crudely put, but we will not fret over this here. The only sorts of sentences we will need to assume are in this category are things like the identity premise of a liar argument—sentences which none doubt the truth of.

With these understandings, we can now formulate the reasoning of Tarski's argument as follows.[2]

Argument for the Exact Indefinability Thesis:

1. Suppose that M is an exactly specified language in which i) the sentences requisite for a liar argument for L are formulable, ii) the identity premise of that liar argument is an assertible sentence of M, and iii) the normal laws of logic hold.[3] [premise]

2. BWOC, suppose there is a formally correct and adequate truth definition, D, for L in M.

3. The identity premise of a liar argument is formulable and assertible in M [from 1i, 1ii]. Let S be the set containing just that identity premise. Note that no term for truth in L is used in the single sentence in S.

4. S is deductively consistent (in M). [from 1iii,3]

5. The T-sentence premise of that liar argument is formulable in M and derivable from D. [from 1i, Princ. of Adequacy]

6. It follows that the conclusion of that liar argument is derivable from $S + D$. [from 3,5,1iii]

---

[2] In §8 of [5, pp. 348–9] Tarski gives the result for which the argument to follow is a reconstruction. Tarski's own statement mixes together a negative result (the indefinability result) and a positive proposal (the specification of a domain of languages in which the *truth definition problem* may yet be solvable). It is the negative result which interests us here. Languages that meet condition (1) of our reconstructed argument are ones in which an adequate and formally correct truth predicate cannot be constructed, and that is why Tarski's positive proposal is very sensibly to restrict our further attention to languages which do not meet all those conditions—semantically open languages, in particular. So, we here wish to formulate and argue for just the negative result—which closely parallels Tarski's indefinability result for semantically-open languages of infinite order [4, Theroem I, p. 247], and has as its historical antecedent the argument of [4, pp. 164–5].

[3] That is, the inference rules of M are classical. This third condition could be weakened considerably. All that we require here is that the inference rules of M underwrite steps (4), (6), and (7).

7. The conclusion of that liar argument is deductively inconsistent in M. [from 1iii]
8. $S + D$ is itself deductively inconsistent. [from 6,7]
9. So, there is an S such that S is deductively consistent, contains only assertible sentences of M which nowhere use the defined term of D, and is such that $S+D$ is deductively inconsistent. [from 3,4,8]
10. Thus, contrary to our supposition, D is not formally correct [from 9, Cond. on Formal Correctness].
11. We conclude, by *reductio ad absurdum*, that there is no formally correct and adequate truth definition in M (for L). [from 2–10]
12. That is, as we may say, truth for L is indefinable in M. [from 11]

It is for the sake of being able to draw such an indefinability conclusion that Tarski introduces the liar argument into his discussion of truth. The resulting theorem, the exact indefinability thesis, has three key antecedent conditions—given in premise (1)—notable among which is the assumption that the identity premise of a liar argument is an assertible sentence of the language in question.

2 Tarski's Use of the Grelling

Tarski suggests that his indefinability result can be strengthened. The premise which we have noted, (1ii), is an evidently *empirical* antecedent condition of the indefinability thesis. It is an empirical condition, because to know that the identity premise is (in Tarski's sense) assertible in a given language would, presumably, require knowing that the identity premise was, in the requisite way, empirically confirmed.[4] But to empirically confirm the identity premise of Tarski's Liar one would presumably have to do things like see which sentence it is that occurs on line such-and-such of page so-and-so of a certain book, and confirm that it is identical to the sentence quoted in the liar argument in question (or, perhaps, ascertain these things from someone who had). Thus, if the indefinability thesis is argued on the

---

[4]The presumption being that this is the only way that a premise of that sort could come to be included among the assertible sentences of the language. Obviously, there are ways to play funny with this Tarskian presumption. One could include the identity premise in the axioms of the language, one could adopt a funny confirmation principle that the identity premise could be seen to pass without actual empirical support, etc. Tarski does not worry himself with formulating things so as to rule such tricks out, and we will follow suit here.

basis of the sort of liar argument Tarski gives, then *to know if that thesis applied to some particular language*, one would have to have a certain kind of background empirical confirmation. Hence, it appears that one could only know *aposteriori* that the indefinability thesis applied to a particular language.

Tarski thinks, however, that a strengthened thesis can be argued which dispenses entirely with the empirical antecedent condition. He suggests several times that one can get just such a strengthened argument using as a basis an appeal to the Grelling instead of the Liar. The idea first appears in [5] and Tarski there also indicates the sort of Grelling argument that he has in mind.

> We have assumed that we can formulate and assert in our language an empirical premise such as the statement (2) [of our liar] argument. It turns out that [this assumption] is not essential, for it is possible to reconstruct the antinomy of the liar without its help.[11] ([11] This can roughly be done in the following way. Let S be any sentence beginning with the words "Every sentence". We correlate with S a new sentence $S*$ by subjecting S to the following two modifications: we replace in S the first word, "Every", by "The"; and we insert after the second word, "sentence", the whole sentence S enclosed in quotation marks. Let us agree to call the sentence S "(self)applicable" or "non(self)applicable" dependent on whether the correlated sentence $S*$ is true or false. Now consider the following sentence: 'Every sentence is nonapplicable'. It can easily be shown that the sentence just stated must be both applicable and nonapplicable; hence a contradiction. It may not be quite clear in what sense this formulation of the antinomy does not involve an empirical premise; however, I shall not elaborate on this point. [5, p. 348]

Also, in a 1956 footnote to [4],[5] Tarski suggests that a Grelling-based indefinability argument does something like the work of his Theorem I— an indefinability result for languages of infinite order which is proved with the aid of tools from Gödel's proof of the incompleteness theorem. Tarski

---

[5] "If we analyse the sketch of the proof [of Theorem I] given below we easily note that an analogous reconstruction could be carried out even on the basis of colloquial language, and that in consequence of this reconstruction the antinomy of the liar actually approximates to the antinomy of the expression 'heterological'. For a rather simple reconstruction of the antinomy of the liar in this direction see [(1944, footnote 11), quoted above]. It seems interesting that in this reconstruction all the technical devices are avoided which are used in the proof of Th. I (such as interpretation of the metalanguage in arithmetic or the diagonal procedure). In connexion with the last paragraph of the text [cf. the concluding remarks of §1, pp. 164 f., and in particular p. 165, note 1.]" (pg. 248 ftnt 19)

represents the proof of Theorem I as also rooted in a Liar-like phenomenon, but suggests that *this* proof has the same virtue that he accorded to the Grelling-based argument alluded to above, because it allows us to avoid "all premisses of an empirical nature which have played a part in the previous formulations of the antinomy of the liar". Still, in the end, Tarski thinks the Grelling-based argument is even yet more general than this Gödel-based argument. So, in the final analysis, the Grelling-based argument holds a certain pride of place for Tarski, over both the Liar-based and Gödel-based arguments.

3   Significance of a Grelling Version

So, to pursue Tarski's suggestion, if we take his exact indefinability thesis, drop the empirical condition and shift to an appeal to a Grelling argument instead of a liar argument, we would expect the resulting strengthened thesis to look something like this.

> *Strong Indefinability:* For exactly specified language L, truth for L is indefinable in any exactly specified language M in which i) a Grelling argument for L is formulable, and ii) the normal laws of logic hold.

Let us consider more closely what might be the significance of obtaining this stronger result.

An obvious virtue that the strengthened thesis might afford has already been mentioned: *some apriori knowledge of the indefinability of truth for particular languages*. Assuming that the two background assumptions used in our argument for the *un*strengthened exact indefinability thesis have the requisite status, that thesis itself is a purely conceptual one—the sort of thesis we count apriori. However, an indefinability conclusion drawn *for some particular language* using that thesis can only be aposteriori. This is because, as we said, application of the thesis to some language requires confirmation of the empirical antecedent condition of the thesis. The strengthened thesis, by dispensing with this empirical condition, could render knowledge in application of the thesis apriori.

In addition, if the indefinability thesis can be strengthened, then a number of related Tarskian theses can also be strengthened in a parallel fashion, Tarski's infamous inconsistency thesis, for example.[6]

---

[6] Just as with the indefinability theses, we also find two distinct inconsistency theses in Tarski. There is a Colloquial Inconsistency Thesis in [4] which is repudiated by Tarski in [5] where he offers the Exact Inconsistency Thesis considered here. This change of view in [5] has evidently been overlooked by Tarski's commentators. I should mention also that Tarski accords no very special significance to his inconsistency theses. They are in fact,

Exact Inconsistency Thesis: For exactly specified languages L and M, language M is inconsistent if it is one in which i) the T-sentence premise of a liar argument for L is formulable, ii) the empirical premise of that liar argument is an assertible sentence, and iii) the normal laws of logic hold.

Where, for any exactly specified language, M, we say that M is an *inconsistent language* just in case some deductively inconsistent sentence is among the assertible sentences of M.

A broader thesis that remains tacit in Tarski would also be affected. Tarski is sometimes said to hold an "inconsistency view of truth"—the view that truth predicates in suitably expressive languages are inconsistent. Once we spell out what it is supposed to mean for a predicate to be inconsistent, the view being attributed is pretty much captured by Tarski's inconsistency thesis stated above. So understood, of course, Tarski does have the inconsistency view of truth, but this attribution does not go very far in telling us about his view of truth, because it does not say anything about what his position is with respect to the *concept* of truth—which is, for most philosophers, ultimately the subject matter of interest. I believe Tarski is best understood as having held an "incoherence view of the concept of truth", and with a little studious extrapolation, it is not hard to articulate and prove a further thesis that we may justly consider Tarskian:

General Incoherence Thesis: The concept of sentential truth is incoherent.[7]

I think that this thesis should form a central part of our understanding of Tarski's theory of truth, but it has only a side-role to play here, so I will limit myself to the following observation. It takes a bit of work to clarify the content of this incoherence thesis and show how it may be argued with basically Tarskian materials. It will suffice to note here that the establishment of this important result depends on establishing that *there is at least one* language with a truth predicate to which Tarski's indefinability thesis applies. And so, it turns out that, if Tarski's indefinability thesis can be strengthened, the incoherency thesis will turn out to be an apriori thesis. In this way, the status of that thesis (whatever exactly it comes to) that

---

in each case, just part of Tarski's chosen way of arguing for his indefinability theorems. My own formulations of the arguments are not routed through these inconsistency claims, because it is not an essential waystation of the argumentation, and Tarski's use of it has been a source of puzzlement and doubt in the literature, and so best avoided in our main discussion.

[7] One can also establish by the same means that the concept of a true sentence of this or that particular language is incoherent.

makes Tarski's view an "incoherence view" (or an "inconsistency view" for that matter) is significantly affected.[8]

Finally, all these differences in apriori status turn out to be significant for an unexpected reason, namely, because they create a difficulty for Tarski's T-strategy of truth definition. So, in a sense, if Tarski is right about the strengthening, then there is a difficulty with the starting point of Tarski's investigation—and the imposition of Convention T in particular. There is already some tension between Tarski's indefinability result and his T-strategy. Strengthening the indefinability result makes this tension especially vexed.

4 Reconstruction of the Grelling Version

With the stakes now firmly in mind, we turn to see if the Grelling can really be marshalled to Tarski's purpose. To begin our exploration of this question, here is a formulation of a Grelling argument patterned in an obvious way on Tarski's sketch (quoted in §2).

> Def: For all S, S is *self-applicable* iff i) S is a sentence of L, ii) it begins with 'Every sentence', and iii) the result of replacing that 'every' by 'the', and inserting S in quotes after 'sentence' is a sentence true in L.

> *Defined Grelling Argument:*
>
> 0. For all S, S is self-applicable iff i) S is a sentence of L, ii) it begins with 'Every sentence', and iii) the result of replacing that 'every' by 'the', and inserting S in quotes after 'sentence' is a sentence true in L. [by definition]
>
> 1. * 'The sentence 'Every sentence is not self-applicable' is not self-applicable' is true in L if and only if the sentence 'Every sentence is not self-applicable' is not self-applicable. [T-sentence premise]
>
> 2. BWOC, suppose 'Every sentence is not self-applicable' is self-applicable.
>
> 3. It follows that, 'The sentence 'Every sentence is not self-applicable' is not self-applicable' is true in L. [from 2,0]
>
> 4. The sentence 'Every sentence is not self-applicable' is not self-applicable. [from 3,1]

---
[8] For a discussion of the Incoherence Thesis, see [2]).

5. Contradiction [from 2,4]
6. So, by *reductio*, 'Every sentence is not self-applicable' is not self-applicable. [from 2-5]
7. 'The sentence 'Every sentence is not self-applicable' is not self-applicable' is true in L [from 6,1]
8. But now we can infer, 'Every sentence is not self-applicable' is self-applicable. [from 7,0]
9. Contradiction [from 6,8]

Here we have an argument apparently of the right sort for Tarski's use, and it has a T-sentence premise, (1), like the Liar argument, but no empirical premise like the Liar did. Yet, this Grelling argument will not work for Tarski's purposes. If we try to construct an argument for indefinability along the lines of the argument we gave earlier, we are led only to the conclusion that truth for L is indefinable in M *or the Grelling definition statement is not formally correct*. Thus, to get an outright indefinability result, we must take on a new antecedent condition to the effect that the Grelling definition *is* formally correct. In short, the Defined Grelling argument only seems to support an indefinability result such as the following.

> *Exact (Def Grelling) Indefinability Thesis:* For exactly specified language L, truth for L is indefinable in any exactly specified language, M, in which i) a Defined Grelling argument for L is formulable, ii) *the definition statement used in that Grelling argument is a formally correct definition*,[9] and iii) the normal laws of logic hold.

While this is a *bona fide* indefinability result and the auxiliary condition is evidently not an empirical one, it is still not the result we were seeking. This thesis is of uncertain significance. We should think that it tells us something directly significant about the indefinability of truth predicates only to the degree to which we think that Grelling definitions are themselves above reproach.[10] Unless we have good reason to think that the

---

[9] Actually, a slightly weaker, but not less confounding, condition could be used here, namely that *there is a formally correct Grelling definition for L in M, if there is a formally correct and adequate truth definiton for L in M*.

[10] To see this more clearly, imagine that this sort of argument was the only one we knew by which to cast doubt on truth definitions. If this were the case, it seems clear that much before we came to doubt the definability of truth, our suspicions would fall upon Grelling definitions—which are, after all, trumped-up just to make trouble. The take-home lesson would not be one about the indefinability of truth, but about what is funny about Grelling arguments. A lesson we might formulate thusly: *For exactly*

'self-applicable' definition is unexceptionable, we fall short of the desired indefinability result. So, the Defined Grelling, though patterned after Tarski's own description, does *not* enable one to argue for Strong Indefinability as Tarski suggested. There might be some concern at this point as to whether, after all, Tarski really meant to lay claim to an argument for something so strong as Strong Indefinability. This concern is, perhaps, mooted by the following demonstration which shows Tarski *can* very well have that strong result.

My strategy is a give a Grelling argument which uses *no* auxiliary definition. The argument I present will look very like what we had before, except the appearance of special terms in it will be understood to be mere abbreviations of presentational convenience, not defined terms. The argument I have in mind is as follows.

> For simplicity of expression, we will present the self-applicability argument in an abbreviated form. The argument itself can be obtained from the abbreviated form below by everywhere replacing occurrences of 'SA' with the expression '*such that the sub of it is a sentence true in L,*' and subsequently replacing (last to first) occurrences of the form ⌜sub of α⌝ with the complex expression ⌜result of concatenating 'The sentence', a word-break, a single-quote mark, an instance of α, a single-quote mark, a word-break, and the result of deleting the first two words of α⌝.[11]

---

specified language, L, there is no formally correct Grelling definition for L in any exactly specified language M in which i) a Defined Grelling argument for L is formulable, ii) truth in L is definable, and iii) the normal laws of logic hold. The original lesson survives only if we have some independent argument for impugning the truth definition rather than the Grelling definition. Of course, we know of such an argument, our Liar-based indefiniability argument, but this employs an empirical antecedent condition, and our current aim is to see if we can construct an argument that does not appeal to any such condition.

[11] Applying these instructions to premise (1) yields the evidently monstrous sentence, *'The sentence 'Every sentence is not such that the result of concatenating 'The sentence', a word-break, a single-quote mark, an instance of it, a single-quote mark, a word-break, and the result of deleting the first two words of it is a sentence true in L' is not such that the result of concatenating 'The sentence', a word-break, a single-quote mark, an instance of it, a single-quote mark, a word-break, and the result of deleting the first two words of it is a sentence true in L' is identical to the result of concatenating 'The sentence', a word-break, a single-quote mark, an instance of 'Every sentence is not such that the result of concatenating 'The sentence', a word-break, a single-quote mark, an instance of it, a single-quote mark, a word-break, and the result of deleting the first two words of it is a sentence true in L', a single-quote mark, a word-break, and the result of deleting the first two words of 'Every sentence is not such that the result of concatenating 'The sentence', a word-break, a single-quote mark, an instance of it, a single-quote mark, a word-break, and the result of deleting the first two words of it is a sentence true in L',*

Abbrev Grelling Argument:

0. * 'The sentence 'Every sentence is not SA' is not SA' is true in L IFF the sentence 'Every sentence is not SA' is not SA. [T-sent premise]
1. * 'The sentence 'Every sentence is not SA' is not SA' is identical to the sub of 'Every sentence is not SA'. [identity premise]
2. BWOC, suppose the sentence 'Every sentence is not SA' is SA.
3. 'The sentence 'Every sentence is not A' is not SA' is true in L. [from 1,2]
4. The sentence 'Every sentence is not SA' is not SA. [from 3,0]
5. Contradiction [from 2,4]
6. So, the sentence 'Every sentence is not SA' is not SA. [from 2-5]
7. 'The sentence 'Every sentence is not SA' is not SA' is true in L. [from 0]
8. 'Every sentence is not SA' is SA. [from 1,7]
9. Contradiction [from 6,8]

It is important for our purposes that we are not using specially-defined terms in this argument. We used some abbreviations in *communicating* the argument in question, but the argument itself does not use terms like 'SA' or 'the sub of', and no definition statements occur in it.

Now, the Abbrev Grelling argument does not employ any definitions, but it does employ an identity premise, (1), just as did the liar argument with which we began. Consequently, it is not hard to see that an indefinability argument based on appeal to such an Abbrev Grelling argument will net us only the following sort of thesis.

Exact (Abbrev Grelling) Indefinability Thesis: For exactly specified language L, truth for L is indefinable in any exactly specified language, M, in which i) an Abbrev Grelling argument for L is formulable, ii) *the identity premise of that Grelling argument is an assertible sentence of the language*, and iii) the normal laws of logic hold.

---

which defies direct comprehension.

If clause (ii) of this thesis turns out to be an empirical condition, then we will have made no headway at all over the Exact (Liar) Indefinability Thesis. So, everything now depends on whether there is any good and interesting sense in which the identity premise of Tarski's liar argument is an empirical premise and the identity premise of the Abbrev Grelling argument is not. There is at least this. To confirm the identity premise of Tarski's liar argument, we have to look into a certain book to see what sentence occurs on a certain line of a certain page. This is very different from what confirmation of the identity premise of the Abbrev Grelling requires. To see that this identity sentence is true requires us to see that the quoted sentence on the one side is in fact the sentence which results from performing a certain syntactical substitution. So, what we need is purely syntactical knowledge. If languages are conceived of as abstract, structured entities, then such syntactic facts about sentences can be reasonably accorded apriori status. Plausibly then, we have here struck upon a Grelling-based indefinability thesis that constitutes a strengthening in just the way Tarski envisioned.

5 Liar Redux

So, we can do what Tarski said, but our result is also disappointing since, if the difference in "empirical status" Tarski pointed to just comes down to the sort of difference in status we see between the identity premises of Tarski's Liar and the Abbrev Grelling, it does not take much to see that this difference was, after all, just an artifact of Tarski's particular choice of liar argument. To see that this is so, first note that a general form for the sort of simple liar arguments of which Tarski's is an instance is as follows.

α is true iff δ is not true
α is identical to δ
$\therefore$ Contradiction

It seems an accident of choice that the definite description that stands in the place of 'δ' in Tarski's liar argument makes reference to token sentences in physical books. Consider instead an instance of the same form, call it the "Modified Liar", which uses a simple name and quote name as follows.

'c is not true' is true iff c is not true.
'c is not true' is identical to c.
$\therefore c$ is true iff c is not true.

The minor premise here does not require that one look in any physical books, and is clearly no more empirical than the identity premise of the Abbrev Grelling. One does have to know (in some sense) what 'c' refers to in order to evaluate the sentence, but this is no more than to require that one understand the sentence in the relevant sense in order to evaluate it, and this is a requirement on any argument we might get up. Thus, it appears that the only difference we can point to as between Liar and Abbrev Grelling arguments for the indefinability thesis is a difference which is wiped out by a trivial variant on Tarski's Liar. Possibly, Tarski thought the difference between the two cases more indissoluble than it turns out to be.

6 Trouble for the T-Strategy

We observed earlier that the most immediate upshot of obtaining (as we now have) an indefinability thesis which had no empirical antecedent condition would be that we could know apriori that certain particular languages satisfied the conditions of the thesis, and hence know apriori that truth was indefinable in those languages.

An important further upshot arises from Tarski's argument, however. We have supposed that the strengthened (aka Abbrev Grelling or Modified Liar) indefinability thesis is reasonably thought apriori, and that the applicability of that thesis to some languages (abstractly conceived) would be likewise apriori. However, inspection of the Tarskian argument shows that a further conclusion may be drawn in regard to any such language. The languages to which the thesis applies are languages in which a certain T-sentence is formulable that leads to a contradiction. Any candidate for a truth definition is scuttled precisely because it must prove all the formulable T-sentences including this one. It stands to reason then that we can infer from this not only that the proposed definition is not formally correct, but also that the trouble-making T-sentence (there may be more than one, of course) is not true.[12] Thus, it now appears, we are in a position to know *apriori* that there is a T-sentence in the language in question which is not true. It should not come as a surprise that some T-sentences are not true, of course, this is an easy upshot of the Liar. The new twist here is the apriori status conferred on this conclusion by dint of Tarski's strengthened indefinability thesis.

Yet, now we have a problem. Let us continue to fix on a language which we can know apriori fits the antecedent conditions of a strengthened indefinability thesis. If we can know apriori that some T-sentences are not true, this draws into question Tarski's whole strategy of truth definition—what we might call the T-*strategy*. Tarski's Convention T insists that any satisfactory truth definition must underwrite (prove) all the T-sentences, but if we can already know apriori that some of those T-sentences are not true, we must ask what legitimates the requirement Convention T imposes? Some

---

[12]In fact, by an easy argument, we can show that that T-sentence is also not false, hence not truth valued.

justify Convention T with the claim that it ensures that the proposed definition makes the defined predicate *extensionally correct*. Could this be right? No. In robust languages, the constraint *ensures disaster*—it would not even make good sense to talk of the extension of a predicate introduced by such a Convention-T-bound definition.[13,14] Evidently, others have thought that T-sentences were *conceptual truths* underwritten by our concept of truth, and, if true, this would give us a clear way to justify Convention T. But this clearly cannot be right, either, for the simple reason that not all the T-sentences are even so much as true.

Still, the idea that T-sentences are in some sense *conceptually underwritten* is a compelling one. If the failure of truth for T-sentences had been knowable only aposteriori, one might have pursued this line by maintaining that T-sentences are indeed (in an as yet unexplicated sense) conceptually underwritten, the failure of truth for those T-sentences not being somehow a conceptual matter at all. Convention T could then be understood as embodying some sort of purely conceptual requirement (albeit an ill-fated one). Given the success of the Abbrev Grelling and Modified Liar versions of Tarski's argument, this way of trying to defend Convention T is no longer open to us. If Convention T can be justified at all, we need a way of seeing how the constraint it imposes can be a legitimate conceptual requirement even though the impossibility of meeting that requirement (in certain languages) is also a bit of apriori knowledge. Tarski's entire T-strategy for the truth definition problem hangs in the balance.

7 Conceptual Status of T-Sentences

I propose below an explicit condition which T-sentences satisfy and which gives precise sense to the idea that T-sentences are underwritten by our concept of sentential truth. Crucially, the sense in which this shows Convention T to be conceptually grounded is not undermined by the ultimate untruth of some T-sentences. The proposal is a sophistication of a certain naive intuition we have about T-sentences. Consider a T-sentence such as

'Neige est blanche' is a true sentence of French if and only if snow is white.

---

[13]This, because if there is such a thing as the extension of the predicate, there would have to be some things that were both in it and not in it, which is absurd.

[14]Some might be tempted to say that the imposition of Convention T is legitimated by the fact that it ensures extensional correctness *in semantically open languages*. This response is inadequate because it fails to address the matter at issue. The claim that truth is indefinable in semantically *closed* languages has been argued with crucial reliance on the assumption that adequate truth definitions must prove all the T-sentences—which is that thing which Convention T insists upon.

Antecedently, we would have said that such a sentence recommends itself to us, because it seems, roughly, that one who has the proper linguistic understanding knows it to be true. Though we know that cannot be strictly correct, there is something to this idea. Let us begin with a case simpler than T-sentences.

DEFINITION 1. For language M and sentence, s, of M, we shall say that s has *simple conceptual warrant in M* iff one who understands s (as a sentence of M), is in a position to know (on non-truth-functional grounds) that if i) each predicate of s is subserved in M by the concept it expresses in M, and ii) each singular referring term of s refers in M, then s is a true sentence of M.

Understanding s as a sentence of M, as used here, is meant to imply of the agent that he or she,

i) for each predicate, p, of s, grasps the concept, c, expressed in M by p and knows of c that it is expressed in M by p, and

ii) associates with each singular referring term of s a condition and knows that it uniquely picks out the referent in M of the term if such there be, and nothing otherwise.

To explain what is intended by saying that a predicate is subserved by a concept, I will avail myself of the useful fiction that concepts come supplied with explicit *application rules* which say what sorts of things are supposed to be included or excluded by the concept.

DEFINITION 2. A concept, c, *subserves* a predicate, p, of language M iff for all x in the domain of discourse of M, i) if the application rules for c imply that x falls under c, then p applies in M to x, and ii) if the application rules for c imply that x fails to fall under c, then p fails to apply in M to x.

Ordinarily, of course, if a predicate expresses a concept, that concept subserves the predicate. However, a concept could subserve a predicate which did not express it, and, just possibly, a predicate could express a concept that did not subserve it.

Sentences with simple conceptual warrant evidently include i) analytically true sentences, ii) sentences free logics treat specially, such as 'if Vulcan is green, then Vulcan is green', as well as iii) some more interesting cases involving vacuous names, such as, 'if Vulcan is a planet, then Vulcan is a heavenly body'. These sentences have exceptional conceptual credentials, though not all are guaranteed to be true. They are all of a sort that we would be entitled to rely on for the purposes of scientific theorizing—at least until such time that it became known that 'Vulcan' fails to refer.

T-sentences do not have simple conceptual warrant, but an extension of the same idea applies to them.[15]

DEFINITION 3. For sentences M and L, and for t, a T-sentence in M for some language, L, (where t has form 'd is a true sentence of L iff p'), we shall say that t has *subtle conceptual warrant in M* just in case one who

  i) understands t as a sentence of M,

  ii) *recognizes that the sentence denoted in M by d is a sentence of the language denoted in M by L*,

  iii) *understands the sentence denoted in M by d as a sentence of the language denoted in M by L*.

is in a position to know (on non-truth-functional grounds) that

> if each predicate of t is subserved in M by the concept it expresses in M, and each singular referring term of t refers, then t is a true sentence of M.

T-sentences have subtle conceptual warrant. The notion of subtle conceptual warrant aims to capture the special sense in which these sentences are conceptually underwritten. It grounds our feeling that example T-sentences are "iron clad". Let us say of a sentence of a language M that it has *full conceptual warrant* in M just in case it has either simple or subtle conceptual warrant in M.

Earlier we asked what was the status of T-sentences such that it could make sense to insist on a truth definition entailing them even though not all those T-sentences are true. The answer to this question is that T-sentences have full conceptual warrant. A T-sentence need not be true to have full conceptual warrant, but such warrant ensures that the sentence is conceptual underwritten in a strong sense. Very roughly speaking, our concept of sentential truth is such as to indicate the truth of all such T-sentences, and indeed it must be so, unless there is something deeply wrong with the concept—something which could prevent some predicates which express that concept from being subserved by it. If a concept was incoherent in this way, even a meaning-giving definition of a predicate which expressed it might well entail untruths, but this would not be grounds for thinking the proffered definition not meaning-giving, nor a reason to think that a meaning-giving definition need not entail just those things. The case of the concept of sentential truth and an adequate truth definition is parallel to

---

[15] Antecedent conditions (i)–(iii) are meant to avoid incidental failures of the sort adumbrated in [3, pp. 62–4].

this. A conceptually warranted definition might be expected to entail all the *T*-sentences, and, though not all of these may be true, this is not grounds for thinking that an *adequate* definition need not entail them.

8 Conclusion

In summary, the results of our investigation are now as follows. First, Tarski's Grelling does not quite serve his purpose, but there is indeed a version of the Grelling that could be used in the context of Tarski's argument, and it would give the resulting indefinability thesis the added strength that Tarski alleges. Second, and somewhat disappointingly, a simple variant of Tarski's Liar would have done just as well. Third, the success in this regard of a Grelling (or Liar) variant of Tarski's argument exacerbates a tension which threatens to undermine Tarski's *T*-strategy of truth definition. In the end, I offered a precise characterization of the conceptual status of *T*-sentences that would resolve this tension.

Appendix

A variant strategy for formulating the Grelling argument that is not considered in the text is the following—which employs just one definition and one abbreviation.

In this approach to the argument, we will use one abbreviation (for simplicity of expression) and one definition. Again our argument will be given in an abbreviated form. The argument itself can be obtained from the abbreviated form below by everywhere replacing occurrences of '*SA*' with the expression '*such that the sub of* it *is a true sentence.*'

DEFINITION 4. For all x and y, y *is a sub of* x iff y is the result of concatenating 'The sentence', a word-break, a single-quote mark, an instance of x, a single-quote mark, a word-break, and the result of deleting the first two words of x.

> *Split Grelling Argument:* The abbreviated presentation we would give for this argument is exactly the same as for the Abbrev Grelling in the text, and is not repeated here.

It is important for our purposes that we keep clearly in view that, while the abbreviated forms of the two arguments are the same, the arguments are different. *This* argument uses a defined term ('is the sub of') that the Abbrev Grelling argument did not.

It may seem that the Split Grelling argument combines the failings of each of our earlier formulations and so that it is the worst candidate, but this is not true. The failure with the Defined Grelling version was that it relied on a definition that was not beyond suspicion (truth-involved as that definition was). This interfered with our ability to draw the desired indefinability conclusion. The Split Grelling argument, however, relies only on a definition that seems quite above suspicion. 'Is the sub of' is defined in purely syntactical terms—expresses a purely syntactical relation.

A Split Grelling version of the indefinability thesis will have as an antecedent condition that the identity premise of a Split Grelling argument is assertible in the language in question. This premise has the same status as in the Abbrev Grelling. Thus, the Split Grelling has no advantage relevant to our concerns here. By the same token it also fares no worse than the Abbrev Grelling, and so suits Tarski's purpose equally well.

In the text, I have identified Tarski's Grelling sketch with something like the Defined Grelling, but it might be that his Grelling could be fairly rendered also as a kind of Reverse Split-Grelling, where 'is SA' is a defined term and 'is the sub of' is an abbreviation. However, the resulting indefinability argument would have just the weakness which we saw with the use of the Defined Grelling.

BIBLIOGRAPHY

[1] Mates, Benson. *Elementary Logic*. 2nd ed. Trans. New York: Oxford University Press, 1972.
[2] Ray, Greg. "Tarski, the Liar and Tarskian Truth Definitions". *A Companion to Philosophical Logic*. Ed. Dale Jacquette. Malden, MA: Blackwell, 2002. pp. 164-176.
[3] Soames, Scott. "*T*-Sentences". *Modality, Morality, and Belief: Essays in Honor of Ruth Barcan Marcus*. Ed. Walter Sinnott-Armstrong, Diana Raffman, and Nicholas Asher. Cambridge: Cambridge Univ Pr, 1995. pp. 250-270.
[4] Tarski, Alfred. "Der Wahrheitsbegriff in den formalisierten Sprachen". *Studia Philosophica* 1 (1935): 261-405. Translated as "On the Concept of Truth in Formalized Languages". *Logic, Semantics, Metamathematics*. 2nd ed. Trans. J. H. Woodger. Indianapolis: Hackett Publishing, 1983. pp. 152-278.
[5] Tarski, Alfred. "The Semantic Conception of Truth and the Foundations of Semantics". *Phil Phen Res* 4 (1944): 341-375.

The Semantics of Denial
EDWIN D. MARES

ABSTRACT. This paper looks at the notion of denial and the semantics of denial predicates. Several contemporary philosophers of language have argued that denial cannot be reduced to assertion and negation, that it is a type of speech act in its own right. One philosophical motive for appealing to denial is to avoid the strengthened liar paradox. But the problem seems to reemerge when we add denial predicates to the language. The paper argues, however, that it is natural to treat denial predicates in a very similar manner to the way in which Barwise and Etchemendy treat truth predicates, and this approach avoids the denial liar.

1 Introduction

This paper is about denial and its relation to the liar paradox. Denial is a type of speech act. It is the negative correlate of assertion. Corresponding to denial is the propositional attitude of *rejection*. That is, denials express rejections just as assertions express beliefs.

The notion of denial goes back at least to Aristotle (see Horn (1989)), but it was itself largely rejected by philosophers in the early twentieth centuries. The reason for the widespread rejection of denial seems to be the widespread acceptance of Frege's argument for the reduction of denials to assertions of negations. Frege argued that we require a negation connective in our logical language in order to formalize imbedded negations. Moreover, since a negation, 'not-A' is true if and only if A can accurately be denied (for any statement A), it is redundant to have both denials and negations. But since we need negation, we should do without denial (Frege (1918-1919)).

With the advent of non-classical logics, Frege's argument for the reduction of denial was no longer acceptable. For a denial of a statement A is accurate if and only if A fails to be true. If our truth condition for 'not-A' is not the same as the "accuracy condition" for denial, then we cannot claim that we can always express the denial of A with the assertion of the negation of A. In particular, if our semantics allows for either truth value gaps or truth value gluts, the correspondence between denials and the assertion of negations will fail in some circumstances. For example, if both A and 'not-A' are neither true nor false, then we can accurately deny A but we cannot accurately assert 'not-A'. Similarly, if both A and 'not-A' are true, then we can accurately assert 'not-A' but we cannot accurately deny A.

Oddly, the requirements of bivalence and consistency for the acceptability of Frege's argument have not always been recognized. In his book, *Frege: Philosophy of Language* (Dummett (1981) pp 316-321), Dummett agrees with Frege's point without seeming to realize that, as an intuitionist, he cannot equate denial and the assertion of negations. This non-equation is particularly striking for intuitionistic logic, for intuitionists (including Dummett) deny particular instances of the law of excluded middle, but cannot assert their negations. The negation of any classical tautology is an intuitionist contradiction.

We will begin our examination of denial by looking at one motivation for its use from the concept of partially defined predicates. We will then look at the semantics of denial and show how we can avoid three apparent paradoxes concerning denial.

2 Partially Defined Predicates

We begin with the notion of a partially defined predicate. A predicate P is *partially defined* if and only if the possible cases in which P can be applied to a thing and those in which $not - P$ can be applied do not exhaust the list of possible cases. Jamie Tappenden (1999) and Scott Soames (1999) claim that natural languages contain partially defined predicates. This might sound like a commonplace, but it needs explanation. For, under the classical theory of negation, the negation of a predicate applies to an object (of the right type) if and only if the predicate itself fails to apply. We will get to the semantic theory itself soon.

Right now, I want to motivate the Tappenden-Soames view. Tappenden and Soames both use invented examples. I will use an invented example of my own and a real example. First, the invented one. In soccer, there are two sorts of free kicks awarded after a foul: an indirect free kick and a direct free kick. An indirect free kick must be touched by a player other than the kicker before it reaches the opposing goal or else the ball's entering the net does not count as a goal. Suppose that just after the rules of soccer were set down a player shot an indirect free kick into his own goal without the ball's touching another player. Let's suppose that at this point there is no rule in the book covering this sort of event. At this time the predicate 'is a goal in soccer' is partially defined. The cases in which 'is a goal' is applicable and the cases in which 'is not a goal' is applicable do not exhaust all possible cases. The players must wait for a ruling from the referee until the score is determined. This reading of events is rather like the understanding of penumbral judgments in law that is found in the legal positivists (such as H.L.A. Hart and Joseph Raz). They claim that when a judge makes a ruling that is not covered by existing legislation, she is inventing new law at that point.

Here is a real-life example. This or something very like it has happened to me many times. I am playing a board game with some friends. At one point, one of the players finds himself in trouble. A second player takes pity on him and lends him some play-money. A third player complains about the actions of the second player saying "that's not allowed". The rules on the inside of the box-top are consulted, but no mention of lending money is made. An argument ensues and a fourth player is called upon to make a ruling. Until this ruling is made, there is no fact of the matter about whether the lending of money is allowed in the game. Hence, until this point in time, the predicate 'is a legal move in the game' is partially defined.

Tappenden treats the truth predicate as a partially defined predicate. He does this to save Kripke's theory of truth (Kripke (1975)) from the strengthened liar paradox. On Kripke's theory of truth, the liar sentence,

> This sentence is false

is neither true nor false. Some philosophers have objected that this move does not help matters, for consider the sentence

> This sentence fails to be true.

This "strengthened liar" sentence, it would seem, is true if and only if it fails to be true even if it is neither true nor false. So it would appear that the paradox is recovered. Tappenden in particular argues that there is something wrong with the strengthened liar sentence. For the phrase 'fails to be true' if taken to mean anything other than 'is false' is a signal of a speech act of denial. But if it is such a signal, then the sentence is not meaningful, because there is nothing being denied. Thus, taking the truth predicate to be partially defined in addition to treating denial as a primitive speech act avoids the strengthened liar paradox.

3 Three Denial Liars

Or so it might seem. The appeal to partially defined predicates and denial avoids one form of the strengthened liar, but it suggests other very similar paradoxes. In this section, we present three such paradoxes.

The first is a simple version of the paradox, viz.,

> (Λ) I deny this sentence.

It would seem that a ideal agent cannot accept Λ without also denying Λ. Nor can she deny Λ without accepting it as well. But she can merely refuse either to accept or deny Λ.

The second is a "normative" version of the paradox. Suppose that we have the resources in our language to talk about what statements we should or should not deny. Then, we could say,

(Σ) I should deny this sentence.

There is an paradox that we seem to be able to derive from Σ. The alleged derivation and my worries about it are presented in the next section. The third paradox is supposed to be derived from the following sentence:

(Δ) This sentence is accurately denied.

The "semantic" denial liar, as I call it, is the most interesting of the three. Our discussion of it below will give us a deeper understanding of the semantics of denial and its relationship to the semantics of negation. I will argue that Δ is in fact not well-formed, that as is Δ cannot express a proposition.

4 The Simple and Normative Denial Liars

The simple and normative versions of the denial liar can be treated in much the same way. We will look at the normative liar in depth and then apply the lessons learned about it to the simple liar.

The "derivation" of the normative liar can be seen as follows. Suppose that we have an ideal agent α. We first prove that α cannot accept Σ, by means of a reductio. Then we prove that the fact that α cannot accept Σ entails that she should reject it. But if she should reject it, then she should also accept it. Hence we have a paradox. In more rigourous form, the derivation is as follows:

1. α accepts Σ (hypothesis).

2. α believes that she should deny Σ (1, meaning of 'Σ').

3. For any statement S if one believes that she should deny S, then she should deny S (general principle).

4. α should deny Σ (2, 3).

5. α is pragmatically inconsistent (1,4), and so not an ideal agent.

6. Thus, α cannot accept Σ (1-5, reductio).

7. Any statement that cannot be accepted should be rejected (general principle).

8. α should reject Σ (6,7).

9. As an ideal agent, α rejects Σ (8).

10. For any statement S, if α realizes that she should reject S, then she should accept the sentence 'I should reject S' (general principle).

8. α accepts 'I should reject Σ' (9,10).

9. 'I should reject Σ' is equivalent to Σ.

10. As an ideal agent, α accepts Σ (11,12).

11. α is pragmatically inconsistent (9,13), and so she is not an ideal agent. (Contradiction!)

There are two moves in this attempted derivation with which I take issue.

First, the principle stated in line three is suspect. One might think that believing that one should do something gives us reason to think that she should do it because otherwise she would be a hypocrite. This is true, but hypocrisy is a minor flaw both in morality and in epistemology. Suppose for example a secret police officer believed that he should torture and kill people but did not do it. He would be a hypocrite, but in that case we would rather that he be a hypocrite than that he follow his moral beliefs. Whether hypocrisy is an important flaw in a person, at least in moral cases, is highly context dependent.

Doxastic hypocrisy is similar. Let us assume for the moment the truth of a reliabilist epistemology. Suppose that an agent believes that she should accept whatever astrology tells her. This belief, according to reliabilists, is insufficient to entail that she should believe in astrology. Astrology's unreliability is, however, sufficient to undercut any such doxastic requirement. Internalist epistemologies like coherentism would have to consider doxastic hypocrisy a more important vice than externalist epistemologies, but even they cannot consider it always to be an overriding concern in deciding cases of warrant. For consider the same agent in a coherentist framework. The belief that she should believe in astrology would have to cohere with many of her other beliefs before she should be compelled to accept what astrology says. A belief by itself, according to coherentism, carries with it very few doxastic requirements.

Second, the principle stated in line seven is also dubious. It is not clear that we should reject a statement even if that statement cannot be accepted.

Perhaps we should just admit that completeness of acceptances and rejections cannot be attained because of paradoxes like this one.

Thus, I believe that this argument does not provide warrant for the claim that the normative denial liar yields a pragmatic contradiction.

Similarly, the difficulty raised by the simple version can be avoided if we reject the claim that we must reject a sentence if we realize that there is some reason that blocks our accepting it. If I neither accept nor reject the sentence, 'I reject this sentence', then it poses no problem. It would seem that *pragmatic completeness* is not as important a virtue as pragmatic consistency. For the latter can be derived from the function of denial itself. Although it would be nice if ideal agents could assert or deny every sentence, it is not worth violating pragmatic consistency to have.

5 The Semantics of "Language Slices"

We now turn our attention to the semantic denial liar. Before we get to the liar sentence itself, we will take a detour through the semantics of partial predicates.

The present semantics gives truth conditions for sentences of a language at a given point in its development. We will call a language at a given time a *language slice*. We will assume a single grammar, which contains the propositional connectives $\wedge$, $\vee$, and $\neg$, predicate constants, names, individual variables, and parentheses.

Our frame includes a set of times (T), a set of possible worlds (W), and a set of individuals. For the sake of simplicity, we will assume that the same individuals are in every world, i.e. this is a constant domain semantics. We also assume a partial order, $\leq$, on times.

Our model includes these frame elements and a set of *valuations*. A valuation is a function from variables and names to individuals and from triples of n-place predicates, worlds, and times to pairs of sets of n-tuples of individuals. That is, for each n-place predicate, if v is a valuation, w is a world, and t is a time, then $v(P, w, t) = (v(P, w, t)^+, v(P, w, t)^-)$ such that $v(P, w, t)^+$ and $v(P, w, t)^-$ are sets of n-tuples of individuals. We will add the stipulation here that $v(P, w.t)^+ \cap v(P, w, t)^- = \emptyset$. This is a consistency assumption. I do not think this assumption is crucial. We could carry out our argument in a paraconsistent context as well, but it is easier if we assume consistency.

Each valuation determines an interpretation, $[-]_{v,t}$. For any wff A and any time t, $[A]_{v,t}$ is an ordered pair of sets of worlds, $([A]^+_{v,t}, [A]^-_{v,t})$, such that the following hold:

- $[P(i_1...i_n)]_{v,t} = (\{w : (v(i_1), ..., v(i_n)) \in v(P, w, t)^+\}, \{w : (v(i_1), ..., v(i_n)) \in v(P, w, t)^-\})$;

- $[A \wedge B]_{v,t} = ([A]^+_{v,t} \cap [B]^+_{v,t}, [A]^-_{v,t} \cup [B]^-_{v,t})$;

- $[A \vee B]_{v,t} = ([A]^+_{v,t} \cup [B]^+_{v,t}, [A]^-_{v,t} \cap [B]^-_{v,t})$;

- $[\sim A]_{v,t} = ([A]^-_{v,t}, [A]^+_{v,t})$.

A language slice, then, is just an interpretation $[-]_{v,t}$.

6 Denial Negation?

A denial negation is a connective '−' such that $[-A]_{v,t} = (W \setminus [A]^+_{v,t}, [A]^+_{v,t})$. Denial negation is a boolean complementation. A worry about adding denial negation is that adding it will seem to saddle us with the semantic denial liar. Luckily we have good reason to reject denial negation in our semantic framework.

The truth condition for denial negation is very different from that of our other connectives. Consider an atomic statement 'the cover of this book is red'. The "internal" negation ($\sim$) of this sentence is true if and only if the cover of this book is in the negative extension of the predicate 'red'. The denial negation of this sentence, on the other hand, is true if and only if the cover of this book fails to be in the positive extension of that predicate. Internal negations (of sentences that do not contain denial negations) express information *contained in* a language slice. Denial negations, other the other hand, express information *about* a language slice.

The picture of language that we want to portray is one that I take from Tappenden (1999). It is a dynamic picture of language developing from language slice to language slice. Languages as they develop come to express more information about the world. On the basis of this picture of language, I suggest the following principle:

Principle 1 (Persistence). If the statement A is true in a language slice s and $s \leq s'$, then A is true in s'.

The persistence principle should be familiar to philosophers who are familiar with the Kripke semantics for intuitionist logic (where it is known as 'hereditariness') and to those who are familiar with situation semantics.

If we accept persistence, we should reject denial negation. There is no direct inconsistency in accepting both, but denial negation trivializes the principle of persistence. For we can only satisfy that principle in the presence of denial negation if $s \leq s'$ only when s and s' make exactly the same statements true. I suggest that we get rid of denial negation. It does not fit well with our picture of language as developing through various slices at various times. On the other hand, persistence, in its non-trivial form, seems to capture this intuition well.

7 A Denial Predicate

Although we reject denial negation, we need some mechanism in our language to express denials within assertions. For we talk about denials – I have been doing so throughout this paper. At first glance, it looks like we need a predicate, D, so that '$D(\ulcorner A \urcorner)$' means '$\ulcorner A \urcorner$ is accurately denied'. But adding this predicate will cause us to trivialize the principle of persistence in the same way that adding denial negation does.

Instead, I suggest we add a binary predicate, δ, that holds between names of sentences and language slices. Thus, we use '$\delta(\ulcorner A \urcorner, s)$' to mean that $\ulcorner A \urcorner$ is accurately denied in s. The content, $[\delta(\ulcorner A \urcorner, s)]_{v,t}$, is a pair of sets of worlds, as usual. In the positive member of the pair (i.e. $[\delta(\ulcorner A \urcorner, s)]_{v,t}^{+}$), we have the set of worlds w such that v at t says that w contains the information that 'A' can be accurately denied. When does w contain this information according to a valuation and a time? It is clearly a *necessary condition* that 'A' fail to be true at w. But it is not obvious that the failure of 'A' to be true is a sufficient condition. Let us consider again one of our examples of a partially defined predicate. Before we come to the realization that there is a gap in the rules of our board game, there is nothing in our language that entails that there is this gap. Rather, when we realize that there is a gap in our language, we add to our language the statement "Lending money is allowed' can be accurately denied [in s]'. On my view, the addition of this statement constitutes the creation of a new language slice.

A language slice s that makes true either '$\delta(\ulcorner A \urcorner, s)$' or '$A$' at every world for every sentence A is called *denial complete*. I hold that no language slice is denial complete. If there were denial complete language slices, they would fall prey to the semantic denial liar. Suppose, for the sake of a reductio, that s is denial complete. And suppose that σ is the sentence 'This statement can be accurately denied in w according to s'. Then we have

$$w \in [\delta(\ulcorner \sigma \urcorner, s)]_{v,t} \text{ if and only if } w \notin [\sigma]_{v,t}$$

Since
$$\sigma \text{ is equivalent to } \delta(\ulcorner \sigma \urcorner, s)$$

(they have the same meaning), the sentences, 'σ' and '$\delta(\ulcorner \sigma \urcorner, s)$' are true according to s in exactly the same possible worlds and false in exactly the same possible worlds. Thus,

$$[\delta(\ulcorner \sigma \urcorner, s)]_{v,t} = [\ulcorner \sigma \urcorner]_{v,t}$$

So we get
$$w \in [\ulcorner \sigma \urcorner]_{v,t} \text{ if and only if } w \notin [\sigma]_{v,t}$$

and this we do not want. Thus we claim that no language slice is denial complete.

8 Supervenience and Denial

The theory of denial that I have put forward is very similar to the "Austinian" theory of truth developed by Jon Barwise and John Etchemendy (in (1987)). In this section, I consider a criticism of Barwise and Etchemendy's view and show how the current theory avoids it.

According to Barwise and Ethemendy's Austinian theory of truth, the truth predicate is a binary predicate that holds of names of statements and situations. Thus, '$T(\ulcorner A \urcorner, \sigma)$' means that $\ulcorner A \urcorner$ is true in σ. Barwise and Etchemendy hold that no situation contains all the truths about what is true in it. The structural similarity between their view of truth and my view of denial is obvious.

Barwise and Etchemendy's view has been criticized by Anil Gupta for violating the principle of the supervenience of truth. According to this principle, all that is necessary for the statement 'it is true that A' to be true is that A itself be true. In other words, the truth of statements about what is true supervenes only on what is true in a situation. And so, all situations are omniscient about what is true in them (Gupta (1989)).

I shall not comment on the force of this criticism against Barwise and Etchemendy's view. Rather, we need to see whether it can be used against my own view of denial. Luckily, I do not think this criticism does apply to my view. The principle of the supervenience of truth gains its plausibility because there is a direct correlation between what information is contained situation and the content of statements about what is true in that context. With denial, on the other hand, the correlation is between what statements are denied of that context (or language slice) and what fails to be true in that context. In order to derive a principle of the supervenience of denial we need to claim that all language slices are denial complete. And there seems to be no good reason to do that. Thus, it would seem that this objection cannot be applied to the present theory of denial.

Acknowledgements

Thanks to the members of the Otago University and Victoria University philosophy departments. In particular, I am grateful to Alan Musgrave for comments.

BIBLIOGRAPHY

[1] Barwise, J. and J. Etchemendy (1987) *The Liar: An Essay on Truth and Circularity*, Oxford: Oxford University Press
[2] Dummett, M. (1981), *Frege: Philosophy of Language*, London: Duckworth
[3] Frege, G. (1918-1919) "Negation" in Frege, Collected Papers on Mathematics, Logic, and Philosophy, Oxford: Blackwell, 1984, pp 373-389

[4] Gupta, A. (1989) "Critical Notice of Jon Barwise and John Etchemendy *The Liar: An Essay on Truth and Circularity*", *Philosophy of Science* 56 pp 697-709
[5] Horn, L. (1989) *A Natural History of Negation*, Chicago: University of Chicago Press
[6] Kripke, S.A. "An Outline of a Theory of Truth" Journal of Philosophy 72 (1975 pp 690-716; reprinted in R.L. Martin (ed.), Recent Essays on Truth and the Liar Paradox, Oxford: Oxford University Press, 1984
[7] Soames, S. (1999) *Understanding Truth*, Oxford: Oxford University Press,
[8] Tappenden, J. (1999) "Negation, Denial, and Language Change in Philosophical Logic" in D. Gabbay and H. Wansing (eds.), *What is Negation?* Dordrecht: Reidel

Truth Translations of Basic Relevant Logics

ROBERT K. MEYER, YOKO MOTOHAMA AND VIVIANA BONO

ABSTRACT. This paper is submitted in memory of Meyer's old friend and longtime collaborator Hugues Leblanc, to whom it is dedicated. It explores the consequences of the classical first-order semantics for the *basic* positive relevant logic **B+** of [44] and its *classical* extension **CB**. We study *entailments* $A \leq C$, where A and C are built up from variables and $\rightarrow, \wedge, \vee, \neg$. The mated classical first-order theory **CBMODEL** has the usual vocabulary, based on a ternary relation symbol 'R' (for the relevant accessibility relation) and, for each propositional variable 'p', a corresponding unary predicate 'P'. There is an infinite run of individual variables 'w', etc. We use the semantical truth-conditions of [44] to define an extended unary predicate $[B]$ for each formula of **B+**, on the following recursive rubric:

$[p]w = Pw$, where P is the unary predicate corresponding to the propositional variable p;
$[C \wedge D]w = [C]w \wedge [D]w; [C \vee D]w = [C]w \vee [D]w, [\neg C]w = \neg([C]w)$
$[C \rightarrow D]w = \forall x \forall y (Rwxy \supset ([C]x \supset [D]y))$

THEOREM. **CB** $\vdash A \rightarrow C$ iff **CBMODEL** $\vdash \forall w([A]w \supset [C]w)$.

The theorem, near enough, is from [44]. But note that it translates relevant PROVABILITY into simple first-order VALIDITY. Put otherwise, **B+** (and its conservative BOOLEAN extension **CB**) reduces RELEVANT LOGIC to CLASSICAL LOGIC *simpliciter*. (The modal analogue is the minimal normal modal logic **K**.)

1 Introduction

A. R. Anderson posed in [2] the question, "Is there a (formal) semantics for the system **E** of (relevant) entailment?" [45] and subsequent papers gave an affirmative answer to this question. The general method was a "worlds semantics", roughly in the style of Kripke's [26]. The major innovation was that, just as modal logicians introduced a *binary* relation to explicate the unary necessity and possibility operators, so we required a *ternary* relation

R to spell out formally the semantics of (irreducibly) binary connectives like the → of relevant implication and entailment.

The relational semantics that Meyer proposed with Routley was (or might as well have been) *classical*. This suggests that the study of propositional relevant logics is also the study of appropriate classical first-order theories. The same can be said of the *theories of types* proposed by researchers into Combinatory Logic (henceforth, **CL**) and Lambda Calculus (henceforth λ). Especially exciting here is the first-order theory **CBMODEL** with *no proper axioms*. We shall show that, on a well-motivated translation, this classical theory *exactly contains* not only relevant logic but also *intersection, union* and *Boolean type theories*.

The original aim of our relational semantical effort was to provide a well-motivated analysis for such famous relevant logics as the Anderson-Belnap systems **R** and **E** of [3]. But even as Kripke moved on from the boyhood delight of taking on **S5** in his [24] to a later plethora of modal logics, just so the supply of relevant logics multiplied. The analogy can be pushed further. There is a *minimal* (normal) modal logic, which has come (in, e.g., Bull and Segerberg [10]) to be called **K** (for Kripke). This is the system *without* special assumptions, save those that arise from the method. Other modal logics arise on adding specific semantic postulates—e.g., that the binary relation be transitive and reflexive, which suffices for **S4**.

There is a similar minimal positive relevant logic. It is the system **B+** of [44]. And **B+** and its conservative Boolean extension **CB** are the systems of relevant entailment that this paper will (mainly) be about. We pause briefly to think of the other positive relevant logics that arise, when *additional* semantical postulates are added to those that produce **B+**. What are these postulates? And what may we take them to say?

2 An Example: R+

As an example, pick the system **R**. More accurately, pick its positive fragment **R+** (the care and feeding of negation being no immediate concern). **R+** stands to **B+** (more or less) as **S4** stands to **K**. As **S4** demands *binary* reflexivity, so **R+** imposes, for all "worlds" w,

Ternary Reflexivity Postulate. $Rwww$ TRP

A further relevant postulate takes a little more work. First, note that, while relational products of binary relations are themselves binary relations, we can build up 4-ary, 5-ary and in general n-ary relations by taking products of 3-ary ones. Not only that, but there are distinct ways of thus relating

4 or more things.[1] We shall distinguish the following:

$$Rxyzw =_{df} \exists a(Rxya \land Razw)$$
$$Rx(yz)w =_{df} \exists b(Rxbw \land Ryzb)$$

The extra **R+** postulate then turns out to be, for all w, x, y, z,

Pasch Postulate. $\quad\quad Rwxyz \Rightarrow Rwyxz \quad\quad$ PP

And **R+** is the system that one gets if one imposes TRP and PP on top of the underlying semantical machinery for **B+** in [44].

Glance again at the special **R+** postulates. Does anything occur to you? In the first place, TRP seems to be doing some *duplicating*. Is there a link, perhaps, to the duplicating combinator $\lambda x.xx$ (alias Δ or **WI** or **SII** for **CL** fans)? If you thought this you're *right*. In the second place, PP seems to be doing some *permuting*. And the permuting that it is doing is, near enough, that induced by Curry's combinator **C** (alias $\lambda wxy.wyx$ for the λ crowd).

These connections between candidate relevant axioms and matching combinators show up also in the formulation of other relevant logics. The principle on which the matching occurs is that the candidate axioms count as the *types*, on the Curry-Howard isomorphism, of the corresponding combinators. (This is the formulas-as-types interpretation, *in spades!*) So pleased were we with these connections that [32] toyed with the thought that **CL** was The Key to the Universe. ([36], of which numerous friends are co-authors, has already been given at a couple of conferences. The written version is in preparation; think of the present essay as an introduction thereto.)

There are, however, *more connections* than were dreamt of in Curry's philosophy. Consider, one more time, the **R+** postulate TRP. Its combinator twin is **WI**. But **WI**, on the analysis of Curry & Feys [17], *has no type*. The reason for this is that Curry-Feys types all correspond to pure $\rightarrow$-formulas. In fact, as Coppo, Dezani, Pottinger, Sallé, Venneri, Barendregt, Ronchi *et al.* saw quite independently[2] (a few years later, but more deeply– cf. [11, 15, 37, 16, 5, 42]), by also making $\land$ *explicit* we get a matching type for $\lambda x.xx$. Thinking propositionally, add the axiom scheme

---

[1] We used to write 4-ary versions of R as R^2. As this would become tedious by about $R^{9541920}$, we elect here (as Dunn also has done) simply to use 'R' again for the various relational products.

[2] After [32], Meyer sought to enlist his friends in the **CL** community in working out the subject matter of the present essay. For a few years, no dice! Then in 1986, as he was dwelling yet again on the combinatory glories of **B+**, he was informed by Hindley, "But that's *already* been done." Thanks to him, accordingly, for calling the Torino work on intersection types to our attention. (And it hadn't *all* been done!)

$$Ax\mathbf{WI}.(A \to B) \wedge A \to B$$

It is well known that, on the extension of the Curry–Howard isomorphism to *intersection types,* AxWI marries the pure duplicating combinator **WI**.

From our present perspective, **R+** is a typical (positive) relevant logic. In its pure implicational part **R→**, it is just Church's *weak* implication [13, 14]. Also unsurprisingly, **R→** mirrors Church's preferred λ**I** version of λ as pure intuitionist implication **J→** mirrors λ**K**.[3] Also, **R+** is just **R→**, dressed up by Anderson and Belnap in the *distributive lattice* clothes that extend **E→** to **E+** via Ackermann [1].[4]

3 A little formal housekeeping

Logic is the *science* of inference. Does Logic then, like other sciences, aim to set out and codify a *body of truths?* We answer "Yes". And "No". No, because the *job* of Logic is to clarify Right Reason. How the biologists, or the astronomers, or the politicians reason correctly from their premises is our first order of business as logicians. But also Yes, since Logic itself is formulated as a deductive discipline, with its own axioms and rules of inference.

The tension between our "Yes" and our "No" is reflected in alternative choices of *formal syntax* for the language of Logic. The first essays in the newfangled *algebra of logic,* by Boole and his successors, were *relational.* Later in the 19th century came Frege and Russell and that crew, who introduced an *assertional* way of stipulating Logic. In particular, when we say that A *implies* B, should we formalize that relationally by writing something like

(ρ) $A \leq B$,

or assertionally with

(α) $\vdash (A \to B)$?

Much ink, not to mention an entire literature about *use-mention confusion,* has been spilled by the strife of (ρ) with (α). Suffice it to say here that the likes of (α) go with our "Yes" above; while (ρ) inclines to our "No". For "Yes" says that Logic is a body of truths—bearing a prefaced turnstile to say so; while getting on in theories is Riding the Rails of a suitable $\leq$.

---

[3] Curry once observed, in commenting on [14], that Church never much liked the combinator K. For Church's λ views, see [12]. For putting meat on the bones of the λ**I** — **R→** connection, see Helman [23]. Should we call this the Church–Helman isomorphism, as the λ**K** — **J→** connection has attained fame as the Curry–Howard isomorphism?

[4] Further *DeMorgan lattice* extensions take **R→** all the way to **R**, as, in effect, [1] took **E→** to **E**.

To set up our truth translations, we recall and adapt some formal machinery in previous papers by Meyer and by Routley, especially [44], [32] and [33]. We invite you to skip (but *not too lightly*) through this section on first reading, since more motivation is coming.

We formulate our logics in two versions. The first, in the sense of Curry's [18], will be *assertional*. We use $\vdash$ as a unary predicate. Where A is a *formula* of our language, $\vdash A$ will be an *(elementary) statement*. Axioms and theorems are all statements. Our second formulations will be, also in the sense of Curry [18], *relational systems*. Where A and C are formulas, $A \leq C$ will be an *(elementary) statement*. Theorems in this formulation will be of the form $A \leq C$. There is a simple translation from the assertional systems to the relational ones, given by $\vdash A \to C$ iff $A \leq C$, for each system. Our main focus here will be on the relational formulations.

In [44], **B+** was axiomatized on p. 193. Given a countable stock of atoms p, q, r, etc., we here[5] specify formulas (i.e., Curry's *obs*) A of its language **L+** by

$$A ::= p | A \wedge A | A \vee A | A \to A$$

Everyone knows that the main business of logic is *entailment*—keeping track of what *follows from* what. In line with motivating remarks above, this gives the relational formulations of our logics *some* priority. We *pronounce* '$A \leq C$' as 'A entails C'.

Against the odds, perhaps, in these licentious times, modern logicians *resist* the temptation to be relational more often than they yield to it. When so resisting, formulas of *any* (well-formed) shape are theorem candidates. The logical grammar that we have in mind, still following Curry [18], is a little different. A formula, standing alone, functions linguistically as a *noun*. But the *theorems* of a system, stated in what Curry calls the *U-language*, are *statements*. To make a sentence from a noun, one requires a *verb*. Our candidate verbs are the prefixed $\vdash$ for the assertional systems, and the infixed $\leq$ for the relational ones.

Nonetheless, we introduce $\leq$ in the assertional systems as an *overloaded* particle. We may *write* a statement of the form $\vdash A \to B$ as $A \leq B$.[6] This facilitates easier reading of formulas. Other advantages of the $\leq$ notation are (a) it makes immediate contact with algebraic counterparts of logics and (b) it stresses the essential unity of relevant logics and intersection (and union) theories of types. In pursuit of these themes, we have introduced relational

---
[5] We ignore, for now, the Ackermann constant **t** and the (contrasting) Church constant **T**.

[6] Including binary particles added or defined below, the full *increasing scope* order is $o, \wedge, \vee, \leftarrow, \to, \leftrightarrow, \supset, \equiv$, otherwise associating to the *left* and using dots as in Curry [18].

systems for which '⊢ A' is *ill-formed;* here the *elementary statements* of our language are themselves *of the form* $A \leq B$.

The full language **L** adds classical ¬ to **L+**. So our Backus-Naur specification for *all* of **L** is

$$A ::= p | \neg A | A \wedge A | A \vee A | A \to A$$

Other particles may be added to taste. We assume definitions in **L** of other connectives—e.g.,

D⊃. $A \supset B$ =df $\neg A \vee B$ D≡. $A \equiv B$ =df $(A \supset B) \wedge (B \supset A)$

We now make *explicit* which are the statements of our systems. When A is a formula, ⊢ A shall be an *elementary statement* of the language we may call **L⊢**. When A and B are formulas, $A \leq B$ shall be an *elementary statement* of **L≤**. We reserve the right to insert '+' into the notation and otherwise decorate it for particular purposes. (We also reserve the right to be sloppy when pedantry would be irksome; readers who catch us will be awarded *3 Mars bars*). For now, note merely that **L≤** may be considered a *sublanguage* of **L⊢** (on the convention that the *entailment* relation holds between A and B just in case the *implication* $A \to B$ is a logical truth. In symbols, $A \leq B$ iff, as a matter of logic, ⊢ $A \to B$.) But **L⊢** is *not* a sublanguage of **L≤** (on which point a pleasant subtlety of our truth translations will eventually rest). Until further notice, we assume that the elementary statements are those of **L⊢**.

A *positive model structure (+ms)* was a triple $\mathbf{K} = \langle 0, K, R \rangle$, where K is a set, $0 \in K$ and R is a ternary relation on K. A binary relation $\subseteq$ was defined by[7]

d⊆. $a \subseteq b$ =df $R0ab$,

and the following postulates were laid down,[8] for all $a, b, c, x \in K$:

p1. $\subseteq$ is *reflexive* and *transitive*.

p2. $a \subseteq x$ and $Rxbc \Rightarrow Rabc$

p3. $b \subseteq x$ and $Raxc \Rightarrow Rabc$

p4. $x \subseteq c$ and $Rabx \Rightarrow Rabc$

---

[7]We have previously used < where we write $\subseteq$ here. But as $\subseteq$ is a semantical notion meaning *subtheory*, near enough, to stick with < now would have invited confusion with $\leq$ (a logical notion meaning *entails*).

[8]These postulates are from [32], which expands on those of [44].

Also important are the notions of *interpretation, verification, and validity*. Let **2** = $\{0,1\}$ be the usual truth-values $\{\mathit{false},\mathit{true}\}$, and let **K** be a +ms. A *possible interpretation* is just any function I from **L+**$\times K$ to **2**. Fixing I and **K** in context, we may write, for a formula A and $w \in K$,

$$[A]w$$

for $I(A,w) = 1$. We use other truth-functional particles and quantifiers over K to continue the story, to specify the conditions on which a *possible* interpretation I is an *interpretation*.

These conditions are of two sorts. First, there are *truth-conditions,* which require (as usual) the value of a compound formula A at w on I to depend on values of its immediate subformulas. For the moment these are $T\wedge, T\vee$ and $T\rightarrow$, spelled out below. Second, there is a *hereditary* condition H, familiar from semantic investigations of other non-classical logics.[9]

$H. \ a \subseteq b \Rightarrow ([A]a \Rightarrow [A]b)$, for all formulas A and $a, b \in K$.

As it turns out, it suffices inductively for the *full* condition H merely to impose it on *atoms,* via

$Hp. \ a \subseteq b \Rightarrow ([p]a \Rightarrow [p]b)$, for all atoms p and $a, b \in K$.

An *interpretation* I of **L+** in the +ms **K** is then any possible interpretation satisfying the truth-conditions and Hp. Since 0 is intended as a *real* (or *logical*) world, we say that A is *verified* on I just in case $A[0]$. A is *valid* in the +ms **K** iff A is verified on all interpretations I in **K**. And finally A is *positively valid* iff A is valid in all +ms. Theorem 2 of [44] delivered the following happy result (among others):

Soundness and completeness of **B+**. $\vdash A$ is a theorem of **B+** iff A is positively valid.

4 Basic relevant logics

When relevant logics first appeared, they were dismissed by many as *deplorably weak*. More lately, systems like **R** have taken flak as *unconscionably strong*.[10] There is a simple remedy for such complaints: if you don't like all the axioms, *change* or *delete* some. This has an obvious semantical counterpart: if you don't like all the *postulates,* change or delete some.[11]

---

[9] In particular, Kripke [27] on intuitionist logic.
[10] Cf., e.g., Brady [9].
[11] You can even, if you would like, *add* some postulates (*with* their corresponding axioms, of course).

But when, you ask, will it *ever* end? The deletion process terminates, we affirm, when *all* the special postulates are gone, and only those principles remain that *belong to the method*. From [45] on, the following have been central:

1. This is a *worlds* semantics.

2. Logical entailment is interpreted as *truth-preservation* across worlds.

3. Extensional particles are interpreted *extensionally*.

4. Intensional particles are interpreted *intensionally*, using the ternary relation R.

5. There is no *universally preferred* relevant logic.

We now say a bit about each of these 5 points.

Ad 1. We follow Leibniz (and Kripke) in referring to the points of our model structures as *worlds*. We insist that they need not be *possible* worlds. And there are many other things to call these points—*theories, states, setups, cases, posets, filters*—in accordance with the ontological predilections, terminological idiosyncrasies and grant applications of various authors.[12]

Ad 2. That A entails B says, on an old story, that B is true *everywhere* that A is true. This is also the *relevant* semantical story.

Ad 3. Belnap has in conversation laid it down, and we have long agreed, that to interpret the *extensional* particles *and, or,* and *not* extensionally is to fix their truth-values *at a world* w on the values of their components *at* w. This motivates the truth-conditions on an interpretation I that we may write as follows:

$$T\wedge. \quad [A \wedge B]w = [A]w \wedge B[w]$$
$$T\vee. \quad [A \vee B]w = [A]w \vee B[w]$$
$$T\neg. \quad [\neg A]w = \neg[A]w$$

The $\neg$ here in question is *Boolean* negation.[13]

---

[12]Even before Kit Fine [22], we leaned to *theories* ourselves. Cf. Routley–Meyer [45].

[13]Boolean negation was a *newfangled* particle in relevant logics, *conservatively* introduced (for **R+** and **R**) by us in [33] and [34] respectively. Original equipment for these logics was the (not exactly extensional) *DeMorgan negation* $\sim$.

Ad 4. The intensional particles are *whatever we want them to be*. Certainly the (relevant) implication → is expected to be among them. In weaker relevant logics, → counts as a *left-to-right* conditional.[14] It is also possible to have a *right-to-left* conditional, which we will symbolize by ←.[15] Other candidates are fusion o, fission $+$, traditional necessity $\square$ and possibility $\lozenge$, etc. If fusion is *commutative*, then $B \leftarrow A$ is *the same* as $A \rightarrow B$. Here are the two most salient semantical truth-conditions on *relevant* particles:

$T\rightarrow.\ [A \rightarrow B]w = \forall x \forall y (Rwxy \Rightarrow ([A]x \Rightarrow [B]y))$
$To.\ [AoB]w = \exists x \exists y (Rxyw \wedge [A]x \wedge [B]y)$

The relevant particles are interpreted *intensionally*. To fix for example the value of $A \rightarrow B$ at w, it is necessary to look at worlds *beyond* w. Somewhere in between is the DeMorgan negation $\sim$. Invoking the Routley $*$ of [47], its truth-condition on the semantics of [45] (etc.) is just

$T\sim.\ [\sim A]w = \neg([A]w*)$

Ad 5. It was once an open question which was the *correct* modal logic. C. I. Lewis (a bit unwillingly), Kripke [26] and their cohorts turned this question on its head, by showing that one could season and salt modal logics to taste. Relevant logics have a similar history. Even [3] introduces a number of relevant logics (a bit unwillingly, since it *claims* to prefer **E**).

Seasoning and salting relevant logics is *not* our present business. That business is rather getting to the *core* of the semantical analysis hitherto laid down. As this is *logic*, the analysis and critique of *inference*, this core will concentrate on the *valid entailments* $A \leq B$. At the *elemental level*, we thus view (relevant) implication (as we have since Meyer [28]) as *essentially relational*.

Appealing to the *Semantic Entailment* lemma of previous papers, which also plays a role below, we lay down

$T\leq.\ [A] \leq [B] = \forall x([A]x \Rightarrow [B]x).$ (SemEnt)

---

[14] We adopt the well-chosen terminology of Restall [41]. This is, as [41] also notes, a *left residual* in the sense of Birkhoff [8]. It is also the *arrow of entailment* in the relevant logic literature.

[15] We *reverse* the arrow with reluctance. The idea is that $B \leftarrow A$ shall be our notation for '*A right-implies B*', a *right residual* in the [8] sense. Dunn, in his [20], accurately notes that *there is no consistency in the literature about which is the "left" residual and which is the "right"*. We follow our [32]. Dunn's [21] (sob!) *misread* [32], intimating that it had assumed that fusion is commutative. [32] made *no* such general assumption, and *very clearly* considered *both* residuals.

The present concentration on semantic entailment, although always a key element in relevant analysis (especially in *soundness* proofs), only became *explicit* in the (so-called) *simplified semantics* of Priest and Routley [39] and Restall [40]. We carry it a little further here, by dropping the "real world" 0 and the set of "logical worlds" to which 0 belongs.

This takes cares of items 1 and 2 above. We turn now to 3, which enjoins us to *respect* whatever truth-functional particles are present. Thinking of worlds as *theories*,[16] the truth-condition $T\wedge$ is built-in. But $T\vee$ (and $T\neg$, when present) require thought. In C.S. Peirce's *long run*, $A \vee B$ needs the support of *at least one* of A, B. In the long run, at least as a *regulative ideal*,[17] we expect $\neg A$ to be *present* iff A is *absent*. So we prefer *prime* theories, which resolve the disjunctions they contain. And we prefer negation *consistent* and *complete* theories, which, when $\neg$ is present, contain *exactly one* of the pair $A, \neg A$, for each formula A.

These preferences have given shape to the ternary *relational* semantics for relevant logics. A simpler *operational* semantics, along the lines of Urquhart [49] or Fine [22], works fine in sorting out the relevant behavior of $\to$ and $\wedge$. But [49] breaks down for **R+** in the presence of $T\vee$. And [22] introduces the prime theory apparatus *too*, after which it is *not pretty*.[18]

We turn now to point 4—the ternary relation R itself, and its role in accounting for the relevant $\to$ and its suite. Many efforts have been made to give *intuitive content* to this relation—to *picture* it and otherwise to get up close and personal. We blush to confess that we have been associated with some of these efforts; as to others, which permute the order of the terms and which attempt binary[19] reductions and the like, our conscience is clear. The intuition that remains is that $T\to$ is the *formal instrument* which looks after the informal operation of *modus ponens*. For what $Rxyz$ says (as the completeness proofs make clear) is that x likes $B \to C$ if and only if, whenever y likes B then z likes C. That is a step, from left to right, of modus ponens for $\to$; a contrapositive move then takes us then from right

---

[16]I.e., *filters*, from the lattice-theoretic viewpoint.

[17]We are *far from suggesting* that such regulative ideals should dominate *logic in practice*. To the contrary, much nonsense has emanated from the insistence that theories be *negation-consistent*, on penalty of concluding *absolutely everything*. But if $\neg$ is Boolean, one had *better be* consistent!

[18]But it is *fine*. While [45] and its suite somewhat anticipated Fine [22], it was (we think) the same *calculus of theories* that provided the mathematical background for his work and ours.

[19]Some binary reductions in fact work well—cf. [4] for Dunn's work on **RM**, for example. But nothing works (at least as we see it) to dispatch the *general* relevant ternary R in favor of what can be cooked up from 2-place relations. Satisfyingly, as both Dunn and R. Wille have called to our attention, C.S. Peirce also took *3-place* relations to be the *most fundamental* ones.

to left.

While ternary R is all about modus ponens for $\to$ (the one rule that you can count on while all others dissolve around you), it gives rise to other (conservatively addable) useful connectives. We have set out To, which provides a *fusion* operator to bunch premises in an *intensional* way as $T\wedge$ bunches them by *extensional* conjunction. Clearly there are several more *fusion-like* connectives o', depending which of w, x, y take the place of $1, 2, 3$ in the rubric

$$\text{To}'. \ [Ao'B]w = \exists x \exists y (R123 \wedge [A]x \wedge [B]y).$$

Just so, there are other *arrow-like* connectives $\to'$, fooling similarly with the rubric

$$T\to'. \ [A \to' B]w = \forall x \forall y (R123 \Rightarrow ([A]x \Rightarrow [B]y))$$

EXERCISE. Locate (what we have called) $\leftarrow$ among the $\to'$.

We have allowed that there may be *many* intensional particles. Some are directly definable in terms of $\to$ and the truth-functions. (Boring exercise: set out $T \leftrightarrow$, where $A \leftrightarrow B = \text{df}(A \to B) \wedge (B \to A)$.) Others result from a little intensional fiddling—cf. T$\sim$ above. Things get more lively if we *mix* relevant and irrelevant particles. Nothing *prevents* (and Anderson–Belnap motivating remarks *suggested*) that the entailment of **E** be parsed as *the strict relevant implication* $\Box(A \to B)$, borrowing an $\to$ from **R** and a $\Box$ from **S4**.[20] The obvious thing to do semantically is to have *two* accessibility relations (as in [43], [31]), a ternary R to look after $\to$ and a binary S to explicate $\Box$. (After that, the sky is the limit.)

Our final point above was that there should be no *preferred* relevant logic. Yet, in a way, we have already come up with one. It is the logic that one gets out of the first-order theory of *any* ternary relation R, merely imposing those that we choose out of the above truth-conditions. (Or so it is our purpose to convince you below.) Without negation, that logic is **B+**. To extend **B+** to any other positive relevant logic, simply impose the additional postulates on R that go with that logic. (Those additional conditions may involve a particular "real world" 0, or a set O of such worlds.) Similarly, there is a natural minimal *classical* relevant logic, imposing T$\neg$ as well. We call that system **CB** in this paper.[21]

---

[20]This thought, though tempting, was only *partially* correct. Kripke [25] *lucked out*, since the $A \to B$ of **E**$_\to$ is exactly translatable in **R**$^\Box_\to$ as $\Box(A \to B)$. The same luck holds when DeMorgan $\sim$ is added. But this luck runs out, as Maksimova demonstrated, when a non-theorem of **E+** is proved on **R**$^\Box$+ translation.

[21]We will apply the technique of our [33] below, which will show **CB** a conservative extension of **B+**.

5 A basic Boolean excursion

In this section, we attend to the claim that the addition of *classical negation* is conservative over **B+** as defined above. This claim has been made before—by ourselves and others. Here, very carefully, we shall *prove* it. And then we shall draw the appropriate corollaries.

Recall from section III the modeling of **B+** in +ms, on which the system is sound and complete. This modeling depends by $p1$ on a reflexive, transitive $\subseteq$ (defined by $R0ab$), equipped with replacement properties by $p2$–$p4$. And every interpretation must satisfy also a (monotone increasing) hereditary condition as well.

We can get *all that* if we simply take the $\subseteq$ in question to be the equality relation $=$. We have $p1$, since equality is reflexive and transitive. We have $p2$–$p4$, since equality licenses replacements. And we have H, since $a = b \Rightarrow I(A,a) = I(A,b)$ trivially. So, for now, let us try out the postulate

$$p0.\ a \subseteq b \text{ iff } a = b.$$

Let us call any appropriate structure $\mathbf{K} = \langle 0, K, R \rangle$ that satisfies $p0$ a b+ms. We have already noted that any b+ms is certainly a +ms. So, by soundness, each theorem $\vdash A$ of **B+** is valid in every b+ms. But what of completeness, relative to the b+ms? This requires, for each *non-theorem* A of **B+**, that there should be some b+ms $\mathbf{K}$ in which A is invalid. And so there is, *massaging* our model theory along the lines of [33]. We recall again, for all interpretations I in all +ms,

Semantic Entailment Lemma (SemEnt). $[A \to B]0$ iff $\forall x([A]x \Rightarrow [B]x)$.

THEOREM 1 (Classical Theorem for B+). *The following conditions are equivalent, for each formula A of $\mathbf{L+}$:*

1. $\vdash A$ is a theorem of **B+**

2. A is valid in all +ms

3. A is valid in all b+ms

Proof. The hard part is to show that (3) implies (2). We proceed by contraposition. *Goal*: A is invalid in some b+ms. *Hypothesis*: A is invalid in +ms $\mathbf{K} = \langle 0, K, R \rangle$. There is an interpretation I in $\mathbf{K}$ such that A is false at 0 on I. We define a b+ms $\mathbf{K}' = \langle 0', K', R' \rangle$ as follows:

(a) $0'$ is a new element disjoint from K

(b) $K' = K \cup \{0'\}$

(c) For all $a, b, c \in K$, we have $R'abc$ iff $Rabc$

(d) For all $a' \in K'$, we have $R'0'a'a'$

(e) Otherwise for $a', b', c' \in K', \neg R'a'b'c'$

We next define an interpretation I' in **K'**, determined by its values on atoms and truth-conditions:

(f) $I'(p, a) = I(p, a)$ for all $a \in K$ and atoms p

(g) $I'(p, 0') = I(p, 0)$ for all atoms p

We now show, by structural induction on D, the generalized

(f') $I'(D, a) = I(D, a)$ for all $a \in K$

(g') $I'(D, 0') = I(D, 0)$

Assume on Inductive Hypothesis (IH) that (f') and (g') hold at all $a \in K'$ for all subformulas of an arbitrary formula D. This is clear by (f) and (g) when D is some atom p. We invoke the (IH) to show the same for *compound* D. The interesting case is $D = B \to C$.

Ad (f'). Let R'' be whichever of R, R' is appropriate. Unpack $T \to$ by $\forall x \forall y (R''axy \Rightarrow ([B]x \Rightarrow [C]y))$. How, given (IH), can this value differ for $a \in K$ on I' as opposed to I? (The quantifiers on the I' side range over K'; on the I side, over K; and R'' is R' on the I' side and R on the I side.) Assume $B \to C$ is *false* at a on I; it must also be false there on I' (since we have the *same* counterexample on (IH), given that R' is an *extension* of R). Assume then for *reductio* that $B \to C$ is *true* at a on I but false at a on I'. Then there are $x', y' \in K'$ such that $R'ax'y'$ and $[B]x'$ but *not* $[C]y'$ on I'. Since this never happens back in K on I, at least one of x', y' must be $0'$. But the "Otherwise" clause (e) above in the definition of R' then enforces $\neg R'ax'y'$ (since a is *old*). Contradiction!

Ad (g'). Again assume (IH). Suppose that $B \to C$ is true at $0'$ on I'. Then, by SemEnt, for all $x' \in K'$ we have $[B]x' \Rightarrow [C]x'$. Since $K \subseteq K'$, we have on IH also $\forall x([B]x \Rightarrow [C]x)$ on I in **K**, whence $[B \to C]0$ on I. For the converse, suppose $B \to C$ false at $0'$ on I'. Then, by SemEnt, there is an $x' \in K'$ such that $[B]x'$ but not $[C]x'$ on I'. If this $x' \in K$, then by (IH) and SemEnt we have $B \to C$ also false at 0 on I. The remaining possibility is $[B]0'$ and not $[C]0'$ on I'. But under (g') of the inductive hypothesis this also sets $I(B, 0)$ true and $I(C, 0)$ false, whence again $B \to C$ is false at 0 on I.

We return to our original formula A, which was false at 0 on I in the +ms **K**. By $(g')A$ is also false at $0'$ on I' in the b+ms $\mathbf{K'} = \langle 0', K', R' \rangle$. In a nutshell, the *denial* of (ii) implies the denial of (iii). Contraposing as promised, (3) implies (2). This concludes what it is necessary to say, and the theorem is *proved*. ∎

Not only is the theorem proved, but also the chief obstacle has been removed to the *relevant* accommodation of classical semantical negation ¬. That obstacle lay in the *hereditary condition* H, which says that if a ⊆b in a +ms then $[A]a \Rightarrow [A]b$ for all formulas A on any interpretation I. Our postulates and truth-conditions for **B+** (and other logics, even those with DeMorgan ∼) sufficed in [45] and elsewhere to establish *all* of H from its assumption Hp above on atoms. But $T\neg$ *resists* the structural induction. Happily it can *no longer resist* in the presence of $p0$, as [33], [34] make clear.

DEFINITION 2 (Classical CB Definition). A statement ⊢ B of **L+** is a theorem of **CB+** iff B is valid in all b+ms.

Adding classical ¬, governed by $T\neg$, to the minimal system **B+** has *done no harm*.[22]

THEOREM 3 (Classical conservation theorem). *CB⊢ is a conservative extension of $B+\vdash$.*

Proof. By the classical theorem for **B+**. Enough said. ∎

6 Basic consecution logics

Confession is good for the soul. For the good of our souls, we make one. The "real world" 0, although it is *not doing very much,* is nonetheless doing *a little* in the basic semantics of this paper. So to keep our promise to drop 0 from the semantics, it is necessary also to take a thoroughgoing *relational view* of what relevant logics are *about*.

That the *ghost* of 0 does not return to *haunt* us with anomalies, we henceforth prefer the *relational language* **L**≤ to the *assertional language* **L** ⊢ that we have assumed until further notice. (This is the further notice.) We also trade in our basic logics like **B+** ⊢ and **CB** ⊢ for *entailment logics* **B+**≤ and **CB**≤.

Another reason for the shift is to find a more perfect union between the *logical* ideas (on which we are concentrating here) and the *type-theoretic* ideas developed by the λ and **CL** communities. For these ideas have been worked out (e.g., in [5]) in terms of a *binary relation* ≤ *on types*.

---

[22] As the late W.V. Quine might have put it. The *Relevantist* of Belnap and Dunn [7] might interject that it has *done no good, either*. For an *anti-relevantist* view, see Meyer [29].

On the interpretation of *types as formulas,* this relation (as far as it goes) is *exactly* **B+≤** entails.

Formulas B of the *Boolean sublanguage* **BL** of **L** have the following Backus-Naur specification:[23]

$$B ::= p \mid \neg B \mid B \wedge B \mid B \vee B$$

A *Boolean tautology* is any formula B of **BL** which is a truth-table tautology. By extension, we also call a formula A of **L** a Boolean tautology if $A = s(B)$ for some substitution s of a Boolean tautology B of **BL**.[24]

We now lay down axioms and rules for **CB≤** and **B+≤**.

B1.	$A \leq C$, when $A \supset C$ is a Boolean tautology	**Bool**
B2.	$(A \to B) \wedge (A \to C) \leq A \to B \wedge C$	**Ax→∧I**
B3.	$(A \to C) \wedge (B \to C) \leq A \vee B \to C$	**Ax→∨E**
R1.	$B \leq C \Rightarrow (A \leq B \Rightarrow A \leq C)$	**RuTrans≤**
R2.	$A' \leq A$ and $B \leq B' \Rightarrow A \to B \leq A' \to B'$	**RuMon→**
R3.	$A \leq B$ and $A' \leq B' \Rightarrow A \wedge A' \leq B \wedge B'$	**RuMon∧**
R4.	$A \leq B$ and $A' \leq B' \Rightarrow A \vee A' \leq B \vee B'$	**RuMon∨**
R5.	$A \leq B \Rightarrow \neg B \leq \neg A$	**RuTransp¬**

Note the redundancy of R4 in the presence of R3 and R5. Clearly these axioms and rules confer a *distributive lattice* structure on **B+≤**, and a *Boolean lattice* structure on **CB≤**.

7 Soundness and Completeness of the Relational Systems

We keep first our promise to drop 0 from the semantics. (In view of SemEnt, and after the classical moves just above, it is evident that 0 isn't really *doing very much* at this basic level.) Combined with our first promise recall that we now view our basic systems as *relational*. A *basic model structure* (henceforth, just *bms*) is then just a pair $\mathbf{K} = \langle K, R \rangle$, where K is a nonempty set and R is a ternary relation on K. A possible interpretation is again a function I assigning one of *true, false* to each formula A at each $w \in K$. Such a function I is an *interpretation* if it satisfies the applicable truth-conditions from among $T\wedge, T\vee, T\neg$ and $T\to$ above. An interpretation I is completely determined by its values on all *atoms* p at all *worlds* $w \in K$.

---

[23] In brief, a formula B of **L** is in **BL** if there are *no arrows* in B.

[24] For **L+**, the Boolean tautologies that count are *instances* of $A \supset B$, where A and B are themselves built up from atoms under just $\wedge$ and $\vee$. They are not *particularly* Boolean, since this fragment is the same for the intuitionist logic **J** and indeed the *first-degree entailments* $\mathbf{D}_{\text{fde}}$ of the relevant logics **R**, **E** and **T** of [3].

More adjustment is required in the vocabulary of *verification*. Since all *statements* of our relational language **L**≤ are now of the form $A \leq C$, all thoughts of a *real world* 0 at which exactly the *logical truths* shall *always* be true are now emphatically beside the point. Even so, we may retain an *imaginary* 0 as a *façon de parler*. And we may still write $[B]0$ for B *is verified* on I. Our *manner of speaking* applies, in the first instance, only to $\to$ formulas, letting $A \to C$ stand in for the honest *statement* $A \leq C$. So, given an interpretation I in a bms **K** we say, in the abbreviated notation introduced above,

$$V\to.\ [A \to C]0 \text{ iff } \forall x([A]x \Rightarrow [C]x)$$

When $A \to C$ is verified on I, we may also say that A *entails* C on I. This is in complete conformity to the SemEnt principle laid down in section 4 above. A *entails* C in a bms **K** iff A entails C on all interpretations I in **K**; and A *basically entails* C iff A entails C in all bms.

We note immediately

THEOREM 4 (Basic soundness theorem). *For all formulas A, C of **L**≤, if $A \leq C$ is a theorem of **CB**≤ then A basically entails C.*

Proof. Consider an arbitrary bms **K** and an interpretation I therein. Show by deductive induction that if $A \leq C$ in **CB**≤ then A entails C on I. Enough said.[25] ∎

Semantical completeness of the basic relational systems requires (as ever) a little more work. We shall treat **B+**≤ and **CB**≤ together in setting out machinery. As ever, a *theory* shall be any set S of formulas closed under *entailment* and *conjunction*. I.e., S is a theory iff, for all formulas A and B in the language, we have both

$$\leq \mathbf{E}) \quad A \leq B \Rightarrow (A \in S \Rightarrow B \in S)$$

and

$$\wedge \mathbf{I}) \quad A \in S \text{ and } B \in S \Rightarrow A \wedge B \in S$$

The *calculus of theories* shall be the structure $\mathbf{CT} = \langle CT, o, \subseteq \rangle$, where CT is the set of all theories, $\subseteq$ is set inclusion, and o is the *fusion* operation defined by

---

[25] Evidently the soundness theorem holds *a fortiori* of **B+**≤.

Do) $SoT = \{B : \exists A(A \to B \in S \text{ and } A \in T\}$[26]

Some theories are more *truth-like* than others. Among the conditions that we might like a theory S to satisfy, for all formulas A and B, are the following:

$\vee$**E)** $A \vee B \in S \Rightarrow A \in S$ or $B \in S$
$\neg$ **E)** $\neg A \in S \Rightarrow A \notin S$
$\neg$ **I)** $A \notin S \Rightarrow \neg A \in S$

Note that the converse $\vee$**I** principle to $\vee$**E** holds automatically by Axiom B1 above. A theory S that admits $\vee$**E** is called *prime;* that admits $\neg$**E**, *consistent;* that admits $\neg$**I**, *complete*. And a prime (and consistent and complete, if $\neg$ is present) S is *truth-like*.[27]

As an exercise, show that the fusion of any two theories is itself a theory. Alas, the fusion of truth-like theories is unlikely to be itself truth-like. We accordingly move to the *canonical relational structure* **CPT** of *prime* theories. **CPT** $= \langle CPT, CTR \rangle$, where CPT is the set of all non-trivial[28] prime theories, and CTR is the *canonical ternary relation* defined on the set CT of *all* theories by

DCTR) $CTRxyz =$ df $xoy \subseteq z$,

for all theories $x, y,$ and z.

Readers, we hope, will see now where we are heading. The canonical structure **CPT** will be the **K** $= \langle K, R \rangle$ for our semantical completeness proofs. At least it is clear that **CPT** is a bms. For CPT is a non-empty set, and CTR is a ternary relation when restricted to that set. We next concoct a *canonical interpretation* CI, by setting, for all formulas A and prime theories x,

DCI) $CI(A, x) = $ *true* iff $A \in x$

Oops—that definition merely makes CI a *possible interpretation*. To make it moreover an *interpretation,* we need the

---

[26] The term *fusion* is due to Fine. But the notion was introduced earlier by Powers in his [38], as *modus ponens product*. And indeed SoT consists of *all results* of applying $\to E$, taking major premisses from S and minor ones from T.

[27] The term *truth-like* comes from [4], to characterize any theory that respects appropriate truth-conditions (e.g., $T\vee$) on such truth-functional particles as belong to its vocabulary. But a *preference* for truth-like theories goes back much further, at least to our [45].

[28] A theory S is *non-trivial* iff S is neither the empty set nor the set of all formulas.

LEMMA 5 (Canonical interpretation lemma). *CI respects the truth-conditions* $T\wedge, T\vee, T\to, T\neg$.

Proof. The members of CPT are non-trivial prime theories. $T\wedge$ and $T\vee$ (and $T\neg$ in the Boolean case) are built into the definition of a truth-like theory. So only $T \to$ requires *serious* verification. We must show on CI, for all formulas B and C and truth-like non-trivial theories w,

(a) $[B \to C]w = \forall x \forall y (CTRwxy \Rightarrow ([B]x \Rightarrow [C]y))$,

where the quantifiers range over CPT. Definitions reduce this to

(b) $B \to C \in w$ iff $\forall x \forall y (wox \subseteq y \Rightarrow (B \in x \Rightarrow C \in y))$.

Left to right is obvious. But the other direction is interesting. Assume $B \to C \notin w$. It will suffice to find x, y in CPT such that (i) $wox \subseteq y$, (ii) $B \in x$ and (iii) $C \notin y$. There are at any rate *theories* x_0 and y_0 in CT that clearly satisfy these conditions: just set $x_0 = \{D : B \leq D\}$, which is the *principal theory* $[B)$ determined by B; and set $y_0 = wox_0$. The final trick is to *blow up* x_0 and y_0 to truth-like theories x and y so that (i)–(iii) continue to hold. The *method* is to start with y_0, extending it to a prime theory y while keeping C *out*. One then applies the *Squeezing lemma* (e.g., of our [44]) to extend x_0 to a *prime* x so that (i) continues to hold.[29] And the lemma is *proved*. ∎

THEOREM 6 (Basic completeness theorem). *The following conditions are equivalent for* **B+≤** *and* **CB≤**:

1. $A \leq C$

2. A entails C on the canonical interpretation CI in the bms **CPT**.

3. A basically entails C.

Proof. (1) $\Rightarrow$ (3) is the content of the basic soundness theorem above. (3) $\Rightarrow$ (2) by the canonical interpretation lemma. We conclude by showing (2) $\Rightarrow$ (1). Assume (2). For *reductio*, assume it a *non-theorem* that $A \leq C$. Consider the principal theory $[A)$ determined by A. On the reductio hypothesis, $C \notin [A)$. But, as in the proof of the last lemma, $[A)$ can be extended to a truth-like theory x such that (i) $A \in x$ and (ii) $C \notin x$. This contradicts (2) and ends the proof. ∎

---

[29] These tasks are most elegantly accomplished using Belnap's *pair-extension lemma*; cf. [4, p. 124].

8 Truth translations

We now introduce our *truth translations* of formulas A of **L** into classical first-order Predicate Logic **PL**. Our classical vocabulary will be as usual, based on a single ternary relation symbol R and countably many monadic predicate symbols P_i, $0 < i < \omega$. We call a formula of **PL** with *exactly one free variable* (but as many bound variables as you like) a *unary predicate expression*. We may write a unary predicate expression A whose free variable is x as $A(x)$.

The underlying idea of our translation is just this. It is customary, in Kripke-style relational semantics for systems **S** of non-classical logics, to parse the *propositions* of such logics as *sets of worlds*. This is, in effect, to interpret the *formulas* of **S** as themselves *propositional functions*—taking worlds $w \in K$ as *arguments* and one of the *truth-values* {false, true} as values. When *curried,* our characterization of a possible interpretation I as a function from $\mathbf{L} \times K$ to **2** conforms; such an I is equivalently a function from **L** to $K \to \mathbf{2}$, where **2** is the 2-element Boolean algebra.

We note (but shall not further explore in the present highly classical environment) that only laziness or undue attachment to prevailing convention makes **2** a *preferred* target algebra for our propositional functions. To the contrary, propositions can have any structure that they *ought to have*—Heyting algebras, DeMorgan monoids, or what you will. But laziness and attachment to convention will prevail in *this* paper.

Having confessed our staid inclinations, and having set out the relational semantics for basic relevant logics, we trust that the rest of our plan of translation will quickly become clear to the reader. Consider an arbitrary formula B of **L**. B has a unique *construction tree,* recording how it has been built up from atoms under the connectives $\wedge, \vee, \neg, \to$ and perhaps others. Working our way from the leaves (or tips) of the tree, which are the atoms, we wish to assign a *unary predicate expression* of **PL** to each subformula C of B. Choosing an appropriate recursive plan, the process will terminate in the assignment of such an expression to B itself.

We mentioned *possible interpretations* in passing a couple of paragraphs ago. What distinguishes genuine, honest interpretations from merely possible ones is the imposition of *truth-conditions* like $T\wedge, T\to$, etc. (There was also a *hereditary condition* H, but the further moves above assure that it is now satisfied *vacuously.*) Fidelity to the truth-conditions will accordingly be the key ingredient in the promised recursive plan.

Let us return to the bracket notation introduced in section 3, where we used '$[A]w$' as shorthand for 'the formula A is true at the world w on the interpretation I'. This looks a lot like *predicating* the formula A *of* the world w. The plot thickens with the truth-conditions of section 4. These say things like $[\neg A]w = \neg[A]w$ and $[A \to B]w = \forall x \forall y (Rwxy \supset ([A]x \supset [B]y))$. Do we not have *in this notation* the central clue as to how our truth translations will work?

Indeed, this is the central clue. To each atom p of **L** we assign a unique monadic predicate symbol $P = \tau(p)$. Making *informal* use of λ notation, and presupposing η-reduction and rewriting of bound variables, we may write this translation as

$$\tau(p) = \lambda x.Px, \text{ for each atom } p.$$

Still using λ notation, we recursively extend this translation τ to take *each formula A of **L*** into an (in general, *defined*) unary predicate expression of **PL**, on the rubric of the following table:

L Formula A	**PL** Unary Predicate $\tau(A)$
$B \wedge C$	$\lambda x. \tau(B)x \wedge \tau(C)x$
$B \vee C$	$\lambda x. \tau(B)x \vee \tau(C)x$
$\neg B$	$\lambda x. \neg \tau(B)x$
$B \to C$	$\lambda x. \forall y \forall z (Rxyz \supset (\tau(B)y \supset \tau(C)z))$

Note how the *truth-conditions* ($T \to$, etc.) have showed up in the $\tau(A)$. We now define an *entailment translation* ν, by setting

Dν) $\quad \nu(A \leq C) = \forall x (\tau(A)x \supset \tau(C)x)$

To show how simple our truth translation is, we institute again our old bracketed notation, slowly churning out the mated formulas of **PL**.
EXAMPLES.

Ax$\wedge$E. $\qquad p \wedge q \leq p \qquad$ (AxB1, since $p \wedge q \supset p$ is a
$\qquad\qquad\qquad\qquad\qquad\qquad\qquad\qquad$ Boolean tautology.)
Translation. $\forall x([p \wedge q]x \supset [p]x) \;=\; \forall x([p]x \wedge [q]x \supset [p]x)$
$\qquad\qquad\qquad\qquad\qquad\qquad\; = \; \forall x(Px \wedge Qx \supset Px)$

Henceforth we leave the prefaced $\forall x$ tacit, to facilitate easier reading of formulas. Next,

Ax$\to \vee$E. $\qquad (p \to s) \wedge (q \to s) \leq p \vee q \to s \quad (Ax$B3$)$
Translation. $[(p \to s) \wedge (q \to s)]x \supset [p \vee q \to s]x =$
$[p \to s]x \wedge [q \to s]x \supset \quad \forall y \forall z (Rxyz \supset$
$([p \vee q]y \supset [s]z)) = \forall y \forall z (Rxyz \supset ([p]y \supset [s]z)) \wedge$
$\forall y \forall z (Rxyz \supset ([q]y \supset [s]z)) \supset \forall y \forall z (Rxyz \supset ([p \vee q]y \supset$
$[s]z)) = \forall y \forall z ((Rxyz \supset (Py \supset Sz)) \wedge \forall y \forall z (Rxyz \supset$
$(Qy \supset Sz)) \supset \forall y \forall z (Rxyz \supset (Py \vee Qy \supset Sz))$

Showing these translations theorems of **PL** is an easy exercise. How about a non-theorem?

AxWI. $(p \to q) \land p \leq q$

Translation. $[(p \to q) \land p]x \leq [q]x = [(p \to q)]x \land [p]x \leq [q]x =$
$\forall y \forall z((Rxyz \supset (Py \supset Qz)) \land Px \supset Qx$

Clearly the translation is *not* a **PL** theorem. That's good, because $AxWI$—though a theorem and even an axiom of very many relevant logics—is *insufficiently minimal* for **B+**.[30]

Verification theorem. Let $A \leq C$ be any statement in the domain of definition of the verification translation ν. Then the following conditions are equivalent for **B+≤** and **CB≤**:

(i) $A \leq C$ is a theorem

(ii) $\nu(A \leq C)$ is a theorem of **PL**

Proof. As the first-order translations merely recapitulate the semantics, the theorem is obvious. ∎

9   CBMODEL (and its kin)

We now take leave to *rename* the first-order logic **PL**, as formulated above with a single ternary R and countably many monadic P_i. Henceforth we call it **CBMODEL**. We take it, as we implicitly did above, as an *assertional* system, whose elementary *statements* are of the form ⊢ A. The *theorems* of **CBMODEL** are just those ⊢ A such that A is *first-order valid* (with axioms and rules, if desired, supplied to the reader's taste). And our main theorem then becomes

THEOREM 7 (Truth translation theorem). *$A \leq C$ in **CB** iff **CBMODEL**⊢ $\forall x([A]x \supset [C]x)$, subject to the definitional schemes introduced above.*

But there is *less* truth than poetry in our claim in the last section to have dropped 0 from the semantics of **B+** and **CB**. For the ghost of 0 *did remain*, via verification conditions that simply mirrored the truth-conditions *at* 0, back when it had as much ontological standing as any other "world" in K. And that ghost would haunt us still further if we proceeded to stronger relevant logics like **R+**, with its semantical *truths* like $Rx0x$, for all $x \in K$.

Nonetheless, 0 *is gone* from our semantical postulates for **B+** and **CB**. Nor does it haunt us even a little where the central assertions of logic are at issue—i.e., the *true entailments*. As these correspond exactly to the type theorists' relational calculi, they too need not mourn for 0.

---

[30]Hey, $AxWI$ is just conjunctive *modus ponens*. What could be wrong with that? Plenty, as it turns out. Cf. our [35] for its *destruction* of a relevantly formulated naïve set theory.

Still, it would be good to accommodate a wider variety of relevant logics on our scheme of truth translation. It might even be good, for those suckled in Intuitionist or Relevantist or other creeds outworn, to provide a wider range of first-order theories *into which* relevant logics might be translated. And it would definitely be good to provide such translations for the original formulations of relevant logics as *assertional* systems.

All of these tasks will involve the *resurrection* of 0, or some surrogate thereof, as an *honest* world. In the full Boolean case, we are pushed not merely to **PL** but to **PL=**, making equality explicit. And in logics stronger than the minimal basic ones, the *targets* of the translations will be *applied* first-order theories, with *proper axioms* doing duty for the semantical postulates.

We illustrate first with a system **CB=MODEL**, which stands to **CB-MODEL** as **CB+** stands to **CB≤**. This too will be a first-order theory, adding a constant 0 and the predicate = to the syntactical equipment of **CBMODEL**. This theory will have a single proper axiom, namely

Ax0. $\quad \forall x \forall y (x = y \equiv R0xy)$,

which recapitulates our Booleanizing maneuvers. This leads immediately to a

Truth translation corollary $\vdash A$ in **CB+** iff **CB=MODEL** $\vdash [A]0$

Corollary to corollary **CB**$\vdash A \to C$ iff **CBMODEL** $\vdash \forall x ([A]x \supset [C]x)$

Proof. Again, the first corollary merely recapitulates the semantics. And it and the theorem imply the second corollary, given the Semantic Entailment lemma SemEnt above. ∎

That was so much fun that we will now propose a first-order theory **CR=MODEL**, which will do for the classical conservative extension **CR** of **R** what our corollary does for **CB**. The language of this theory adds the unary (Routley) function symbol ∗ to the primitives of **CR=MODEL**, with extra postulates **Ax0**, $\forall x Rxxx$ (TRP), $\forall x \forall y \forall z \forall w (\exists v (Rxyv \land Rvzw) \equiv \exists v (Rxzv \land Rvyw))$ (PP), $\forall x (x** = x), \forall x \forall y \forall z (Rxyz \supset Rxz*y*)$. These last 2 postulates look after DeMorgan ∼, eliminated via the truth-condition T∼ of section 4.

CR is just the system introduced as **CR*** in our [34], as a *conservative extension* of **R**.

Truth translation for CR $\vdash A$ in **CR** iff **CR=MODEL** $\vdash [A]0$

Similar results hold generally for relevant and other substructural logics, *mutatis mutandis*. And, as noted, we may *forswear* Boolean simplifications (but why?) by making other choices for the first-order logics of the *target* theories.[31]

10 Summing Up

We present this paper as very much a *work in progress*. Its main idea—that relevant logics can be recast in terms of (as it is put) a *classical first-order metalogic*—has long been evident to workers in the field. Nor is that idea quite so attractive as once it was. Other concerns—such as minimizing the *computational complexity* of proof searches—have come to the fore. (*Not many* of our best friends will shower us with praise for having "reduced" the almost trivial logic **B+** to the seriously undecidable **CBMODEL**.)[32]

Nonetheless, we take the present project to be *worth pursuing*. It was, after all, *unknown*, in the early days of relevant semantical investigation, that these logics could be furnished so smoothly (and indeed conservatively) with a full Boolean classical negation ¬. Even the choice of **B+** as *the* minimal positive relevant logic was, in [44] and [32] days, not so clear.

It is clearer now, on several grounds. One is simply the lovely connections between **B+** (or at least its →, ∧ fragment) that have been worked out independently in the λ community.[33] More relevant here is that, as we have recast the basic semantics, the *partial order* relation ⊆ and its special properties are *no longer required*. At root there is just a primitive ternary relation R on the semantic side, with *no* special properties.

Yet much remains to be done. We have exempted (at least so far) the Ackermann and Church sentential constants, fusion o and the right-to-left conditional ← from our classical theories.[34] On the verification side, ← is

---

[31]There is a painfully *simple* argument, set out by Meyer in [30], that the semantics of [45] is sound and complete for **R** when expressed in a theory **RMODEL** based on the first-order logic $\mathbf{R}^{\forall \exists x}$ of [4].

[32]The triviality of **B+** is *most evident* in its pure → fragment **B→**. For a formula in this fragment is a theorem iff it is of the form $A \to A$. On the **PL** side, the theory of even a single *binary* relation is paradigmatically undecidable. We have a *ternary* one, and all those monadic predicates to boot.

[33]Intersection type theorists also add a constant ω, which is relevantly translatable as the (optionally added) Church constant **T**. (There has been some confusion between Church **T** and the hitherto more relevantly important Ackermann **t**.) Church **T** is readily got by Boolean definition as $p \vee \neg p$. So defined, **T** satisfies on semantic grounds *both* the postulates $A \le \mathbf{T}$ and the (more mysterious) $\mathbf{T} \le \mathbf{T} \to \mathbf{T}$ of [5].

[34]In fact, there is *less* to accommodating such extra particles than one might fear. In view of the semantical completeness results, extra particles like ← are easy to add conservatively. An earlier draft of this paper showed that fusion o also can find a sleeping bag within the tent of classical conservative extension of **B+**. The result depended on this: for **B+o**, we can adapt a [33] "metavaluation" argument to show BoC a theorem

interested in relations of the shape $Ra0b$, as opposed to those of the form $R0ab$ (which $p0$ trivializes to $a = b$) that look after its left-to-right mate $\rightarrow$. And we have done hardly anything with DeMorgan $\sim$, the *original* relevant negation. To be sure, [32] proposed one system there called **B**. Routley preferred *another* **B** in [46].[35] Finally, the elimination of 0 is still incomplete. It *becomes complete* (and is more consonant both with the work on type theories and with logicians' insistence that their subject is first and foremost about the *relation* of entailment) on the above plan which *presents* the systems with a primitive binary $\leq$ rather than a unary $\vdash$.

Probably the most likely applications are to *theories of types*, in the λ logicians' sense.[36] Already Dezani *et al.* have noted in [19], as a consequence of [5], that there is a nice model of λ in the class of non-empty *theories* based on the **B+** fragment (*cum* extension) **B**$\wedge T$ (in $\rightarrow, \wedge,$ **T**).[37] And it is of course crashingly obvious that classical logic (as here formulated, with ternary R) models λ. For the relation $Rabc$ admits in particular the interpretation $r(a, b) = c$, where r is any binary operation. Well, the application operation of Combinatory Logic is a binary operation; and λ, which is definable within a system of combinators, has more models these days than one can shake a stick at. Any of these will do.

Still, one would like something a little more *sui generis*—which *illuminates* and which does not merely *copy* known results. To this too we pledge our best endeavours.

BIBLIOGRAPHY

[1] Ackermann, W., *Begründung einer strengen Implikation*, Journal of Symbolic Logic, 21 (1956), 113-128.

[2] Anderson, A.R., Some open problems concerning the system E of entailment, *Acta philosophica fennica 16* (1963), 7-18.

[3] Anderson, A.R. and N.D. Belnap, **Entailment (vol. I)**, Princeton, 1975.

[4] Anderson, A. R., N. D. Belnap and J. M. Dunn, **Entailment (vol. II)**, Princeton, 1992.

[5] Barendregt, H.P., M. Coppo and M. Dezani-Ciancaglini, A filter lambda model and the completeness of type assignment, *Journal of Symbolic Logic*, 48 (1983), 931-940.

---

iff both B and C are theorems.

[35] "Will the *real* **B** please stand up?" is not such a pressing question at our minimal level. In **R**, by contrast, DeMorgan goes for $A \rightarrow B \leq\ \sim B \rightarrow \sim A$, while Boole counters with $A \wedge \neg A \leq B$ and $A \leq B \vee \neg B$. Boole stands firm even at **CB**. But DeMorgan transposition has been reduced from an axiom to a rule. And, anyway, **CB** is a *proper extension* of everyone's **B**. (For the record, Meyer now prefers the Routley **B** to his own, for a *minimal* relevant logic.)

[36] Meyer makes this admission through clenched teeth. He doesn't really *believe* in types, save as useful fictions. So it would be a fine irony if his work were taken up by those of *another view*.

[37] [19] proposes another model using *all* of **B+**, but it is *not so nice*.

[6] Belnap, N.D., Display logic, *Journal of Philosophical Logic*, 11 (1982), 375-417. Discussed also in [4].
[7] Belnap, N.D. and J.M. Dunn, Entailment and the disjunctive syllogism, in G. Fløistad and G.H. von Wright, eds., *Philosophy of language/philosophical logic*, The Hague, 1981, 337-366. An edited version appears in [4, pp. 488–506].
[8] Birkhoff, G., *Lattice Theory*, Providence, 1948 (3rd edition, 1967).
[9] Brady, R.T., *Universal logic*, Centre for the Study of Language and Information - Lecture Notes, 2006.
[10] Bull, R., and K. Segerberg, Basic modal logic, in D.M. Gabbay and F. Günthner, eds., *Handbook of Philosophical Logic (vol. 2)*, Dordrecht, 1984, 1-88.
[11] Coppo, M. and M. Dezani-Ciancaglini, An extension of the basic functionality theory for the λ-calculus, *Notre Dame Journal of Formal Logic*, 21 (1980), 685-693.
[12] Church, A., The calculi of lambda conversion, Number 6 in *Annals of Mathematical Studies*, Princeton, 1941.
[13] Church, A., The weak positive implicational propositional calculus, abstract, *Journal of Symbolic Logic*, 16 (1951), 239.
[14] Church, A., The weak theory of implication, in A. Menne, A. Wilhelmy and H. Angsil, eds., *Kontrolliertes Denken*, Munich, 1951, 22-37.
[15] Coppo, M., M. Dezani-Ciancaglini and P. Sallé, Functional characterization of some semantic equalities inside λ-calculus, in *ICALP'79*, vol. 71 of Springer Lecture Notes in Computer Science, Berlin, 1979, 133-146.
[16] Coppo, M., M. Dezani-Ciancaglini and B. Venneri, *Principal type schemes and λ-calculus semantics*, in [48], 535-560.
[17] Curry, H.B. and R. Feys, *Combinatory logic I*, N. Holland, Amsterdam, 1958.
[18] Curry, H. B., *Foundations of Mathematical Logic*, McGraw-Hill, N.Y., 1963.
[19] Dezani-Ciancaglini, M., R. K. Meyer and Y. Motohama, The semantics of entailment omega. *Notre Dame Journal of Formal Logic*, 43(3):129–145, 2002.
[20] Dunn, J. M., Gaggle theory: an abstraction of Galois connections and residuation with applications to negation and various logical operations, in *Logics in AI*, vol. 478 of Springer Lecture Notes in Computer Science, 1991, 31-51.
[21] Dunn, J. M., Partial gaggles applied to logics with restricted structural rules, in P. Schroeder-Heister and K. Došen, eds., *Substructural logics*, Oxford, 1993, 63-108.
[22] Fine, K., Models for entailment, *Journal of Philosophical Logic*, 3 (1974), 347-372. An edited version appears in [4, pp. 208–231].
[23] Helman, G., *Restricted lambda abstraction and the interpretation of some non-classical logics*, Ph. D. thesis, U. of Pittsburgh, 1977. See also Helman's chapter, *Relevant implication and relevant functions*, in [4, pp. 202–222].
[24] Kripke, S.A., A completeness theorem in modal logic, *Journal of Symbolic Logic*, 24 (1959), 1-15.
[25] Kripke, S.A., The problem of entailment, *Journal of Symbolic Logic*, 24 (1959), abstract, 324.
[26] Kripke, S.A., Semantical analysis of modal logic I, *ZML*, 9 (1963), 67-96.
[27] Kripke, S.A., Semantical analysis of intuitionist logic I, in J. N. Crossley and M. A. E. Dummett, eds., *Formal systems and recursive functions*, N. Holland, Amsterdam, 1965, 92-129.
[28] Meyer, R. K., *Topics in modal and many-valued logic*, Ph. D. thesis, Pittsburgh, 1966.
[29] Meyer, R. K., *Why I am not a relevantist*. Research paper no. 1, Australian National University Logic Group, Philosophy, RSSS, Canberra, 1979.
[30] Meyer, R.K., Proving relevant semantical completeness relevantly, typescript, ANU, 1990.
[31] Meyer, R. K. and E. D. Mares, The semantics of entailment 0, in P. Schroeder-Heister and K. Došen, eds., *Substructural logics*, Oxford, 1993, 239-258.
[32] Meyer, R. K. and R. Routley, Algebraic analysis of entailment I, *Logique et analyse*, n.s., 15 (1972), 407-428.

[33] Meyer, R. K. and R. Routley, Classical relevant logics I, *Studia logica 32* (1973), 51-68.
[34] Meyer, R. K. and R. Routley, Classical relevant logics II, *Studia logica* 33 (1974), 183-94.
[35] Meyer, R. K., R. Routley and J. M. Dunn, Curry's paradox, *Analysis 39* (1979), 124-128.
[36] Meyer, R.K., and others, *The Key to the Universe*, in preparation.
[37] Pottinger, G., A type assignment for strongly normalizable λ-terms, in [48, pp. 561–57].
[38] Powers, L., On P-W, *Relevance logic newsletter 1* (1976), 131-142.
[39] Priest, G. and R. Sylvan, Simplified semantics for basic relevant logics, *Journal of Philosophical Logic*, 21 (1992), 217-232.
[40] Restall, Greg, Simplified semantics for relevant logics (and some of their rivals), *Journal of Philosophical Logic*, 22 (1993), 481-511.
[41] Restall, Greg, *An Introduction to Substructural Logics*, Routledge, London, 2000.
[42] Ronchi della Rocca, S. and B. Venneri, Principal type schemes for an extended type theory, *Theoretical computer science* 28 (1984), 151-169.
[43] Routley, R., and R. K. Meyer, The semantics of entailment II, *Journal of Philosophical Logic*, 1 (1972), 53-73.
[44] Routley, R., and R. K. Meyer, The semantics of entailment III, *Journal of Philosophical Logic*, 1 (1972), 192-208.
[45] Routley, R. and R. K. Meyer, The semantics of entailment (I), in H. Leblanc, ed., *Truth, syntax and modality*, North Holland, Amsterdam, 1973, 194-243.
[46] Routley, R., with V. Plumwood, R. K. Meyer and R. T. Brady, RLR1, *Relevant Logics and their Rivals 1*, Ridgeview, 1982.
[47] Routley, R., and V. Routley, Semantics of first degree entailment, *Nous* 6 (1972), 335-359.
[48] Seldin, J.P. and J.R. Hindley, eds., *To H. B. Curry: Essays on Combinatory Logic, Lambda Calculus and Formalism*, London, 1980.
[49] Urquhart, A., Semantics for relevant logics, *Journal of Symbolic Logic*, 37 (1972), 159-169. An edited and expanded version appears in [4].

Part II
Probability and Induction

The Reference Class Problem is Your Problem Too!

ALAN HÁJEK

Well may we say, with Bishop Butler, that "probability is the very guide of life". But 'probability' is a multifarious notion, while the aphorism implies that there is exactly one such guide. What sort of probability, then, is it?

We may think of probability theory as having two levels: axiomatization and interpretation. At the level of axiomatization Kolmogorov's theory clearly reigns. He began by axiomatizing unconditional probability, and he later defined conditional probability as a ratio of unconditional probabilities according to the familiar formula:

$$\text{RATIO} \quad P(A|B) = \frac{P(A \cap B)}{P(B)} \quad (P(B) > 0).$$

At the level of interpretation we have an embarrassment of riches. Still, for better or for worse, some version of frequentism — the view that probabilities are suitably defined relative frequencies — seems still to have the ascendancy among scientists. To be sure, among philosophers it is moribund — rightfully so, in my opinion, and for many reasons (see [14]). However, I would like to revisit one of the best known arguments against frequentism, one that many consider fatal to it: the so-called *reference class problem*. For if it is fatal to frequentism, it is also fatal to most of the leading interpretations of probability. I will argue that versions of the classical, logical, propensity and subjectivist interpretations also fall prey to their own variants of the reference class problem. Other versions of these interpretations apparently evade the reference class problem. But I contend that they are all 'no-theory' theories of probability, accounts that leave quite obscure why probability should function as a guide to life. The reference class problem besets those theories that are genuinely informative and that plausibly constrain our inductive reasonings.

However, there is a sense in which the reference class problem is not really a *problem* for these interpretations at all. Rather, it reveals something important about the fundamental nature of probability: it is essentially a two-place notion. All probability statements of any interest are at least tacitly, and often explicitly, relativized. So rather than try to solve the reference class problem, I propose that we *dissolve* it: accept the fact that probabilities are essentially reference class-dependent, and honor that fact by taking conditional probabilities as basic. I have argued elsewhere [15] that we should reject Kolmogorov's axiomatization of probability, and in particular his taking unconditional probability as primitive; instead, conditional probability is the proper primitive of probability theory, and it should be axiomatized directly. The ubiquity of the reference class problem only drives home the essential relativity of probability assignments.

The conference on which this volume is based, and the volume itself, were conceived as tributes to Hughes Leblanc, who among other things was a champion of primitive conditional probabilities. I like to think of him as an ally in this campaign.

1 What is the reference class problem?

It is not surprising that the reference class problem originates, as far as I am aware, with Venn [38] — the Venn of 'diagram' fame. After all, the problem is generated by the fact that any particular thing or event belongs to various sets. He observes: "It is obvious that every individual thing or event has an indefinite number of properties or attributes observable in it, and might therefore be considered as belonging to an indefinite number of different classes of things..." (p. 194). Then, he discusses how this leads to a problem in assigning probabilities to individuals, such as the probability that John Smith, a consumptive Englishman aged fifty, will live to sixty-one. He concludes: "This variety of classes to which the individual may be referred owing to his possession of a multiplicity of attributes, has an important bearing on the process of inference..." (p. 196). An important bearing, indeed.

Reichenbach [29] uses the term for this problem that has now become standard: "If we are asked to find the probability holding for an individual future event, we must first incorporate the case in a suitable reference class. An individual thing or event may be incorporated in many reference classes, from which different probabilities will result. This ambiguity has been called the *problem of the reference class*." (p. 374)

With such clear statements of the problem by two of the most famous frequentists, it is perhaps also not surprising that the reference class problem has traditionally been regarded as a problem for *frequentism*; I think, moreover, that many people consider it to be the most serious problem that frequentism faces. What *is* surprising is that it is unrecognized that something akin to the reference class problem besets versions of *all* of the other leading interpretations of probability: the classical, logical, subjectivist, and propensity interpretations.[1]

The reference class problem arises when we want to assign a probability to a single event, E, which can be regarded as a token of various event types, E_1, E_2, ..., yet its probability can change depending on *how* it is typed. *Qua* event of type E_1, its probability is p_1; *qua* event of type E_2, its probability is p_2, where $p_1 \neq p_2$; and so on; and perhaps, typed still another way, its probability does not exist at all. Now, there would be no problem worth speaking of if one way of typing E, say E_k, stood out from the rest as being the 'correct' one; then it seems the probability of E would simply be p_k. The problem grows teeth to the extent that this is not the case — to the extent that there are apparently equally good claimants for the probability of E. For it would seem that E can only have one (unconditional) probability. Nor, perhaps, would there be a problem worth speaking of if all the p_i's were roughly equal; then at least the probability of E could be confined to a small interval. The teeth grow sharper to the extent that these probabilities differ significantly from one another.

This is really a special case of a more general problem that one might still call 'the reference class problem'. Let E be a proposition — it might correspond to an event-token, or an event-type, or statement in some language, or a set of possible worlds. It seems that there is *one unconditional* probability of E; but all we find are *many conditional* probabilities of the form $P(E$, given $A)$, $P(E$, given $B)$, $P(E$, given $C)$, etc. Moreover, we cannot recover $P(E)$ from these conditional probabilities by the law of total probability, since we likewise lack unconditional probabilities for A, B, C, etc.. Relativized to the condition A, E has one probability; relativized to the condition B, it has another; and so on.

We have here both a metaphysical problem and an epistemological problem. The former arises because it seems that there should be a fact of the matter about the probability of E; what, then, is it? The latter arises as an immediate consequence: a rational agent apparently can assign only one (unconditional) probability to E: what, then, should that probability be? So perhaps we strictly should not speak of *the* reference class problem, as if there were only one problem. But these two problems are so closely related that I will not worry about distinguishing them unless I explicitly say otherwise. I will now argue that these problems will not go away simply by jettisoning frequentism.

---

[1] Hild [16] does a fine job of arguing that the reference class problem arises for the propensity theorist and for the subjectivist who is constrained by the Principle of Direct Probability (see below). My discussion of those interpretations is inspired by and indebted to him.

2 The reference class problem and the leading interpretations of probability

Guidebooks to the interpretations of probability ritually list the following: frequentist, classical, logical, subjectivist, and propensity interpretations. This taxonomy is fine as far as it goes, but I will find it useful to refine it, dividing each of these species into two sub-species:

1. Frequentism: (i) actual and (ii) hypothetical.

2. Classical: (i) finite sample spaces, and (ii) infinite sample spaces.

3. Logical: (i) fully constrained and (ii) less constrained.

4. Propensity: (i) frequency or symmetry-based and (ii) not frequency or symmetry-based.

5. Subjectivism: (i) radical and (ii) constrained.

We will find that most of these accounts face their own version of the reference class problem. However, those that do not, achieve a hollow victory — they say precious little about what probability *is*, or leave mysterious why it should guide us. I will call them 'no-theory theories' to convey my dissatisfaction with them.[2]

2.1 Frequentism

Let us begin where the reference class problem supposedly begins, with frequentism. (Again, it is underappreciated that it does not *end* there.) Versions of frequentism, as I have said, identify probability with relative frequency, differing in the details of how this is to be done. But the word 'relative' is already a warning that they will all face a reference class problem.

(i) Actual frequentism

Actual frequentists such as Venn [38] in at least some passages and, apparently, various scientists even today,[3] identify the probability of an attribute or event A in a reference class B with the relative frequency of actual occurrences of A within B. Note well: *in a reference class B*. By changing the reference class we can typically change the relative frequency of A, and thus the probability of A. In Venn's example, the probability that John Smith,

---

[2]I borrow this term from Sober [32] and Hild [16], although I think my usage of it may differ slightly from each of theirs.

[3]Witness Frieden [8, p. 10]: "The word 'probability' is but a mathematical abstraction for the intuitively more meaningful term 'frequency of occurrence' ".

a consumptive Englishman aged fifty, will live to sixty-one, is the frequency of people like him who live to sixty-one, relative to the frequency of all such people. But who are the people "like him"? It seems there are indefinitely many ways of classifying him, and many of these ways will yield conflicting verdicts as to the relative frequency.

(ii) Hypothetical frequentism

Hypothetical frequentists such as Reichenbach [29] and von Mises [39] are inspired by the dictum that probabilities are *long-run* relative frequencies, and are well aware that the actual world may not deliver a long run of trials of the required sort. No matter — we can always consider instead a *hypothetical* sequence of trials that is as long as we want, and the longer, the better. In particular, an infinite sequence is as good as it gets.

Consider Reichenbach's formulation. We begin with two sequences of event-tokens: $\{x_i\}$, some members of which may belong to a class A, and $\{y_i\}$, some members of which may belong to a class B. Let $F^n(A, B)$ be shorthand for the ratio of two frequencies: the denominator is the frequency of x's out of the first n that belong to A, while the numerator is frequency of (x_i, y_i) pairs out of the first n pairs for which x_i belongs to A and y_i belongs to B. We can now state Reichenbach's definition:

> If for a sequence pair $x_i y_i$ the relative frequency $F^n(A, B)$ goes toward a limit p for $n \to \infty$, the limit p is called the probability from A to B within the sequence pair. (p. 69)

What of the probability of an event-token? As we have seen, Reichenbach says that we must incorporate it in "a suitable reference class". Suppose that we are interested in the probability that a given coin lands heads on a given toss. Suppose further, following Reichenbach, that we toss our coin repeatedly, interspersing it with tosses of another coin. All the tosses, in order, constitute our sequence $\{x_i\}$, some members of which belong to the class A of all tosses of our coin. Let $\{y_i\}$ be the sequence of outcomes of all the tosses, some members of which belong to the class B of 'heads' outcomes. Given this specification of $x_i y_i$, A and B, we may suppose that the probability from 'all tosses of our coin' to 'heads' is well-defined (non-trivial though the supposition is). But we could have specified our event differently — for example, as a toss of our coin with such-and-such angular momentum, or within a certain time period. That is, there are various candidates for A. *Qua* member of one candidate for A, we get one answer for our event's probability; *qua* member of another, we get another. What, then, is *the* probability of our event?

This is already enough of a reference class problem, but there is more to come. For a sequence has more structure than a set: its members are *or-*

dered. So even fixing the set of outcomes (our first reference class problem), there is the further problem of choosing among infinitely many orderings of its members. Probabilities must be relativized not merely to a reference *class* (a set), but to a *sequence* within the reference class. We might call this the *reference sequence problem*.

The beginnings of a solution to this problem would be to restrict our attention to sequences of a certain kind, those with certain desirable properties. Von Mises restricts his to what he calls *collectives* — hypothetical infinite sequences of attributes (possible outcomes) of specified experiments that meet certain requirements. Call a *place-selection* an effectively specifiable method of selecting indices of members of the sequence, such that the selection or not of the index i depends at most on the first $i-1$ attributes. The axioms are:

> *Axiom of Convergence:* the limiting relative frequency of any attribute exists.
>
> *Axiom of Randomness:* the limiting relative frequency of each attribute in a collective ω is the same in any infinite subsequence of ω which is determined by a place selection.

Church [4] renders precise the notion of a place selection as a recursive function. The probability of an attribute A, relative to a collective ω, is then defined as the limiting relative frequency of A in ω. Nevertheless, the reference sequence problem remains: probabilities must always be relativized to a collective, and for a given attribute such as 'heads', or 'dying by age 61' there are infinitely many. Von Mises embraces this consequence, insisting that the notion of probability only makes sense relative to a collective. In particular, he regards single case probabilities as "nonsense". For example: "We can say nothing about the probability of death of an individual even if we know his condition of life and health in detail. The phrase 'probability of death', when it refers to a single person, has no meaning at all for us" (p. 11).[4] But does this solve the reference class problem, or merely ignore it?

On the other hand, Venn and Reichenbach face the problem head on, and do go on to give similar prescriptions for choosing a privileged reference class, and thus a privileged probability. Reichenbach puts it this way: "We then proceed by considering the narrowest class for which reliable statistics can be compiled" (p. 374). But this prescription is patently inadequate.

---

[4]He should also say that the phrase 'probability of death' has no meaning at all even when it refers to a million, or a billion, or any finite number of people, since they do not a collective make.

When are statistics "reliable"? This suggests more than just sufficiently large sample size (for example, unbiasedness) — and even that notion is all too vague. Worse than that, there may be many equally narrow classes for which "reliable" statistics can be compiled. Suppose that there are reliable statistics on the deaths of Englishmen who visit Madeira, and of consumptives who visit Madeira, but not on consumptive Englishmen who visit Madeira. John Smith is a consumptive Englishman visiting Madeira. In which class should we place him?

2.2 Classical probability

The classical interpretation [23] converts information about numbers of *possibilities* into information about *probabilities*. It is assumed that we can partition the space of possible outcomes into a set of 'equipossible' outcomes. When this set is finite, the probability of E is simply the fraction of the total number of these possibilities in which E occurs; when the set is infinite, we may finitely partition it into equipossible sets, which can still be regarded as outcomes. Outcomes are equipossible if there is no evidence to the contrary — no evidence that favors some outcomes over others. This is the infamous 'principle of indifference'. We have two cases here: outcomes for which we have *no evidence at all*, and outcomes for which we have *symmetrically balanced evidence*. We will see that the reference class problem looms either way.

Note the structural resemblance of classical probability to frequentism. A set of outcomes is chosen; probability is identified as a ratio of the number of favorable outcomes to the total number of outcomes. The only significant difference is in the nature of the outcomes: in frequentism they are the outcomes of a repeated experiment, while in the classical interpretation they are the possible outcomes of a single experiment. Small wonder, then, that classical probabilities will face a reference class problem much like frequentism's.

(i) Finite sample spaces

There can be no set of equipossibilities without a set of possibilities. In applications of the classical theory in which the sample space is finite, they are invariably one and the same. Thus, the two possible ways a coin might land or the six possible ways a die might land are identified as exactly the *equi*possibilities of the respective spaces; landing on an edge, for instance, is not even considered as a possibility in the first place. A reference class problem arises for the classical theory in the choice of a sample space — in the very modeling of a random experiment.

If there is such a thing as a situation in which we literally have no evidence at all, then presumably there is nothing to distinguish various competing choices of sample space. We should then be indifferent between expanding the original space to include further possibilities (when that original space was not logically exhaustive), and indifferent between various refinements of the original space. For an example of the former case, if we really have *no* evidence regarding coin-tossing, then we should be indifferent between adopting the sample space {heads, tails} and {heads, tails, edge}, and even {heads, tails, edge, heads-edge-of-edge, tails-edge-of-edge}. For an example of the latter case, we should likewise be indifferent between adopting various spaces that refine the 'heads' outcome according to its final orientation. We could partition 'heads' according to the various angles from north in which that face could end up oriented:

{heads oriented within $[0, 180^0)$ of north, heads oriented within $[180^0, 360^0)$ of north, tails},

{heads within $[0, 120^0)$, heads within $[120^0, 240^0)$, heads within $[240^0, 360^0]$, tails}

and so on ad infinitum. Thus, if we really have *no* evidence, then we have the reference class problem in spades, for all probabilities will be determined by an apparently arbitrary choice of sample space. In practice we choose the {heads, tails} space, of course, because we have *some* evidence: we know enough about the physics of coin-tossing or about the frequencies of outcomes to know, among other things, that 'edge' is far less probable than 'heads' or tails, that 'heads' is equally likely to point in each direction, and so on. We rarely enter a random experiment in a state of total epistemic innocence. When we do, however, the reference class problem is unavoidable. To adapt a well-known example from physics, Bose-Einstein statistics, Fermi-Dirac statistics, and Maxwell-Boltzmann statistics each arise by considering the ways in which particles can be assigned to states, and then partitioning the set of alternatives in different ways. (See, e.g., [7].) Someone ignorant of which statistics apply to a given type of particle (and this state of mind is *not* hard to imagine!) can only make an arbitrary choice and hope for the best. And yet the classical interpretation is purported to be the one that applies in the face of ignorance!

In typical applications of the classical theory, the work is really done by the 'symmetrically balanced evidence' clause of the definition. There are two potential sources of a reference class problem here: in the 'symmetry', and in the 'evidence'. The most obvious characterization of symmetrically balanced evidence is in terms of equality of conditional probabilities: given evidence E and possible outcomes $O_1, O_2, \ldots, O_n$, the evidence is symmetrically balanced iff $P(O_1|E) = P(O_2|E) = \ldots = P(O_n|E)$.[5] (One might

---

[5] One might use a non-probabilistic account of evidential support here — for example,

reasonably wonder how *these* probabilities are determined.) Be that as it may, it is clear that classical probabilities are acutely sensitive to the evidence — not in the sense that they might *change* if the evidence changes, but in the sense that they might *vanish!* That is, if the evidence is *unbalanced*, favoring some outcomes over others, then classical probabilities are not merely revised, they are *destroyed*. This is a particularly interesting form of reference class problem, and it occurs with equal force in both finite and infinite sample spaces. The problem of competing respects of symmetry, however, occurs most strikingly in infinite sample spaces, to which we now turn.

(ii) Infinite sample spaces

When the space of possibilities is infinite, the equipossibilities must be distinct from them. In fact, they must be a finite partition of equivalence classes of the space — otherwise their probabilities could not all be the same *and* sum to 1. The reference class problem arises immediately, then, in the choice of partition: among the infinitely many possible, one is chosen as the basis for the assignment of classical probabilities. But which?

This would not be a problem if one partition stood out among all of them. However, as Bertrand's paradoxes [1] teach us, this need not be the case. They turn on conflicting applications of the principle of indifference, each of which seems equally compelling. Some presentations of this species of paradox are needlessly arcane: I would like to conduct a poll to determine how many philosophers can correctly define 'specific gravity', as found in famous presentations by von Kries, Keynes and Nagel among others. Length and area suffice. Suppose that we have a square with side-length between 0 and 1 foot. What is the probability that its side-length is between 0 and $\frac{1}{2}$ a foot? You have been told so little that ignorance over the possible sidelengths is guaranteed. In particular, it would seem that the intervals $[0, \frac{1}{2})$ and $[\frac{1}{2}, 1]$ are equipossible for containing the side-length. Applying the principle of indifference, then, the answer appears to be $\frac{1}{2}$. But the question could be equivalently formulated: we have a square with area between 0 and 1 square foot. What is the probability that its area is between 0 and $\frac{1}{4}$ square feet. Now the intervals $[0, \frac{1}{4})$, $[\frac{1}{4}, \frac{1}{2})$, $[\frac{1}{2}, \frac{3}{4})$ and $[\frac{3}{4}, 1]$ appear to be equipossible for containing the area. Applying the principle of indifference, then, the answer appears to be $\frac{1}{4}$. *Qua* one specification of the problem, we get one answer, *qua* another specification we get another. And we could have asked the question equivalently in terms of the cube of the side-length, and the seventeenth root of the side-length, and so on.

---

plausibility theory. (See Hild [17].) The danger is that we won't recover *probabilities* at any stage. Whatever else the classical theory might be, it is at least supposed to be a theory of *probability*.

Note that in continuous cases such as this, the problem does not lie with differently weighting the individual outcomes, the infinitely many possible side-lengths or areas, for if it makes sense to speak of their weight at all, they are uniformly 0 on each of the formulations. Rather, the problem lies with the different ways in which the infinite space can be finitely partitioned, both 'symmetric' by some reasonable criterion. The reference class problem, then, is created by the simultaneous membership of a given outcome in multiple partitions which are not simply refinements of a fixed partition. The outcome that the length lies in the interval $[0, \frac{1}{2}]$ just *is* the outcome that the area lies in the interval $[0, \frac{1}{4}]$, but construed the first way it is an equal partner in a 2-membered partition, whereas construed the second way it is an equal partner in a 4-membered partition. And that's just the beginning. Classical probabilities must thus be relativized to a reference class.

2.3 Logical probability

Logical theories of probability retain the classical interpretation's insight that probabilities can be determined a priori by an examination of the space of possibilities. However, they generalize it in two important ways: the possibilities may be assigned *unequal* weights, and probabilities can be computed whatever the evidence may be, symmetrically balanced or not. Indeed, the logical interpretation, in its various guises, seeks to codify in full generality the degree of support or confirmation that a piece of evidence E confers upon a given hypothesis H, which we may write as $c(H, E)$.

Keynes [22], Johnson [21], Jeffreys [20], and Carnap [2; 3] all consider probability theory to be a generalization of logic. They regard statements of the form $c(H, E) = x$ as being either logically true or logically false. Moreover, Keynes, Johnson, Jeffreys, and the early Carnap think that there is exactly one correct measure of such support, one 'confirmation function'. The later Carnap gives up on this idea, allowing a family of such measures. We thus distinguish two versions of logical probability.

(i) Fully constrained logical probability

Let us concentrate on the early Carnap, since his is the most complete development of a fully constrained logical probability. While he allows logical probabilities to be determined even when the principle of indifference does not apply, symmetries are still essential to the determination of probabilities. This time, the objects to which probabilities are assigned are sentences in a formal language, and it will be symmetries among them that will hold the key to the assignment of logical probabilities. The language contains countably many names, denoting individuals, finitely many one-place predicates, denoting properties that the individuals may or may not have, and the usual logical connectives. The strongest statements that can be made in a given language are called *state descriptions*: each individual is described in as much detail as the language allows (that is, the application of each predicate to each individual is either affirmed or denied). Equivalence classes of such state descriptions can be formed by permuting the names; these equivalence classes are called *structure descriptions*. We can then determine a unique measure $m*$ over the state descriptions, which awards equal measure to each structure description, and divides this in turn within a structure description equally among its state descriptions. This induces a confirmation function, $c*$, defined by:

$$c(H, E) = m^*(H \& E)/m^*(E), \text{where} \quad m^*(E) > 0.$$

This is the confirmation function that Carnap favors.

And thus is born a reference class problem. There is no such thing as the logical probability of H, simpliciter, but only the probability of H evaluated in the light of this or that evidence. The relativity to an evidence statement is essential: change the evidence, and the degree of confirmation of H typically changes. So we can putatively determine, say, the logical probability that the next emerald observed is green, *given* the evidence that a hundred (observed) emeralds were all green or *given* the evidence that three (observed) emeralds are purple and one is vermilion, and so on. But what about the probability that the next emerald is green, *sans qualification?*

Carnap's recommendation for the determination of the degree of confirmation of a hypothesis, in the face of this plurality of possible evidence statements to which it might be relativized, is that one should use one's *total evidence*, that is, the maximally specific information at one's disposal, the strongest proposition of which one is certain. This is at best a pragmatic, methodological point, for all of the various conditional probabilities, with their conditions of varying strengths, are well-defined, and logic/probability theory is indifferent among them. Logic, of course, cannot dictate what your total evidence is, so it cannot dictate the probability of H.

In any case, when we go beyond toy examples it is unclear whether there really is such a thing as 'the strongest proposition' of which one is certain. Suppose you are playing a real life version of the Monty Hall problem. A prize lies behind one of three doors; you guess that it is behind door 1. Monty Hall, who knows where the prize is and is careful not to reveal the prize, reveals door 2 to be empty. It is a familiar point that you did not just learn that door 2 was empty; you also learned that Monty chose to reveal door 2 to be empty. But you also learned a host of other things: as it might be, that Monty opened the door with his right hand AND at a particular time on a particular date, AND with the audience gasping in a particular way .... Call this long conjunction X. Moreover, it seems that you also learned a potentially infinite set of *de se* propositions: 'I learned that X' , 'I learned that I learned that X' and so on. Perhaps, then, your total evidence is the infinite intersection of all these propositions, although this is still not obvious — and it is certainly not something that can be represented by a sentence in one of Carnap's languages, which is finite in length.

But even this concedes too much to Carnap. The total evidence criterion goes hand in hand with positivism, and a foundationalist epistemology according to which there are such determinate, ultimate deliverances of experience. But perhaps learning does not come in the form of such 'bedrock' propositions, as Jeffrey [19] has argued — maybe it rather involves a shift in one's subjective probabilities across a partition, without any cell of the partition becoming certain. In that case, the strongest proposition of which one is certain is expressed by a tautology T. (Indeed, it might be tempting to think that in any case, the unconditional logical probability of a hypothesis, H, is just the probability of H, given T.) But a reference class problem still remains. For H and T will have to be formulated in some language or other. Which one will it be? Carnap's logical probabilities are acutely sensitive to the choice of language: change the language, and you change the values of the confirmation function. So there is no single value of $c^*(H,T)$, but a host of different answers corresponding to different choices of the language. And more generally, the notation $c^*(H,E)$ is somewhat misleading, suppressing as it does the dependence of c^* on the language L for all H and E. This is a second reference class problem: a hypothesis and evidence statement must be incorporated into a *set* of hypotheses (the set of state descriptions and disjunctions thereof), and the logical probability linking them can only be evaluated relative to that set. Thus Carnap's logical probabilities are doubly relativized: first to the specification of the evidence proposition, and second to the choice of language.

(ii) Less constrained logical probability

And they eventually become triply relativized. Carnap later generalizes his confirmation function to a continuum of functions c_λ. Define a *family* of predicates to be a set of predicates such that, for each individual, exactly one member of the set applies, and consider first-order languages containing a finite number of families. Carnap [3] focuses on the special case of a language containing only one-place predicates. He lays down a number of axioms concerning the confirmation function c, mostly symmetry principles. They imply that, for a family $\{P_n\}$, $n = 1, ..., k$, $k > 2$:

c_λ (individual $s+1$ is P_j, s_j of the first s individuals are P_j) = $\dfrac{s_j + \lambda/k}{s + \lambda}$,
where λ is a positive real number.

The higher the value of λ, the less impact evidence has: induction from what is observed becomes progressively more swamped by a classical-style equal assignment to each of the k possibilities regarding individual $s+1$.

A new source of relativization thus appears: logical probabilities now depend also on λ, on how 'cautious' is our inductive system. But nothing in logic, probability theory, or anything else for that matter seems to dictate a unique setting of λ. Three things now determine the reference class of a hypothesis H whose probability we might seek: the language in which H is formulated, the evidence relative to which it is evaluated, and λ.

2.4 Propensity interpretations

Propensity theorists think of probability as a physical propensity, or disposition, or tendency of a given type of physical situation to yield an outcome of a certain kind, or to yield a long run relative frequency of such an outcome. Popper [27], for example, regards a probability p of an outcome of a certain type to be a propensity of a repeatable experiment to produce outcomes of that type with limiting relative frequency p. Giere [10], on the other hand, attributes propensities to single events: probability is just a propensity of a repeatable experimental set-up to produce sequences of outcomes. We may thus usefully distinguish *frequency-based* propensity theories from *non-frequency-based* propensity theories: the former appeal to relative frequencies in the characterization of propensities, while the latter do not. Frequency-based propensity theorists include Popper and Gillies [11]; non-frequency-based propensity theorists include Giere, Mellor [25], Miller [26] and Fetzer [6].

Frequency-based propensity theories will immediately inherit frequentism's reference class problem. After all, the relativization of frequencies to a set of trials, or to an ordered sequence of trials, or to a collective, will transfer to whatever propensities are based on these relative frequencies.

What about non-frequency-based propensity theories? Some of them clearly invite a reference class problem in their very formulation. Consider Giere's [10, p. 471], formulation, which takes as given a chance setup, CSU. He interprets the statement "$P(E) = r$" as follows: "The strength of the propensity of CSU to produce outcome E on trial L is r". Propensities, then, are relativized to a chance setup. There are other terms for much the same idea: relativization of propensities to 'experimental arrangements', or 'test conditions', or what-not. Some other non-frequency-based propensity theories face the reference class problem less obviously, but face it nonetheless. Here it is useful to introduce another distinction: between *symmetry-*

based propensity theories, which ground propensities in more basic physical symmetries, and *non-symmetry-based* theories, which don't. The former will meet the reference class problem in the specification of the appropriate respect of symmetry; the latter may avoid it, but I suspect only at the cost of being no-theory theories: 'dormative virtue' theories in which the nature of probability remains obscure.[6]

I take Mellor [25], for example, to be offering a symmetry-based propensity theory. A coin might be pronounced to be fair in virtue of its *physical* symmetries — its symmetric shape, its symmetric mass distribution, or what have you — with no regard for what the results of tossing it happen to be, or indeed for whether or not it is even tossed. More complicated systems, such as dice and roulette wheels, function as well as they do as gambling devices in virtue of other symmetries (or near-symmetries), albeit more complicated. Indeed, Strevens [34] shows how much high-level simplicity, in the form of stable probabilities, inevitably arises out of low-level complexity, *in virtue of symmetries*. (Think, for example, of how microscopic chaos gives rise to macroscopic order in thermodynamics, or how capricious behaviors of the individual organisms in an ecological system give rise to stable probabilities at the population level.)

Symmetry-based propensities look a fair bit like classical probabilities. Indeed, Mellor's "principle of connectivity" can be thought of as a counterpart to the principle of indifference. The idea is simple: propensities of outcomes are the same unless there is a difference in their causes. But this leads to a reference class problem, much as the principle of indifference did. If the outcomes of coin-tossing are genuinely indeterministic, with the outcomes 'heads' and 'tails' *uncaused*, then the principle of connectivity applies, and they must have the same propensity, $\frac{1}{2}$. So far, so good. (Make the example quantum mechanical if you think that the results of coin tosses are caused by initial conditions.) But now suppose that various refinements of the outcomes are also uncaused. Recall the example of the various possible final orientations of 'heads'. Suppose that both heads-oriented-within $[0, 180^0)$ of north and heads-oriented-within $[180^0, 360^0)$ of north are also uncaused. So by the principle of connectivity, these too should get the same probability as heads, namely $\frac{1}{2}$. But then we have a violation of additivity ($\frac{1}{2} + \frac{1}{2} \neq \frac{1}{2}$), and propensities are not really probabilities at all. We could drop the principle of connectivity to avoid such unwelcome results, but then we would be left with a no-theory theory. Better to relativize its application. Relative to one partition of outcomes, all of which have the same causes (or lack thereof), we have one set of propensities; relative to another, we have another.

---

[6]Sober likewise speaks of 'dormative virtue' theories of objective probability.

What about non-frequency-based, non-symmetry-based propensity theories? What, for example, of theories that claim that propensities are intrinsic properties of chance set-ups, or inherent dispositions, or unanalyzable tendencies, or graded modalities, or ... — and say no more? Here I suspect we are entering 'no-theory theory' territory. For we are told all too little about what exactly propensities *are*, or how they are to be determined even in principle. In fact, it is unclear why they should even obey the probability calculus. I fear then that "propensity", like "dormative virtue", is just a resonant name for something that we do not really understand.

2.5 Subjectivism

Subjectivists regard probabilities as degrees of belief, and see the theorems of probability as rationality constraints on degrees of belief.

(i) Radical subjectivism

Radical subjectivists such as de Finetti [5] regard them as the *only* such constraints. Your degrees of belief can be whatever you like, as long as they remain probabilistically coherent. It thus appears that there is not any interesting reference class problem for the radical subjectivist. The probability that you assign to E is whatever it is. *Qua* nothing.

This is a benefit, if that's the right word for it, of the radical subjectivist's permissive epistemology. But it comes at a cost. The epistemology is so *spectacularly* permissive that it sanctions opinions that we would normally call ridiculous. For example, you may without any insult to rationality assign probability 0.999 to George Bush turning into a prairie dog, provided that you assign 0.001 to this not being the case (and that your other assignments also obey the probability calculus). And you are no more worthy of praise if you assign it 0,[7] or 0.17485, or $\frac{1}{e}$ or whatever you like. Being saddled with such unwelcome results is the price that the radical subjectivist pays for offering a no-theory theory of probability: there is so little constraining probability assignments that I wonder what interest is left in them. In particular, the assignments can be completely at odds with the way the world is. If you want exclusively to assign extremely high probabilities to contingent propositions that are in fact false, and extremely low probabilities to contingent propositions that are in fact true, you have the radical subjectivist's blessing. (Just stay coherent!) Probability theory becomes autobiography rather than epistemology.

---

[7]Some otherwise radical subjectivists impose the requirement of *regularity* — only a priori falsehoods get assigned probability 0 — in order to allow learning by repeated conditionalization on evidence. But then, staggeringly, an assignment of 0 to Bush's turning into a prairie dog is judged *irrational*, while an assignment of 0.999 is judged *rational*.

(ii) Constrained subjectivism

But many subjectivists are more demanding of their subjects — and their further demands will bring reference class problems in their train. There are various proposals for extra constraints on rational opinion. I find it most perspicuous to present them all as instances of a certain canonical form. Gaifman [9] coins the terms "expert assignment" and "expert probability" for a probability assignment that a given agent strives to track: "The mere knowledge of the [expert] assignment will make the agent adopt it as his subjective probability" (p. 193). The guiding idea is captured by the equation

(*) $P(A|pr(A) = x) = x$

where 'P' is the agent's subjective probability function, and '$pr(A)$' is the assignment that the agent regards as expert. For example, if you regard the local weather forecaster as an expert on matters meteorological, and he assigns probability 0.1 to it raining tomorrow, then you may well follow suit:

$P(rain|pr(rain) = 0.1) = 0.1$

More generally, we might speak of an entire probability function as being such a guide for an agent. Van Fraassen [36], extending Gaifman's usage, calls pr an "expert function" for P if (*) holds *for all x* such that $P(pr(A) = x) > 0$, so that the conditional probability is defined. We should keep in mind the distinction between an expert function and an expert assignment, because an agent may not want to track *all* the assignments of her 'expert'. (If your forecaster gives probability 0 to it raining in Los Angeles tomorrow, you may think that he's gone too far, and may not want to follow him there.)

Various candidates for expert functions for rational agents have been proposed:

The *Principle of Direct Probability* regards *relative frequencies* that way. (See Hacking [13] for a presentation of it.) Let A be an event-type, and let $relfreq(A)$ be the relative frequency of A. Then for any rational agent with probability function P, we have

$P(A|relfreq(A) = x) = x$, for all A such that $P(relfreq(A) = x) > 0$.

Lewis [24] posits a similar role for the *objective chance function, ch,* in his *P*rincipal Principle:

$P(A|ch(A) = x) = x$, for all A such that $P(ch(A) = x) > 0$.[8]

A frequentist who thinks that chances just *are* relative frequencies would presumably think that the Principal Principle just *is* the Principle of Direct Probability; but Lewis' principle may well appeal to those who have a very different view about chances — e.g., propensity theorists.

---

[8] I ignore complications due to Lewis' notion of "admissibility".

Van Fraassen [35; 37], following Goldstein [12], argues that one's *future probability assignments* play such a role in constraining one's present assignments in his *R*eflection Principle:

$$P_t(A|P_{t+\Delta}(A) = x) = x.$$

The idea is that a certain sort of epistemic integrity requires you to regard your future self as 'expert' relative to your current self.

One might also give conditionalized versions of these already-conditional principles, capturing the idea that an agent might want to track certain conditional probability assignments of her expert. (See van Fraassen [36, pp. 201–2].) For example, the Principal Principle might be amended in such a way:

$$P(A|ch(A|B) = x \cap B) = x.$$

Finally, if Carnap is to be believed, then *logical probability* plays such a role as expert — perhaps the ultimate one.

With various expert assignments in place, the reference class problem is poised to strike. In fact, it can now strike in two different, though closely related, ways: firstly, if the expert assignments *disagree* with one another; secondly, if the expert assignments themselves are susceptible to a reference class problem. Let's take these points in order.

All is well if all your experts speak in unison — as it might be, your two favorite weather forecasters both assign a probability of 0.1 to it raining tomorrow, 10% of days 'like' tomorrow were rainy days, your own research (perhaps on meteorological symmetries?) convinces you that the chance of rain is 0.1, your current probability assignments to your future probability assignments concur, and (somewhat fancifully) it turns out that the logical probability of rain tomorrow, given your putative total evidence, is the same again. But all may not be well. Suppose some of these numbers differ. You can't serve all your masters at once, so you have to play favorites. But who trumps whom, which trumps which? You have no difficulty forming a series of conditional probabilities, each of the form (*), with different functions playing the role of *Pr* in each case. Your difficulty arises in combining them to arrive at a single unconditional probability assignment.

Now of course you can simply weight your various experts' assignments and combine them in some way in order to come up with your own assignments. But what are the weights to be? If they are totally unconstrained, then you risk collapsing into radical subjectivism, and its no-theory theory: make the weights 0.999, or 0, or 0.17485, or $\frac{1}{e}$, or whatever you like as long as the weights add up to 1. (Just stay coherent!) But if the weights are constrained by something external — some *expert* — then you find yourself with further conditional probabilities, and no respite. For example, you might give more weight to one of your favorite forecasters than the other because he is better *calibrated:* his probability assignments in the past have been better vindicated by the relevant relative frequency data. But by now I hardly need to point out that any relative frequency data is *relativized.* Moreover, Simpson's paradox teaches us of the perils you can face when you mix conditional probability assignments: correlations that all of the experts see may be washed out or even reversed. Worse still, these correlations may be reversed again when we partition our probability space more finely — which is to say, when we refine our reference classes. Enter the reference class problem again.

A further, related problem arises when the expert functions assignments are susceptible to a reference class problem — and it seems to me that *they invariably are.* Consider again the Principle of Direct Probability: given its dependence on relative frequencies, it immediately inherits frequentism's reference class problem. Likewise, if the assignment by the chance function 'ch' is susceptible to a reference class problem, so will be the corresponding assignment by the subjective probability function 'P'. We simply have the previous case if we identify 'ch' with relative frequency, à la Venn, or à la Reichenbach. (Not à la von Mises, since he eschews single case chances, so the Principal Principle is never instantiated according to him.) This point generalizes to any account of 'ch' that is thus susceptible — e.g., symmetry-based propensities, accounts that appeal to 'chance set-ups', and what-not. There may be no reference class problem if 'ch' is a no-theory theory propensity; but then we would be left wondering why the Principal Principle should have any claim on us, and how ever to apply the Principle.

As for human 'experts' (weather forecasters, your future selves) and their subjective probabilities, we have a dilemma: either they are constrained by something external to *them* or they are not. In the former case, the reference class problem looms, for presumably something else is playing the role of 'expert' for *them* — frequencies, symmetries, logical probabilities, or what have you. In the latter case it is dubious whether they have earned their title as 'experts'; we would be left with a no-theory theory of expertise.

The two problems just discussed — that of conflicting experts, and that of inheriting the reference class problem from your experts — are closely related. In a sense, the reference class problem just *is* the problem of conflicting experts. When an event is typed one way, or relativized to one background assumption, any one of your experts — relative frequency information, chance, your weather forecaster, your future self, logical probability — assigns it one probability; when it is typed another way, or relativized to another background assumption, the same expert assigns it another probability. A single expert is conflicted with itself. Or looked at another way, any given expert fissions into *many* experts, one for each reference class. For each way of typing tomorrow, we have a relative frequency 'expert', a chance 'expert', and so on. The problem of conflicting experts is far worse than we might have thought, because we have so *many* of them. And this means that the reference class problem for the non-radical subjectivist is far worse than we might have thought.

3 Conditional probability as primitive

3.1 The ratio analysis

We have found the reference class problem bobbing up in important versions of every major interpretation of probability. A pessimistic conclusion that one might draw is that all of the interpretations are somehow incomplete: that they each need to be supplemented with a further theory about what are the 'right' reference classes on which probability statements should be based. Yet the prospects for such theories (e.g., in terms of 'narrowest classes for which reliable statistics can be compiled', or 'total evidence') are dim. And those interpretations that appear to escape it do so by being no-theory theories. Among theories that make substantive claims about what probabilities are and how they may be determined — that might be genuine *guides to life* — it is seemingly inescapable.

But perhaps we should stop trying to escape it. Where we seek unconditional, single-case probabilities we keep finding conditional probabilities instead. Maybe there's a hint there to be taken. For there is a sense in which the reference class problem is not really a *problem* for these interpretations at all, any more than the relativity of simultaneity is a *problem* for time. If the reference class problem is a problem for anything, it is for Kolmogorov's treatment of conditional probability.

As I noted in the introduction, the orthodox Kolmogorov theory identifies conditional probability with a ratio of unconditional probabilities:

$$\text{RATIO} \quad P(A|B) = \frac{P(A \cap B)}{P(B)} \quad (P(B) > 0).$$

Thus, all probabilities are unconditional probabilities or ratios thereof, and conditional probabilities are undefined whenever their antecedents have zero unconditional probability. Let us call the identification of conditional probabilities with ratios of unconditional probabilities the *ratio analysis* of conditional probability. In the next section, I will argue that it is inadequate.

3.2 Problems with the ratio analysis

We have already noted that conditional probabilities are undefined whenever their antecedents have zero unconditional probability. It is not without reason that (RATIO) has its proviso. Now, perhaps the proviso strikes you as innocuous (as it does, for example, Jackson [18]). To be sure, we could reasonably dismiss probability zero antecedents as 'don't cares' if we could be assured that all probability functions of any interest are *regular* — that is, they assign zero probability only to logical impossibilities.

Unfortunately, this is not the case. As probability textbooks repeatedly drum into their readers, probability zero events need not be impossible, and indeed can be of real interest. Yet these very same textbooks seem to forget these examples when they adhere to the ratio analysis of conditional probability. Indeed, interesting cases of conditional probabilities with probability zero antecedents are manifold. Consider the perfectly random selection of a real number from the unit interval: The probability that either the point $\frac{1}{4}$ or the point $\frac{3}{4}$ is selected is zero; still, the conditional probability that $\frac{1}{4}$ is selected, *given* that either $\frac{1}{4}$ or $\frac{3}{4}$ is selected, is surely $\frac{1}{2}$. Kolmogorov's approach to conditional probability thus cannot deliver the intuitively correct answer. Obviously there are uncountably many problem cases of this form.

The difficulties that probability zero antecedents pose for the ratio formula for conditional probability are well known; so much so that I am left wondering why they aren't paid more attention. In any case, less familiar are the difficulties posed by *vague* probabilities. Many Bayesians relax the requirement that probabilities are single real numbers, allowing them to be intervals or sets of such numbers. For example, your probability that there is intelligent life elsewhere in our galaxy need not be a sharp number such as 0.7049570000..., but might instead be '0.7-*ish*', represented by a suitable set of numbers around 0.7. Yet even then, various corresponding conditional probabilities can be sharp — for example, the probability that there is such life, *given* that there is such life, is clearly 1, and more interestingly, the probability that this fair coin lands heads, *given* that there is such life, is $\frac{1}{2}$.

The problem of vague unconditional probabilities is bad enough, but the problem of undefined unconditional probabilities is worse. Conditional probabilities of the form $P(A, \text{given } B)$ can be defined even when $P(A \cap B)$ and $P(B)$ are undefined, and hence their ratio is undefined. Here is an urn with 90 red balls and 10 white balls, well mixed. What is the probability that Joe draws a red ball, given that Joe draws a ball at random from the urn? 0.9, of course. According to the ratio analysis, it is:

$$\frac{P(\text{Joe draws a red ball } \cap \text{ Joe draws a ball at random from the urn})}{P(\text{Joe draw a ball at random from the urn})}$$

Neither the numerator nor the denominator is defined. For example, there is no fact of the matter of the probability that Joe draws a ball at random from the urn. *Who is this Joe, anyway?* None of that matters, however, to the conditional probability, which is well-defined (and obvious). By analogy, we can determine that the argument:

Joe is a liar

Therefore,

Joe is a liar

is valid, even though there is no fact of the matter of the truth value of the statement 'Joe is a liar'.[9]

I conclude that it is time to rethink the foundations of probability. It is time to question the hegemony of Kolmogorov's axiomatization, and in particular the conceptual priority it gives to unconditional probability. It is time to follow heterodox probability theorists such as Popper [28], Renyi [30], Spohn [33], Roeper and Leblanc [31], (among others), to take conditional probability as the fundamental notion in probability theory, and to axiomatize it directly.

4 The reference class problem and conditional probability

Let us return to our discussion of the reference class problem. We have only seen more examples of conditional probabilities that cannot be identified with ratios of unconditional probabilities, because the required unconditional probabilities simply aren't there to be had.

Various frequentists could tell us the conditional probability that John Smith will live to age sixty-one, *given* that he is a consumptive Englishman aged fifty. But they could not identify this with the ratio:

$$\frac{P(\text{John Smith will live to 61} \cap \text{John Smith is a consumptive Englishman aged 50})}{P(\text{John Smith is a consumptive Englishman aged 50})}$$

Neither term in the ratio is defined, but let us focus on the denominator. According to frequentism, this is another relative frequency. But there's the rub: another *relative* frequency. The reference class problem strikes again! *Qua* one way of classifying John Smith, we get one relative frequency for his being a consumptive Englishman aged fifty; *qua* another way of classifying him, we get another relative frequency. Indeed, in a universe with infinitely

---

[9] In my [15] I canvas — and reject — various proposals for rescuing the ratio analysis in the face of such counterexamples.

many things — quasars, quarks, space-time points all included in their number — almost all of which are *not* consumptive Englishmen aged fifty, this relative frequency could be as small as 0. Hardly comforting for the ratio analysis! But in any case, we only get further relative frequencies — or as I would prefer to put it, we get further conditional probabilities. Moreover, the conditions, in turn, have various relative frequencies, but yet again, relative to still further reference classes. And so the regress goes. The process never 'bottoms out' with unconditional probabilities. To paraphrase an old joke, it's conditional probabilities all the way down.

And so it goes for the other interpretations as well. One can assign classical *conditional* probabilities *given* a specification of a set of equipossibilities; but one cannot assign a classical unconditional probability to this *being* the set of equipossibilities. One can assign a logical *conditional* probability to the next emerald being green, *given* the evidence of ten observed green emeralds; but one cannot assign a logical unconditional probability to this evidence. This coin may have a *conditional* propensity of landing heads, *given* a specification of an experimental set-up or what-not, but there is no propensity for this experimental set-up or what-not itself. And various subjectivists could assign various *conditional* probabilities, *given* corresponding expert assignments; but they could only assign unconditional probabilities to these assignments themselves by becoming no-theory theorists.

How, then, should conditional probability be analyzed? Answer: *it shouldn't*. We should regard conditional probability to be the fundamental notion of probability theory. Conditional probability is the very guide of life.

Acknowledgements

I thank especially Mark Colyvan, Branden Fitelson, Matthias Hild, Chris Hitchcock, and Jim Woodward for extremely helpful discussions.[10]

BIBLIOGRAPHY

[1] Bertrand, J. (1889): *Calcul des Probabilités*, 1st edition, Gauthier-Villars.
[2] Carnap, Rudolf (1950): *Logical Foundations of Probability*, University of Chicago Press.
[3] Carnap (1963): "Replies and Systematic Expositions", in P. A. Schilpp (ed.), *The Philosophy of Rudolf Carnap*, Open Court, La Salle, Ill, 966-998.
[4] Church, A. (1940): "On the concept of a random sequence", *Bulletin of the American Mathematical Society* 46, 130–135.

---

[10] An updated version of this paper will appear as "The Reference Class Problem Is Your Problem Too" (no exclamation mark!), forthcoming in a special volume of *Synthese* edited by Stephan Hartmann.

[5] De Finetti, Bruno (1937): "Foresight: Its Logical Laws, Its Subjective Sources", translated in H. E. Kyburg and H. E. Smokler (eds.) (1964), Studies in Subjective Probability, Robert E. Krieger Publishing Company.
[6] Fetzer, James (1977): "Reichenbach, Reference Classes, and Single Case 'Probabilities'", Synthese 34: 185-217; Errata, 37: 113-114.
[7] Fine, Terrence (1973): Theories of Probability, Academic Press.
[8] Frieden, B. R. (1991): Probability, Statistical Optics and Data Testing,Springer-Verlag.
[9] Gaifman, Haim (1988): "A Theory of Higher Order Probabilities", in Causation, Chance, and Credence, eds. Brian Skyrms and William L. Harper, Kluwer.
[10] Giere, R. N. (1973): "Objective Single-Case Probabilities and the Foundations of Statistics", in P. Suppes et al. (eds.), Logic, Methodology and Philosophy of Science IV, North Holland 467-83.
[11] Gillies, Donald (2000): "Varieties of Propensity", British Journal of Philosophy of Science 51, 807-835.
[12] Goldstein, Michael (1983): "The Prevision of a Prevision" Journal of the American Statistical Association 78, 817–19.
[13] Hacking, Ian (1965): Logic of Statistical Inference, Cambridge University Press.
[14] Hájek, Alan (1997): " 'Mises Redux' — Redux: Fifteen Arguments Against Finite Frequentism", Erkenntnis, 45:209–227. Reprinted in Probability, Dynamics and Causality. Essays in Honor of Richard C. Jeffrey, D. Costantini and M. Galavotti, eds, Kluwer.
[15] Hájek, Alan (forthcoming): "What Conditional Probability Could Not Be", Synthese 137 (3), 273–323.
[16] Hild, Matthias (2003)): Introduction to The Concept of Probability: A Reader, MIT Press.
[17] Hild, Matthias (in preparation): An Introduction to Induction.
[18] Jackson, Frank (1987): Conditionals, Blackwell, Oxford.
[19] Jeffrey, Richard (1992): Probability and the Art of Judgment, Cambridge University Press.
[20] Jeffreys, Harold (1939): Theory of Probability; reprinted in Oxford Classics in the Physical Sciences series, Oxford University Press, 1998.
[21] Johnson, W. E. (1932): "Probability: The Deductive and Inductive Problems", Mind 49, 409-423.
[22] Keynes, J. M. (1921): Treatise on Probability, Macmillan, London. Reprinted 1962, Harper and Row, New York.
[23] Laplace, Pierre Simon de (1814): "Essai Philosophique sur les Probabilités", Paris. Translated into English as A Philosophical Essay on Probabilities, New York, 1952.
[24] Lewis, David (1980): "A Subjectivist's Guide to Objective Chance", in Studies in Inductive Logic and Probability,l Vol II, ed. Richard C. Jeffrey, pp. 263–293, University of California Press. Reprinted in Philosophical Papers, Volume II, Oxford University Press, 1986.
[25] Mellor, D. H. (1971): The Matter of Chance, Cambridge University Press, Cambridge.
[26] Miller, D. W. (1996): "Propensities and Indeterminism", in A. O'Hear (ed.), Karl Popper: Philosophy and Problems, Cambridge University Press 121-47
[27] Popper, Karl (1959a): "The Propensity Interpretation of Probability", British Journal of Philosophy of Science 10, 25-42.
[28] Popper, Karl (1959b): The Logic of Scientific Discovery, Basic Books.
[29] Reichenbach, Hans (1949): The Theory of Probability, University of California Press.
[30] Renyi, Alfred (1970): Foundations of Probability, Holden-Day, Inc.
[31] Roeper, Peter and Hughes Leblanc (1999): Probability Theory and Probability Semantics, Toronto Studies in Philosophy.
[32] Sober, Elliott (2000): Philosophy of Biology, Westview Press, 2nd ed.

[33] Spohn, Wolfgang (1986): "The Representation of Popper Measures", *Topoi* 5, 69-74.
[34] Strevens, Michael (2003): *Bigger than Chaos*, Harvard University Press.
[35] van Fraassen, Bas (1984): "Belief and the Will", *Journal of Philosophy* 81, 235-256.
[36] van Fraassen, Bas (1989): *Laws and Symmetry*, Clarendon Press, Oxford.
[37] van Fraassen, Bas (1995): "Belief and the Problem of Ulysses and the Sirens", *Philosophical Studies* 77, 7-37.
[38] Venn, John (1876): *The Logic of Chance*, 2nd ed., Macmillan and co.
[39] von Mises, Richard (1957): *Probability, Statistics and Truth*, revised English edition, New York.

A Formal Model of Holistic Epistemic Coherence

CHARLES B. CROSS

I am pleased and honored to participate in this volume celebrating the memory of Hugues Leblanc—an outstanding logician, a delightful conversational companion, and a most exact philosopher!

According to Laurence BonJour's Coherence Theory of Justification,[1] a subject's set of beliefs is epistemically justified in part by its satisfying a requirement of *holistic epistemic coherence*. BonJour gives the following informal description of the property of coherence on which his theory relies:

> Intuitively, coherence is a matter of how well a body of beliefs "hangs together": how well its component beliefs fit together, agree or dovetail with each other, so as to produce an organized, tightly structured system of beliefs, rather than either a helter-skelter collection or a set of conflicting subsystems. It is reasonably clear that this "hanging together" depends on the various sorts of inferential, evidential, and explanatory relations which obtain among the various members of a system of beliefs, and especially on the more holistic and systematic of these. [BonJour 1985, p. 93]

This essay presents a formal model of holistic epistemic coherence in the context of the theory of nonmonotonic consequence. My model is based on the account in [Cross 2003] of *nonmonotonic inconsistency*: a defeasible property which is a counterpart of logical inconsistency in the context of nonmonotonic reasoning. In Section 1, I shall examine the informal conception of coherence on which my formal model is based and present a key example to illustrate this conception. In Section 2, I shall provide some background on nonmonotonic inference and define the notions of unresolved conflict and nonmonotonic inconsistency. Finally, in Section 3, I shall provide analyses of the notions of anomaly and epistemic coherence and explain

---
[1] See [BonJour 1985].

how these notions are illustrated by the example to be considered in Section 1.

1 Coherence and anomalies

Coherence is a matter of degree, for BonJour, and in order to evaluate the degree of coherence of a given set of beliefs one must take measurements along a number of dimensions. A belief system's degree of coherence is therefore determined by a vector, and one of the components of this vector is logical consistency:

> A system of beliefs is coherent only if it is logically consistent. [BonJour 1985, p. 95]

Another concerns explanatory anomalies within a belief system:

> The coherence of a system of beliefs is decreased in proportion to the presence of unexplained anomalies in the believed content of the system. [BonJour 1985, p. 99]

An anomaly relative to a given a belief system, for BonJour, is an item of believed content that is incapable of being explained or predicted on the basis of other beliefs in the system. The notion of an anomaly is well-illustrated by the following example, due originally to Klein and Warfield[2] but as formulated by Merricks:

> Now consider two belief sets. The first, B, includes the following beliefs:
>
>> b1. Dunnit had a motive for the murder.
>> b2. Witnesses claim to have seen Dunnit do it.
>> b3. A credible witness claims to have seen Dunnit two hundred miles from the scene of the crime at the time of the murder.
>> b4. Dunnit committed the murder.
>
> Now consider B^* which has the members of B, plus the following:
>
>> b. Dunnit has an identical twin which was seen by the credible witness two hundred miles from the scene of the crime during the murder.
>
> B^* is more coherent than B. [Merricks 1995, p. 308]

---

[2]See [Klein and Warfield 1994].

Why is B^* more coherent than B? Both are logically consistent, so that is not the problem. The problem is that relative to B, b3 counts as an *anomaly*: Nothing in B can be used to explain why a credible witness would claim to have seen Dunnit two hundred miles from the scene of the crime at the time of the murder, for, according to B, Dunnit did it, had a motive, and according to credible witnesses was seen doing it. In the context of B^*, however, b3 is not anomalous: the fact that Dunnit's identical twin was seen by the credible witness explains why the credible witness would say that he or she saw Dunnit two hundred miles from the scene of the crime during the murder. So B^* is more coherent than B because b3 is no longer an anomaly when B is expanded to obtain B^*.

In the next section we introduce the apparatus that we shall use to make the notion of an anomaly rigorous.

2 Nonmonotonic consequence and unresolved conflict

2.1 A few basics about nonmonotonic consequence

A relation '$\vdash$' of *logical* consequence is recognizable as such in part because it satisfies such conditions as reflexivity, monotonicity, and transitivity:[3]

Ref($\vdash$) If $p \in X$ then $X \vdash p$.

Mono($\vdash$) If $X \subseteq Y$ and $X \vdash p$, then $Y \vdash p$.

Trans($\vdash$) If $X \cup \{p\} \vdash q$ and $X \vdash p$ then $X \vdash q$.

For the past twenty-five years or so, there has been increasing interest within the fields of artificial intelligence and philosophical logic in *nonmonotonic* consequence relations, i.e. consequence relations for which the second of the above conditions fails.[4] A nonmonotonic consequence relation '$\vdash\!\!\!\sim$' represents what a philosopher would think of as a mechanism for inductive inference—a defeasible form of reasoning taking one beyond the strictly logical consequences of the set to the left of the turnstile.[5] The commonsense inductive reasoning that real epistemic subjects do on an everyday basis is nonmonotonic, and the past twenty-five years of research on nonmonotonic consequence in the artificial intelligence community has shown that a proof-theoretic approach to inductive reasoning is not only possible but fruitful.

---

[3] I shall use 'p' and 'q' as variables ranging over sentences and 'X' and 'Y' as variables ranging over sets of sentences.

[4] For a survey, see [Makinson 1994].

[5] I shall use '$\vdash\!\!\!\sim$' to range over consequence relations that may or may not be monotonic.

To call a consequence relation nonmonotonic is to characterize it in a negative way—to identify a condition that it does not satisfy. Can nonmonotonic reasoning be characterized in a positive way? If we replace monotonicity in the above list of conditions with the weaker condition of cautious monotony (CM), the resulting three conditions characterize what Dov Gabbay calls *cumulative inference*.[6]

Ref($\mid\sim$) If $p \in X$ then $X\mid\sim p$.

CM($\mid\sim$) If $X\mid\sim p$ and $X\mid\sim q$, then $X \cup \{p\}\mid\sim q$.

Trans($\mid\sim$) If $X \cup \{p\}\mid\sim q$ and $X\mid\sim p$ then $X\mid\sim q$.

Not every nonmonotonic consequence relation discussed in the artificial intelligence literature is cumulative, but some of the more appealing ones are, including Poole systems (with or without constraints) and stopped preferential entailment.[7] Many other systems of nonmonotonic consequence discussed in the literature satisfy at least reflexivity and transitivity, including general preferential entailment, Reiter-style default logic, justification-based truth maintenance systems in the style of Doyle, and skeptical inference using a logic program with negation in the style of Gelfond and Lifschitz.[8]

Now, some systems combine classical logical consequence ($\vdash$) with a nonmonotonic consequence relation ($\mid\sim$). In such systems it is natural to suppose that nonmonotonic consequence obeys the principles of supraclassicality and right absorption:

SupNC If $X \vdash p$ then $X\mid\sim p$.

RightAbs For all X, $C(X) = C(Cn(X))$

where $Cn(X)$ (the closure of X under logical consequence) and $C(X)$ (the closure of X under nonmonotonic consequence) are defined as follows:

DEFINITION 1. $Cn(X) =_{df} \{p : X \vdash p\}$.

DEFINITION 2. $C(X) =_{df} \{p : X\mid\sim p\}$.

Supraclassicality amounts to a decision to treat classical consequence as a special case of nonmonotonic consequence. Right absorption is the principle that the nonmonotonic consequences of a set are a function of the set's logical consequences, so that two sets with the same logical consequences cannot

---
[6] See [Gabbay 1985] and [Makinson 1989].
[7] See [Poole 1988] and [Makinson 1994, p. 88].
[8] See [Reiter 1980], [Doyle 1979], [Gelfond and Lifschitz 1988], and [Makinson 1994, p. 88].

have different nonmonotonic consequences. When a relation of nonmonotonic consequence satisfies right absorption it also satisfies weak cautious monotony and weak transitivity for nonmonotonic consequence:

WeakCMNC If $X \mathrel{|\!\sim} q$ and $X \vdash p$, then $X \cup \{p\} \mathrel{|\!\sim} q$.

WeakTrNC If $X \cup \{p\} \mathrel{|\!\sim} q$ and $X \vdash p$, then $X \mathrel{|\!\sim} q$.

Some examples of systems which satisfy both supraclassicality and right absorption (and therefore also WeakCMNC and WeakTrNC) are Reiter-style default logic (with or without non-normal defaults), Poole systems (with or without constraints), and classical preferential entailment (with or without stopping).[9]

2.2 Nonmonotonic inconsistency

While the theory of nonmonotonic consequence has been thoroughly investigated for the past twenty-five years, the idea of a nonmonotonic counterpart of logical inconsistency—the idea of a property representing conflict of an inductive, evidential, or defeasible nature—received its first explicit attention only recently in [Cross 2003]. The account of nonmonotonic inconsistency developed in [Cross 2003] can be formulated in terms of the notion of a *point of unresolved conflict* for a given nonmonotonic consequence relation '$\mathrel{|\!\sim}$':

DEFINITION 3. A statement p is a *point of unresolved conflict* for a set X iff for some $Y_1, Y_2 \subseteq \mathrm{Cn}(X)$, $Y_1 \mathrel{|\!\sim} p$ and $Y_2 \mathrel{|\!\sim} \neg p$, and $X \mathrel{|\!\sim} p$ iff $X \mathrel{|\!\sim} \neg p$.

A statement p is a point of unresolved conflict for a set X iff $\mathrm{Cn}(X)$ contains subsets Y_1 and Y_2 which provide conflicting evidence regarding the truth of p (Y_1 supports p, whereas Y_2 supports $\neg p$) but where X itself does not resolve this conflict in favor of *exactly one* of the alternatives. X may fail to resolve the conflict in one of two ways: by supporting both p and $\neg p$, or by supporting neither p nor $\neg p$. Let us call the former species of unresolved conflict type (i) and the latter type (ii).

The simplest example of an unresolved conflict of type (i) would be a set X that contains some statement and its negation, e.g. $X = \{p, \neg p\}$. If '$\mathrel{|\!\sim}$' satisfies reflexivity, then p is a point of unresolved conflict for X, where $Y_1 = \{p\}$ and $Y_2 = \{\neg p\}$. If '$\mathrel{|\!\sim}$' is not only reflexive but also supraclassical, then every logically inconsistent set has a point of unresolved conflict and every sentence is a point of unresolved conflict for any logically inconsistent set.

An example of an unresolved conflict of type (ii) would be the so-called *Nixon Diamond*. We are given the following facts: Nixon is a Republican

---
[9] See [Makinson 1994, p. 88].

(Rn), but Nixon is a Quaker (Qn). We are given the following rules for making nonmonotonic inferences from the facts: Republicans are normally non-pacifists ($r1$), but Quakers are normally pacifists ($r2$). So is Nixon a pacifist (Pn), or is he a non-pacifist ($\neg Pn$)? Relative to our rules, Nixon's being a Quaker supports the conclusion that he is a pacifist, i.e. $\{Qn\}\mathrel{\mid\!\sim} Pn$, but his being a Republican supports the contradictory conclusion that he is not a pacifist, i.e. $\{Rn\}\mathrel{\mid\!\sim} \neg Pn$. Considering all and only the facts we have, and in the absence of a policy which orders the rules by priority (e.g. a policy saying that when $r1$ and $r2$ both apply, only $r2$ may be used), an appropriately skeptical system of nonmonotonic reasoning will come to no conclusion concerning whether Nixon is a pacifist. In other words, for such a system, $\{Qn, Rn\}\mathrel{\not\mid\!\sim} Pn$ and $\{Qn, Rn\}\mathrel{\not\mid\!\sim} \neg Pn$. Thus in the Nixon example, p is a point of unresolved conflict for X, where $X = \{Qn, Rn\}$, $Y_1 = \{Qn\}$, $Y_2 = \{Rn\}$, and $p = Pn$.

According to the account developed in [Cross 2003], a set X is nonmonotonically inconsistent ($X\mathrel{\mid\!\sim}$) iff it has at least one point of unresolved conflict:[10]

DEFINITION 4. $X\mathrel{\mid\!\sim}$ iff for some p, p is a point of unresolved conflict for X.

Thus, for example, for an appropriately skeptical definition of nonmonotonic consequence, the facts of the Nixon Diamond form a nonmonotonically inconsistent set in the context of rules $r1$ and $r2$, since the claim that Nixon is a pacifist is a point of unresolved conflict for those facts. At the intuitive level, it is clear that the facts of the Nixon Diamond, while not logically inconsistent, are in a state of inductive or evidential conflict. It is precisely this kind of conflict that [Cross 2003] aims to formalize.

Given Definition 4, the general principles governing nonmonotonic inconsistency will be determined to a great extent by the properties of the underlying nonmonotonic consequence relation. Let us turn to a brief survey of some results illustrating this.

First, we have this result relating WeakTrNC and WeakCMNC to certain counterpart conditions on nonmonotonic inconsistency:

PROPOSITION 5. *If WeakTrNC and WeakCMNC hold for all X, p, and q, then WeakCMNI and WeakTrNI hold for all X and p:*[11]

WeakCMNI *If $X\mathrel{\mid\!\sim}$ and $X \vdash p$ then $X \cup \{p\}\mathrel{\mid\!\sim}$.*

WeakTrNI *If $X \cup \{p\}\mathrel{\mid\!\sim}$ and $X \vdash p$ then $X\mathrel{\mid\!\sim}$.*

---
[10]See [Cross 2003, Proposition 15].
[11]See [Cross 2003, Proposition 13].

Weak cautious monotony for nonmonotonic inconsistency (WeakCMNI) states that if a set is nonmonotonically inconsistent, then this inconsistency is preserved if one of the set's logical consequences is added. Weak transitivity for nonmonotonic inconsistency (WeakTrNI) states that if a set is nonmonotonically consistent (i.e. not nonmonotonically inconsistent), then this consistency is preserved if one of the set's logical consequences is added.

Next we have a result relating Trans($\mid\!\sim$) and a principle of consistency preservation for nonmonotonic consequence to a strong cautious monotony principle for nonmonotonic inconsistency:

PROPOSITION 6. *If CP, SupNC, and Trans($\mid\!\sim$) hold for all X, p, and q, then StrongCMNI holds for all X and p, where CP and StrongCMNI are as follows:*[12]

CP *If $X\mid\!\sim p$ and $X\mid\!\sim \neg p$, then $X \vdash$.*

StrongCMNI *If $X\mid\!\sim$ and $X\mid\!\sim p$ then $X \cup \{p\}\mid\!\sim$.*

StrongCMNI is the thesis that the nonmonotonic inconsistency of a set is preserved when one of its nonmonotonic consequences is added. Consistency preservation (CP) is the thesis that the nonmonotonic consequences of a set are classically inconsistent only if the set itself is classically inconsistent. Some examples of systems which satisfy CP are default logic with normal defaults,[13] Poole systems without constraints,[14] and complete classical stoppered preferential entailment.[15]

Finally, let us note this result, which relates a strong transitivity principle for nonmonotonic inconsistency to a transitivity assumption about points of unresolved conflict:

PROPOSITION 7. *If TrUC holds for all X, p, and q, then StrongTrNI holds for all X and p, where TrUC and StrongTrNI are as follows:*[16]

TrUC *For all p, q, and X, if q is a point of unresolved conflict for $X \cup \{p\}$ and $X\mid\!\sim p$, then q is a point of unresolved conflict for X.*

StrongTrNI *If $X \cup \{p\}\mid\!\sim$ and $X\mid\!\sim p$ then $X\mid\!\sim$.*

The idea behind TrUC is that if $X\mid\!\sim p$ and if q is a point of unresolved conflict for $X \cup \{p\}$, then removing p from $X \cup \{p\}$ should not be sufficient to resolve the conflict.

---

[12] See [Cross 2003, Proposition 14].
[13] See [Reiter 1980] and Makinson's discussion of consistency preservation for default logic in [Makinson 1994, p. 59].
[14] See [Poole 1988] and [Makinson 1994, p. 68].
[15] See [Makinson 1994, p. 81].
[16] See [Cross 2003, Proposition 17].

For proofs of the above results (and others), see [Cross 2003] and [Cross 2004]. Meanwhile, let us move on to consider how the notion of unresolved conflict can be applied to the problem of formalizing epistemic coherence.

3 Unresolved conflict and epistemic coherence

The theory of nonmonotonic inconsistency presented in [Cross 2003] can help make the notions of coherence and incoherence more rigorous because the important notion of an anomaly is a close cousin of the notion of a point of unresolved conflict. Recalling the Dunnit example described above in Section 1, consider the set $B \sim \{b4\}$, i.e. the result of deleting b4 from belief set B. Assuming a plausible mechanism for inductive reasoning (i.e., a reasonably chosen '$\hspace{1pt}\mid\hspace{-4pt}\sim$'), it would follow that b4 is a point of unresolved conflict for $B \sim \{b4\}$. This is so because $B \sim \{b4\}$ supports neither b4 nor its negation, yet there are subsets of $B \sim \{b4\}$ that point to conflicting inductive conclusions concerning b4. In particular, the set $\{b1, b2\}$ supports b4 (i.e., $\{b1, b2\}\mid\hspace{-4pt}\sim b4$), whereas $\{b3\}$ supports ¬b4 (i.e., $\{b3\}\mid\hspace{-4pt}\sim \neg b4$). $B \sim \{b4\}$ is therefore nonmonotonically inconsistent ($B \sim \{b4\}\mid\hspace{-4pt}\sim\bot$). The same cannot be said of $B^* \sim \{b4\}$, however, since $B^* \sim \{b4\}$ supports b4 ($B^* \sim \{b4\}\mid\hspace{-4pt}\sim b4$). Inspired by this example, I tentatively offer the following analysis of anomalies in coherentist epistemology. Since the process of deleting a statement from a set may not be as simple as subtracting it set-theoretically, I shall assume some operation of *theory contraction*. The set X_q^- in Definition 8 is the set that results from performing some given operation of contraction on $\text{Cn}(X)$ to remove q:[17]

DEFINITION 8. p is an *anomaly* relative to a set of statements X iff there exist q and Y such that $X \vdash q$ and $p \in X_q^-$ and $Y \subseteq X_q^-$ and $X_q^- \not\mid\hspace{-4pt}\sim q$ and $X_q^- \not\mid\hspace{-4pt}\sim \neg q$ but $Y\mid\hspace{-4pt}\sim q$ and $\{p\}\mid\hspace{-4pt}\sim \neg q$.

The Dunnit example illustrates the definition thusly:

$$
\begin{aligned}
p &= b3 = \text{'A credible witness claims to have seen Dunnit two hundred miles from the scene of the crime at the time of the murder.'} \\
q &= b4 = \text{'Dunnit committed the murder.'} \\
X &= B = \{b1, b2, b3, b4\} \\
X_q^- &= \text{Cn}(\{b1, b2, b3\}) \\
Y &= \{b1, b2\}
\end{aligned}
$$

---

[17] I make no assumptions about how contraction should work, except that (1) $q \notin X_q^-$ whenever $\not\vdash q$; and (2) $X_q^- \subseteq \text{Cn}(X)$. For more on contraction, see [Gardenfors 1988] and [Hansson 1999].

There is a clear connection between having an anomaly and having a point of unresolved conflict, but a set's having an anomaly does not imply that it has a point of unresolved conflict. Indeed, the set B in the Dunnit example contains an anomaly but has no point of unresolved conflict. This is no coincidence. The presence in B of the claim that Dunnit did it [b4] is precisely what makes b3 an anomaly rather than merely a piece of evidence that competes with other evidence [b1–b2]. Note, however, that b3 is an anomaly for B *only because* the set B^-_{b4} has a point of unresolved conflict, namely b4. In general, we have this result:

PROPOSITION 9. *If there is a p such that p is an anomaly for X, then there is a q such that $X \vdash q$ and X^-_q has a point of unresolved conflict.*

The coherence of a belief system, for BonJour, is determined in part by its anomalies. Since nonmonotonic inconsistency is defined in terms of unresolved conflict, Proposition 9 establishes that in certain cases epistemic *in*coherence is a matter of a set's having nonmonotonically inconsistent subsets of a certain kind. What about the notion of coherence itself? I offer the following analysis:

DEFINITION 10. A set X of sentences is *coherent* iff (i) no sentence is an anomaly for X; and (ii) $X \not\mid\!\sim$; and (iii) $X = C(X)$.

This definition captures the idea that coherence involves (on the negative side) (i) freedom from anomalies as well as (on the positive side) (iii) the maximum degree of inductive "hanging together," in the form of closure under nonmonotonic consequence. Assuming CP and SupNC both hold, requirement (ii) (nonmonotonic consistency) in Definition 10 captures two of BonJour's necessary conditions of epistemic coherence, since, by Proposition 11,[18] CP and SupNC imply that a nonmonotonically consistent set must be, first, logically consistent and, secondly, free of inductively "conflicting subsystems", i.e. subsets Y_1 and Y_2 which, respectively, support conflicting conclusions p and $\neg p$ neither of which is supported by X.

PROPOSITION 11. *Given CP and SupNC, $X \mid\!\sim$ iff either $X \vdash$ or there is a p such that, for some Y_1 and Y_2, where $Y_1 \subseteq Cn(X)$ and $Y_2 \subseteq Cn(X)$, $Y_1 \mid\!\sim p$ and $Y_2 \mid\!\sim \neg p$ but $X \not\mid\!\sim p$ and $X \not\mid\!\sim \neg p$.*

It might be thought an objection to Definition 10 that it does not capture the notion that coherence is a matter of degree. This deficiency is easily remedied. An ordering with respect to degree of coherence can be obtained as follows:

DEFINITION 12. *For sets X and Y, X is more coherent than Y iff either*

---

[18]For proof, see [Cross 2003, Proposition 7].

(i) X and Y have exactly the same points of unresolved conflict, but X's anomalies are a proper subset of Y's anomalies; or

(ii) X and Y have exactly the same anomalies, but X's points of unresolved conflict are a proper subset of Y's points of unresolved conflict; or

(iii) $C(X) = C(Y)$, and X and Y have the same anomalies and points of unresolved conflict, but Y is a proper subset of X.

Clause (i) ensures that if X has the same points of unresolved conflict as a competing set Y while Y's set of anomalies includes X's anomalies and then some, then X is the more coherent of the two sets. Clause (ii) ensures that if X has the same anomalies as a competing set Y while Y's points of unresolved conflict include X's points of unresolved conflict and then some, then, again, X is the more coherent of the two sets. Finally, clause (iii) ensures that if two sets have the same anomalies, points of unresolved conflict, and nonmonotonic consequences, but one of the two sets is a superset of the other, then the superset is the more coherent, since it is strictly nearer to being closed under nonmonotonic consequence than the subset.[19]

Note that Definition 12 does not result in a total ordering of sets with respect to degree of coherence, but this is as it should be. Intuitively, orderings with respect to coherence seem most intelligible when, as in the Dunnit example, the two belief sets being compared are extremely similar.

Note also that Definition 12 yields the correct ordering of belief sets for the Dunnit example, since B^* counts as more coherent than B in virtue of clause (i): B^* and B have exactly the same points of unresolved conflict (namely, none), but B^*'s set of anomalies (namely the empty set) is a proper subset of B's set of anomalies.

Finally, note that given Definition 12, coherence as defined in Definition 10 is the highest possible degree of coherence in the sense that no set can be more coherent than a set that satisfies Definition 10:

PROPOSITION 13. *Assuming $Ref(\hspace{-0.5mm}\mid\hspace{-1mm}\sim)$ holds, if X is coherent then there is no Y such that Y is more coherent than X.*

Proof: Assume $Ref(\hspace{-0.5mm}\mid\hspace{-1mm}\sim)$ holds and suppose that some set Y is more coherent than X. By Definition 12, there are three cases:

---

[19] It would not work to add to clause (i) that $C(X) = C(Y)$, since this might be ruled out by the presence of additional anomalies in Y. Similarly, it would not work to add $C(X) = C(Y)$ to clause (ii), since this might be ruled out by the additional points of unresolved conflict in Y.

(i) Suppose that Y's anomalies are a proper subset of X's. Then X has at least one anomaly, in which case X is not coherent, since a coherent set has no anomalies.

(ii) Suppose that Y's points of unresolved conflict are a proper subset of X's. Then X has at least one point of unresolved conflict, in which case X is not coherent, since a coherent set has no points of unresolved conflict.

(iii) Suppose that X is a proper subset of Y, but $C(X) = C(Y)$. By Ref($\vdash$), $Y \subseteq C(Y)$; hence X is a proper subset of $C(Y)$. If X is coherent, then $X = C(X)$, in which case, contrary to hypothesis, $C(X)$ is a proper subset of $C(Y)$. So X is not coherent in this case, either.

In each of the three cases, then, X is not coherent. Our result follows by contraposition. ∎

Conclusion

We have seen that the notion of an anomaly in coherentist epistemology can be given a formal analysis in terms of nonmonotonic consequence, and we have seen that, under this analysis, the notion of an anomaly is closely related to that of a point of unresolved conflict in the sense of [Cross 2003]. The aptness of our analysis of anomalies is confirmed by our application of it to Klein and Warfield's Dunnit example. Based on the notions of anomaly, nonmonotonic inconsistency, and closure under nonmonotonic consequence we have provided in Definition 10 a formal analysis of epistemic coherence and in Definition 12 a means of ordering sets with respect to their degree of coherence. The formal precision of Definitions 10 and 12 shows that holistic coherentist epistemology can indeed be made rigorous.

Acknowledgements

This essay originated as a section of a longer paper presented at the 2001 annual meeting of the Society for Exact Philosophy hosted by the Université de Montréal (June 2001) and honoring the memory of Hugues Leblanc. The rest of that longer paper was published separately as [Cross 2003], with a correction published as [Cross 2004].

This research was supported in part by a grant from the University of Georgia Research Foundation.

BIBLIOGRAPHY

[BonJour 1985] L. BonJour, *The Structure of Empirical Knowledge*, Harvard University Press, Cambridge (USA), 1985.

[Cross 2003] C. Cross, Nonmonotonic inconsistency. *Artificial Intelligence* 149 (2) (2003) 161–178.

[Cross 2004] C. Cross, A correction to 'Nonmonotonic inconsistency'. *Artificial Intelligence* 160 (1–2) (2004) 191–192.

[Doyle 1979] J. Doyle, A truth-maintenance system. *Artificial Intelligence* 12 (3) (1979) 231–272.
[Gabbay 1985] D. Gabbay, Theoretical foundations for non-monotonic reasoning in expert systems, in: K. Apt (Ed.), *Logics and Models of Concurrent Systems*, Springer-Verlag, Berlin, pp. 439–457.
[Gardenfors 1988] P. Gärdenfors, *Knowledge in Flux*, The MIT Press, Cambridge (USA), 1988.
[Gelfond and Lifschitz 1988] M. Gelfond and V. Lifschitz. The stable model semantics for logic programming, in: K. Bowen and R. Kowalski, (Eds.), *Fifth International Conference Symposium on Logic Programming 2*, The MIT Press, Cambridge, MA, 1988, pp. 1070–1080.
[Hansson 1999] S.O. Hansson, *A Textbook of Belief Dynamics: Theory Change and Database Updating*, Kluwer, Dordrecht, 1999.
[Klein and Warfield 1994] P. Klein and T. Warfield, What price coherence? *Analysis* 54 (3) (1994) 129–132.
[Makinson 1989] D. Makinson, General theory of cumulative inference, in: M. Reinfrank, J. de Kleer, M.L. Ginsberg, and E. Sandewall, (Eds.), *Lecture Notes in Artificial Intelligence 346: Nonmonotonic Reasoning*, Springer-Verlag, Berlin, 1989, pp. 1–18.
[Makinson 1994] D. Makinson, General patterns in nonmonotonic reasoning, in: D.M. Gabbay, C.J. Hogger, and J.A. Robinson, (Eds.), *Handbook of Logic in Artifical Intelligence and Logic Programming, Volume 3: Nonmonotonic Reasoning and Uncertain Reasoning*, Oxford University Press, Oxford, 1994, pp. 35–110.
[Merricks 1995] T. Merricks, On behalf of the coherentist, *Analysis* 55 (4) (1995) 306–309.
[Poole 1988] D. Poole, A logical framework for default reasoning, *Artificial Intelligence* 36 (1) (1988), 27–47.
[Reiter 1980] R. Reiter, A logic for default reasoning, *Artificial Intelligence* 13 (1–2) (1980), 81–132.

How do the Harper and Levi Identities Constrain Belief Change?

OLIVER SCHULTE

ABSTRACT. Belief revision is the process of revising beliefs in light of new information. Belief contraction is the process of giving up beliefs to make them consistent with new information. The Levi and Harper Identities provide constructions of revisions and contractions in terms of each other. This paper gives necessary and sufficient conditions for when revisions can be constructed from contractions, and contractions from revisions. I relate these conditions to other well-known principles for belief revision and contraction.

1 Minimal Belief Change and the Levi and Harper Identities

Belief revision is the process of incorporating new information into a body of extant beliefs. This process is clearly of central epistemic importance. Viewed in suitable generality, it encompasses scientific and inductive reasoning and many forms of everyday reasoning, for example causal and default reasoning. Another important epistemic process is belief contraction. Roughly, to contract one's beliefs on some proposition p is to "give $\neg p$ a hearing"—to transform one's beliefs, if necessary to weaken them, so that they not longer entail p. One reason why belief contraction has been interesting to philosophers of science is that it seems to model the situation of a scientist who holds a theory but opens her mind enough to consider alternatives [2].

Quine made famous the idea that rational belief revision should be minimal belief revision, the "minimal mutilation" of one's web of beliefs. Since then, philosophers and logicians have devoted much effort to determining general principles of minimal belief change [6]. One early proposal by Levi was to link the notion of minimal belief revision to belief contraction. He suggested that a theory change from the current theory T on new information p ought to proceed in two stages [4]. First, we may contract the theory T on the assertion $\neg p$. This yields a theory T' that does not entail $\neg p$, and hence is consistent with p. Then we add the new information p to T'. This recipe for deriving belief revision from belief contraction is known as the *Levi Identity*.

In this paper I investigate what constraints on belief revision result from the very idea of revision proceeding via contraction. Are there revision functions that violate Levi's proposal, in that they cannot be derived from contraction functions? If so, which revision functions are consistent with belief contraction and which aren't? I show that not all revision functions follow Levi's recipe. With mild assumptions about the operative notion of logical consequence, the following criterion is necessary and sufficient for a revision function to be derivable from a contraction function: the revision must be logically weaker than, or the same as, the result of simply adding the new information. In symbols, if $T * p$ represents the revision of a theory T given new information p, then $T \cup \{p\}$ must entail $T * p$. This is the AGM postulate K*3 [1, Ch.3.3]. Gärdenfors showed that any revision function that satisfies his "basic postulates for revision"—K*1 through K*6—can be constructed via the Levi Identity [1, p.71]. The result in this paper strengthens Gärdenfors' observation by providing necessary conditions as well as sufficient ones. We will see that in particular Gärdenfors' postulates K*5 (the "success postulate") and K*4 (the "preservation principle") are not necessary for satisfying the Levi Identity.

It turns out that there are strong independent grounds to hold that K*3, the main postulate for satisfying the Levi Identity, is a fundamental principle of minimal belief change. First, it is the characteristic condition of a constraint on belief change that I have called *Pareto-minimality*. Roughly, a belief revision $T * p$ is Pareto-minimal if it cannot be made more minimal by retracting fewer beliefs from T without adding more, or by adding fewer beliefs to T without retracting more.[1] Second, there is a standard way of translating belief revision postulates into axioms for conditionals known as the *Ramsey test*. Given the Ramsey test, the K*3 postulate corresponds exactly to a plausible and widely accepted principle of conditional logic, namely that $(p > q) \to (p \to q)$, where $\to$ stands for material implication and $>$ stands for a conditional connective ("if-then") [1, Lemma 7.3]. It is remarkable that four independently motivated ideas—the conditional axiom mentioned, Pareto-minimality, Levi's proposal of defining revision in terms of contraction, and the AGM postulate K*3—should amount to essentially the same constraint on belief revision.

Harper proposed a definition of belief contraction in terms of belief revision [2] that Gärdenfors refers to as the *Harper Identity* [1, p.70]. Briefly, the idea is that a belief q should be part of the contraction $T \dot{-} p$ just in case q is a member of T and of $T * \neg p$, the revision of T on the negation of p. As

---

[1] Pareto-minimality corresponds to Rott's symmetric-difference criterion [7].

with the Levi Identity and belief revision, we can ask what constraints the Harper Identity imposes on belief contraction. Which contraction functions can be derived from revision functions via the Harper Identity? It turns out that under mild assumptions about the operative notion of logical consequence, a contraction function is derivable from a revision function if and only if the contraction function satisfies the "recovery principle" [1, p.62]. Intuitively, the recovery principle asserts the following. Consider an agent who contracts her beliefs on a proposition p so that her contracted beliefs no longer entail p. Suppose that after giving $\neg p$ "a hearing", the agent decides to include p among her beliefs after all. Then according to the recovery principle, she should return to the epistemic state she was in before contracting her beliefs on p. In symbols, if $T \dot{-} p$ stands for the contraction of a theory T on an assertion p, then the recovery principle says that $T \dot{-} p \cup \{p\}$ entails $T \cup \{p\}$, and vice versa.

As with the Levi Identity, this result strengthens Gärdenfors' observation that his basic postulates for belief contraction suffice to guarantee that contraction functions can be constructed via the Harper Identity [1, p.71], by giving necessary as well as sufficient conditions for contraction functions to satisfy the Harper Identity.

So we find that two independently motivated ideas—the Harper Identity and the recovery principle—turn out to give equivalent constraints on belief contraction. One may take this equivalence to support both ideas. On the other hand, the recovery principle has been subject to some objections (see Section 6 below). It follows from the equivalence of the Harper Identity and the recovery principle that if we reject the recovery principle as a constraint on belief contraction, then we cannot assume that contraction functions are associated with revision functions as the Harper Identity stipulates, and we must be careful about "going back and forth between revision and contraction" (see also [5]).

The paper is organized as follows. I begin with the formal assumptions concerning the logical language and consequence relations. Then I introduce the Levi and Harper Identities. The next section characterizes the revision functions that satisfy the Levi Identity. I outline the related results concerning conditionals and Pareto-minimal belief change. The equivalence between the recovery principle and the Harper Identity is the final topic.

2 Theories

I begin with the representation of an agent's current beliefs as a deductively closed *theory* expressed in a formal language. As is usual in belief revision theory, my assumptions about the structure of the language in which an agent formulates her beliefs are sparse; essentially, all I assume is that the language features the usual propositional connectives. I take as given a suitable consequence relation between sets of formulas in the language, obeying the standard Tarskian properties. The formal presuppositions are as follows.

A **language** L is a set of formulas satisfying the following conditions.

1. L contains a **negation operator** $\neg$ such that if p is a formula in L, so is $\neg p$.

2. L contains a **conjunction connective** $\wedge$ such that if p and q are formulas in L, so is $p \wedge q$.

3. L contains an **implication connective** $\rightarrow$ such that if p and q are formulas in L, so is $p \rightarrow q$.

A **consequence operation** $Cn : 2^L \rightarrow 2^L$ represents a notion of entailment between sets of formulas from a language L. A set of formulas Γ **entails** another set of formulas Γ', written $\Gamma \vdash \Gamma'$, iff $Cn(\Gamma) \supseteq \Gamma'$. A set of formulas Γ entails a formula p, written $\Gamma \vdash p$, iff $p \in Cn(\Gamma)$. I assume that Cn satisfies the following properties, for all sets of formulas Γ, Γ'.

Inclusion $\Gamma \subseteq Cn(\Gamma)$.

Montonicity $Cn(\Gamma) \subseteq Cn(\Gamma')$ whenever $\Gamma \subseteq \Gamma'$.

Iteration $Cn(Cn(\Gamma)) = Cn(\Gamma)$.

A **theory** is a deductively closed set of formulas. That is, a set of formulas $T \subseteq L$ is a theory iff $Cn(T) = T$.

The entailment relation $\vdash$ is related to the propositional connectives as follows.

Modus Ponens If $\Gamma \vdash p$, $(p \rightarrow q)$, then $\Gamma \vdash q$.

Implication If $\Gamma \vdash q$, then $\Gamma \vdash (p \rightarrow q)$.

Deduction $\Gamma \cup \{p\} \vdash q$ iff $\Gamma \vdash (p \rightarrow q)$.

Conjunction $\Gamma \vdash (p \wedge q)$ iff both $\Gamma \vdash p$ and $\Gamma \vdash q$.

Consistency Suppose that $\Gamma \not\vdash p$. Then $\Gamma \cup \{\neg p\} \not\vdash p$.

Inconsistency $\{p \wedge \neg p\} \vdash L$.

Double Negation $\Gamma \vdash p$ iff $\Gamma \vdash \neg\neg p$.

For the remainder of this paper, assume that a language L and a consequence relation Cn (and hence an entailment relation $\vdash$) have been fixed that satisfy the conditions laid down above.

For example, suppose that we have a formal language for describing a very simple situation: there are three objects and one table. Our language has three propositional letters a, b, c. To provide some intuition, we interpret a to mean "the first object is on the table", b to mean "the second object is on the table", and c as "the third object is on the table". I will use the scenario throughout the paper to illustrate definitions.

Next, I state without proof two simple lemmas about theories and consequence relations that will be useful later.

LEMMA 1. *Let T_1, T_2 be two theories. Then $T_1 \cap T_2$ is a theory.*

We will have occasion to consider the logical consequences of adding a formula p to a theory, that is $Cn(T \cup \{p\})$. In belief revision theory, this operation is called **expansion**. Introducing a special symbol for expansion will simplify the notation in what follows.

DEFINITION 2. *For all sets of formulas Γ and formulas p define $\Gamma + p = Cn(\Gamma \cup \{p\})$.*

Note that in this notation, the Deduction Principle is expressed as $\Gamma \vdash p \to q$ iff $\Gamma + p \vdash q$.

A useful fact is that, given our assumptions about the consequence relation Cn, expansion distributes over the intersection of two theories.

LEMMA 3. *Let T_1, T_2 be two theories. For any formula p it is the case that $(T_1 \cap T_2) + p = (T_1 + p) \cap (T_2 + p)$.*

3 Belief Revision, Belief Contraction and The Levi and Harper Identities

A belief revision function represents the agent's disposition to change her beliefs in light of new evidence represented by a formula p.

DEFINITION 4. *A belief revision function is a function $* : \mathbf{T} \times L \to \mathbf{T}$ such that for all formulas p, it is the case that $T * p \vdash p$.*

A complete list of the AGM postulates K*1 through K*8 for revision functions may be found in [1, Ch.3.3]. In terms of the AGM axioms, Definition 4 restricts attention to belief revision functions satisfying K*1 and K*2.

A major part of the theory of minimal belief change is the analysis of belief contraction, which is formally represented by a belief contraction function.

DEFINITION 5. *A belief contraction function $\dot{-}$ is a function $\dot{-} : \mathbf{T} \times L \to$*

T such that for all theories T and for all formulas p, it is the case that $T \vdash T \dot{-} p$.

Thus a belief contraction only retracts beliefs, but does not add any. Usually belief revision theorists require that a belief contraction on a formula p yields a theory that is consistent with the negation of p (provided that p is not a theorem). It turns out that we can characterize the content of the Harper and Levi Identities without that requirement, so to obtain the strongest possible result, I do not impose it.

Gärdenfors introduces eight postulates K^-1 through K^-8 for belief contraction, which may be found in [1, Ch.3.4]. In my usage, the postulates K^-1 and K^-2 define a belief contraction function.

One of the early ideas about belief revision was Levi's proposal for constructing revisions out of contractions [4]. Gärdenfors formalizes Levi's idea via the following definition [1, p.69].

DEFINITION 6 (The Levi Identity). Let $\dot{-}$ be a belief contraction function. The belief revision function $*$ associated with $\dot{-}$ is defined by $T * p = T \dot{-} \neg p + p$.

I write levi($\dot{-}$) to denote the belief revision function associated with $\dot{-}$. To illustrate the Levi Identity, consider again the belief contraction $Cn(\{a, \neg b\}) \dot{-} \neg b = Cn(\{a\})$. The associated belief revision is $Cn(\{a, b\}) * b = (Cn(\{a, b\}) \dot{-} \neg b) + b$, which is $Cn(\{a\}) + b = Cn(\{a, b\})$. In words, we can think of the revision as first withdrawing nothing but the negation of the new information b, and then adding the new belief b.

How should we define a belief contraction function given a revision function $*$ for a theory T? Harper made the following proposal (translated into our syntactic framework) [2]. Consider the revision $T * \neg p$. If $T * \neg p$ is a minimal revision of T on $\neg p$, then the difference between $T * \neg p$ and T is minimal, and so $T * \neg p$ has as much in common with T as possible given the requirement of accommodating $\neg p$. Thus the overlap $T \cap T * \neg p$ ought to be as large as it can be while conforming with $\neg p$. This means that $T \cap T * \neg p$ is a plausible candidate for a minimal retraction of T that makes room for $\neg p$, that is, a contraction of T on p. Hence the following definition.

DEFINITION 7 (The Harper Identity). Let $*$ be a belief revision function for T. The contraction function associated with $*$ is defined by $T \dot{-} p = T \cap T * \neg p$.

As the Levi Identity yields a contraction function given a revision function, the Harper Identity defines a revision function from a contraction function; see Figure 1.

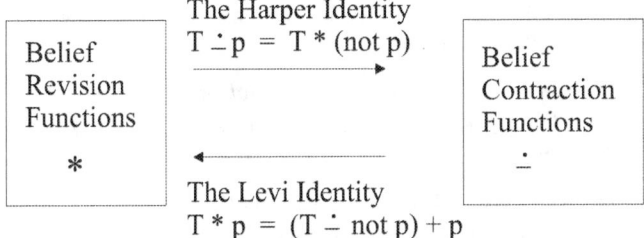

Figure 1. The Levi and Harper Identity

I write harper(∗) to denote the belief contraction function associated with ∗.

To illustrate the Harper identity, suppose that we have a revision $Cn(\{a, \neg b\}) * b = Cn(\{a, b\})$. (The agent initially believes that the first object is on the table and the second is not. On learning that the second is on the table, her new beliefs are that the first two objects are on the table.) Assume that the revision function treats b and $\neg\neg b$ identically, such that $Cn(\{a, \neg b\}) * \neg\neg b = Cn(\{a, b\})$. The associated belief contraction is $Cn(\{a, \neg b\}) \dot{-} \neg b = Cn(\{a, \neg b\}) \cap (Cn(\{a, \neg b\}) * \neg\neg b)$, which is $Cn(\{a, \neg b\}) \cap Cn(\{a, \neg b\}) * b = Cn(\{a, \neg b\}) \cap Cn(\{a, b\})$. It is possible to show that $Cn(\{a, \neg b\}) \cap Cn(\{a, b\}) = Cn(\{a\})$. All told, we have that $Cn(\{a, \neg b\}) \dot{-} \neg b = Cn(\{a\})$.

Note that in this case, the Levi and Harper Identities invert each other. If we start with the revision $Cn(\{a, \neg b\}) * b = Cn(\{a, b\})$, the Harper Identity yields the contraction $Cn(\{a, \neg b\}) \dot{-} \neg b = Cn(\{a\})$. And as we saw above, applying the Levi Identity to the contraction $Cn(\{a, \neg b\}) \dot{-} \neg b = Cn(\{a\})$ yields the revision $Cn(\{a, \neg b\}) * b = Cn(\{a, b\})$.

4 Necessary and Sufficient Conditions for Satisfying the Levi Identity

The Levi Identity stipulates a constraint on revision functions for minimal belief change by connecting them to belief contraction. What is the content of this constraint? That is, what properties must belief revision functions satisfy if they follow the Levi Identity? The answer is that the Levi Identity picks out those revision functions that satisfy K*3—the requirement that the expansion $T + p$ must be at least as strong as the revision $T * p$. Let us say that a function ∗ **satisfies the Levi Identity**, or is **generated by the Levi Identity**, if there is a belief contraction function $\dot{-}$ such that ∗ is the function associated with $\dot{-}$ (i.e., ∗ = levi($\dot{-}$)) (cf. [5, p.386]). It is easy to see that if a belief revision function satisfies the Levi Identity, then it also satisfies K*3. (Proof omitted.)

LEMMA 8. *Let $\dot{-}$ be a belief contraction function with associated belief revision function $*$. Then for all theories T and for all formulas p, it is the case that $T + p \vdash T * p$.*

What about the converse of Lemma 8? The converse requires us to show that if a belief revision function $*$ satisfies K*3, then there is some contraction function $\dot{-}$ that generates $*$ via the Levi Identity. The obvious candidate for such a contraction function is the function harper($*$) that the Harper Identity associates with the revision operator. It turns out that indeed, applying the Levi Identity to harper($*$) yields the original belief revision function $*$; in other words, the Levi Identity inverts the Harper Identity, but only with some provisos. The first proviso is that $*$ must satisfy K*3, as Lemma 8 requires. The second is that $*$ must treat doubly negated formulas like unnegated formulas. Thus I say that a belief revision function $*$ for T respects **double negation** if for all formulas p, we have that $T * p = T * \neg\neg p$. Respect for double negation is much weaker than the AGM postulate K*6 which requires that the respective results of revising on logically equivalent formulas be the same. With these conditions in place, the postulate K*3 is a necessary and sufficient condition for the Levi Identity to invert the Harper Identity.

PROPOSITION 9. *Let $*$ be a belief revision function that respects double negation. Then the Levi Identity inverts the Harper Identity applied to $* \iff$ for all theories T and formulas p, it is the case that $T + p \vdash T * p$.*

From both a mathematical and a philosophical point of view, it is desirable to have this tight connection between the two identities. Gärdenfors puts it like this:

> But we also want the two definitions to be *interchangeable* in the sense that, if we start with one definition to construct a new contraction (or revision) function and after that use the other definition to obtain a revision (or contraction) function again, then we ought to get the original function back. If this can be proved, we will have shown that contractions and revisions are interdefinable in a strong sense. [1, p.70]

Proposition 9 characterizes the revision functions for which the Levi and Harper Identity are interchangeable in this sense. The proposition also immediately yields a characterization of the belief revision functions that are consistent with the Levi Identity.

COROLLARY 10. *A belief revision function $*$ that respects double negation can be generated by the Levi Identity $\iff$ for all theories T and formulas p, it is the case that $T + p \vdash T * p$.*

5 Discussion and Related Results

The fact that the postulate K*3 is equivalent to the Levi Identity, viewed as a constraint on belief revision, suggests that K*3 expresses a fundamental principle of minimal belief change. There are a number of other considerations that bring out the importance of K*3.

The Update Postulates. K*3 is one of the key principles of Katsuno and Mendelson's well-known *Update* theory of belief change, which they present as an account of belief change in a dynamically changing environment [3].

Conditional Logic. Gärdenfors introduced a formal connection between belief revision axioms and axioms for conditionals, known as the Ramsey test because Gärdenfors credited the basic idea to Frank Ramsey. The proposal is that an agent should accept a conditional $p > q$ just in case she accepts q after revising her beliefs on p; in symbols, the condition is that $T \vdash p > q \iff T * p \vdash q$. Gärdenfors showed that under the Ramsey test, K*3 corresponds exactly to the conditional axiom $(p > q) \to (p \to q)$, which is part of Lewis' system VC (for the details, see [1, Lemma 7.3]).

Pareto-minimal theory change. It turns out that K*3 characterizes another very plausible constraint on belief revision functions. For a given theory T and possible revision T', consider the symmetric difference $T \triangle T' = (T - T') \cup (T' - T)$. For example, if $T = Cn(\{a\})$ and $T' = Cn(\{a, b, c\})$, then $T \triangle T' = \emptyset \cup Cn(\{b, c\}) = Cn(\{b, c\})$.

Say that a theory T' satisfies the **symmetric difference criterion** for T iff for all theories T^* it is not the case that $T \triangle T^* \subset T \triangle T'$ ([7, Sec.II], [9, Sec.4]). In our example, $T' = Cn(\{a, b, c\})$ does *not* satisfy the symmetric difference criterion because if we take $T^* = Cn(\{a, b\})$, we have that $T \triangle T^* = Cn(\{b\})$, whereas $T \triangle T' = Cn(\{b, c\})$, so $T \triangle T^* \subset T \triangle T'$.

Roughly speaking, the symmetric difference criterion rules out a theory change $T * p$ if some other possible theory change T^* retracts less from T without adding more, or if T^* adds less to T without retracting more (see [9, Sec.4]). In our example, the revision $Cn(\{a\}) * b = Cn(\{a, b\})$ adds fewer beliefs to $Cn(\{a\})$ than $Cn(\{a, b, c\})$ does, and retracts no more, so $Cn(\{a, b, c\})$ is clearly not a minimal theory change. If we think of retractions and additions as a kind of cost to be minimized in theory change, this means that the symmetric difference criterion is an instance of the basic decision-theoretic principle of Pareto-optimality for choosing among objects with multiple attributes. That is, the symmetric difference criterion selects exactly those theory changes that are (weakly) Pareto-optimal with respect to the two "cost dimensions" retractions and additions. For this reason, Schulte [9, Sec.4] refers to theory changes satisfying the symmetric difference criterion as *Pareto-minimal theory revisions*. In the context of belief revision, we want to restrict attention to theory changes that entail a given piece of new information p. This leads to the following definition.

DEFINITION 11. Let T be a theory and let p be a formula. Then $T * p$ is a **Pareto-minimal** revision of T on p $\iff$

1. $T * p$ entails p, and

2. for all theories T' entailing p, it is not the case that $T \triangle T' \subset T \triangle T*p$.

It seems clear that Pareto-minimality is a necessary condition for a theory change $T * p$ to count as minimal. The next theorem gives an explicit characterization of Pareto-minimal belief revision functions; the proof is in [9, Th.5].

THEOREM 12. *Let T be a theory and let p be a formula. A theory revision $T * p$ is a Pareto-minimal revision of T on p* $\iff$

1. $T * p \vdash p$, and

2. $T + p \vdash T * p$, and

3. *if $T \vdash p$, then $T * p = T$.*

Clause 1 simply states the basic property of incorporating the new evidence, and Clause 3 says that if a theory T already incorporates the new evidence, no change at all should occur. Since no change is clearly the smallest change, Condition 3 is a trivial requirement for minimal belief change. Thus it is Clause 2 that captures the force of Pareto-minimality in theory change—and this condition is just the familiar postulate K*3.

So we have the striking result that three principles with independent strong motivations—the Levi Identity as a constraint on belief revision, the conditional axiom $(p > q) \to (p \to q)$, and Pareto-minimality—are basically equivalent to K*3.

6 Necessary and Sufficient Conditions for Satisfying the Harper Identity

This section investigates the content of the Harper Identity. Let us say that a function $\dot{-}$ **satisfies the Harper Identity**, or is **generated by the Harper Identity**, if there is a belief revision function $*$ such that $\dot{-}$ is the function associated with $*$ (i.e., $\dot{-} = \mathrm{harper}(*)$). It is not hard to prove that the following condition is necessary for a belief contraction function to be generated by the Harper Identity. (Proof omitted.)

LEMMA 13. *Suppose that $*$ is a belief revision function, and that $\dot{-}$ is the contraction function associated with $*$. Then for all theories T and for all formulas p, it is the case that $T\dot{-}p + p = T + p$.*

To illustrate the lemma, let us consider an example of a contraction that does not satisfy the Harper Identity. For example, let $T = Cn(\{a,b\})$, and suppose that $T\dot{-}a = Cn(\emptyset)$ (to withdraw the belief that the first object is on the table, contract to being uncertain about all three objects). Then $T\dot{-}a + b = Cn(\{b\})$, which is different from $T + b = Cn(\{a,b\})$. Hence Lemma 13 entails that $T\dot{-}a$ does not satisfy the Harper Identity.[2]

In the case in which $T \vdash p$, the condition that $T\dot{-}p + p = T + p$ is essentially equivalent to Gärdenfors' postulate K$^-$5, viz. $T\dot{-}p + p \vdash T$. Since $T + p = T$ if $T \vdash p$, the condition of Lemma 13 entails K$^-$5. And since $T \vdash T\dot{-}p$ for any contraction function $\dot{-}$, it is immediate that $T + p \vdash T\dot{-}p + p$.

The postulate K$^-$5 is often referred to as a **recovery postulate** because it asserts that after first contracting on p and then adding p "back in", the agent recovers all of the beliefs in her original theory T. The condition of Lemma 13 is a slightly different formulation of the recovery principle. The intuition behind the recovery principle is this. To contract beliefs on p means to "give $\neg p$ a hearing", or to entertain the possibility that p may be false. If the agent gives $\neg p$ a hearing, but then finds that p is correct after all, the agent should restore confidence in any proposition q that he may have believed but called into doubt along with q.

Before establishing a converse to Lemma 13, I ask under what circumstances the Harper Identity inverts the Levi Identity, as before in the case of the Levi Identity. The recovery postulate turns out to be sufficient as well as necessary, provided that the consequence relation satisfies two more conditions.

First, as with belief revision functions, I say that a belief contraction function for a theory T **respects double negation** if for all formulas p, it is the case that $T\dot{-}\neg\neg p = T\dot{-}p$. Respect for double negation is an instance of Gärdenfors' postulate K$^-$6. Second, a consequence relation Cn **satisfies disjunctive syllogism** if for all sets of formulas Γ it is the case that if $\Gamma \vdash p \to q$ and $\Gamma \vdash \neg p \to q$, then $\Gamma \vdash q$. With these conditions in place, the recovery principle is a necessary and sufficient condition for the Harper Identity to invert the Levi Identity.

---

[2]To verify this fact directly, consider any revision $T * \neg a$ and apply Lemma 3 to $(T \cap T * \neg a) + a$.

PROPOSITION 14. *Assume that the consequence relation Cn satisfies disjunctive syllogism, and let $\dot{-}$ be a belief contraction function that respects double negation. Then the Harper Identity inverts the Levi Identity for the belief contraction function associated with $\dot{-}$ $\iff$ for all theories T and for all formulas p, it is the case that $T \dot{-} p + p = T + p$.*

Proposition 14 immediately yields a characterization of the belief revision functions that are consistent with the Harper Identity.

COROLLARY 15. *If the consequence relation Cn satisfies disjunctive syllogism, a belief contraction function $\dot{-}$ that respects double negation can be generated by the Harper Identity $\iff$ for all theories T and for all formulas p, it is the case that $T \dot{-} p + p = T + p$.*

Corollary 15 shows that two independently motivated principles for theory contraction, the Harper Identity and the Recovery Principle, turn out to be equivalent. There are several objections to the recovery principle, which by our result are also objections to the Harper Identity. It is not my purpose in this paper to adjudicate the status of the recovery principle; several authors have discussed the pros and cons of this principle—see [1, Ch.3.4], [5], [10], [8] and the references in these papers. The mathematical results apply whether one accepts the principle or not.

7 Conclusion

We may view the Levi Identity as a constraint on belief revision: revisions should be such that they can be constructed from a contraction function as directed by the Levi Identity. I showed that a revision function satisfies this constraint just in case it satisfies the AGM postulate K*3. Via the Ramsey test, the postulate K*3 in turn is equivalent to the conditional axiom $(p > q) \to (p \to q)$. Finally, K*3 is the characteristic axiom of Pareto-minimal theory change, a basic requirement for minimal belief revision. The fact that four independently motivated constraints on belief revision turn out to be essentially equivalent reinforces each of them, and provides strong evidence that K*3 is a basic principle of minimal theory change.

As with the Levi Identity, it is possible to view the Harper Identity as a constraint on belief contraction: contractions should be such that they can be constructed from a revision function as directed by the Harper Identity. I showed that a contraction function satisfies this constraint just in case it satisfies the recovery principle. The fact that the Harper Identity and the recovery principle turn out to be equivalent, though independently motivated, would seem to support both.

On the other hand, some belief revision theorists have objected to the recovery principle; if the recovery principle is objectionable, then so is the

Harper Identity, and there is only a limited extent to which we can make use of the Harper and Levi Identities to translate from revision to contraction and vice versa.

8 Proofs

Proof of Proposition 9. Let $\dot{-}$ be the belief contraction function $harper(*)$ defined by $T\dot{-}p = T \cap T*\neg p$. First we have that (a) $T\dot{-}\neg p + p = (T \cap T*\neg\neg p) + p = (T \cap T*p) + p$ by the assumption that $T*\neg\neg p = T*p$. By Lemma 3 we have that $(T \cap T*p) + p = T + p \cap T*p + p$, which is equal to $T + p \cap T*p$ since $T*p$ is a theory entailing p. Together with (a), this shows that (b) $T\dot{-}\neg p + p = T + p \cap T*p$. Thus $T\dot{-}\neg p + p = T*p$ if and only if $T + p \supseteq T*p$; in other words, if and only if $T + p \vdash T*p$. □

Proof of Proposition 14. Let $*$ be the belief revision function $levi(\dot{-})$ defined by $T*p = T\dot{-}\neg p + p$.

($\Rightarrow$) If $\dot{-}$ is the result of applying the Harper Identity to the belief revision function $*$, it follows from Lemma 13 that for all formulas p, it is the case that $T\dot{-}p + p = T + p$.

($\Leftarrow$) Suppose that it is the case that $T\dot{-}p + p = T + p$. We want to show that $T\dot{-}p = T \cap T * \neg p$. By the definition of $*$, we must show that $T\dot{-}p = T \cap (T\dot{-}\neg\neg p + \neg p)$, which is equal to $T \cap (T\dot{-}p + \neg p)$ if $\dot{-}$ respects double negation. It is easy to see that $T\dot{-}p \subseteq T \cap (T\dot{-}p + \neg p)$. For if q is a formula in $T\dot{-}p$, then $q \in T$ since $T\dot{-}p \subseteq T$, and by Monotonicity $T\dot{-}p + \neg p \vdash q$. For the converse, let q be a formula in $T \cap (T\dot{-}p + \neg p)$. Then $q \in T + p$, and so by hypothesis $q \in T\dot{-}p + p$. Thus by Deduction, $T\dot{-}p \vdash p \to q$. Also $T\dot{-}p \vdash \neg p \to q$ since $q \in T\dot{-}p + \neg p$. So if Cn satisfies disjunctive syllogism, then $q \in T\dot{-}p$; since q is an arbitrary formula, this establishes that $T\dot{-}p = T \cap (T\dot{-}p + \neg p)$ and hence that $T\dot{-}p = T \cap T * \neg p$. Since this holds for any formula p, the Harper Identity inverts the Levi Identity for the belief contraction function $\dot{-}$, which was to be shown. □

BIBLIOGRAPHY

[1] Peter Gärdenfors. *Knowledge In Flux: Modeling the Dynamics of Epistemic States.* MIT Press, Cambridge, Mass., 1988.

[2] William L. Harper. Rational conceptual change. In *Proceedings of the Meeting of the Philosophy of Science Association*, volume 2, pages 462–494, East Lansing, Mich., 1975. Philosophy of Science Association.

[3] H. Katsuno and A. O. Mendelzon. On the difference between updating a knowledge base and revising it. In *Proceedings of the Second International Conference on Principles of Knowledge Representation and Reasoning*, pages 387–394, Los Altos, CA, 1991. Morgan Kaufmann Publishers.

[4] Isaac Levi. Subjunctives, dispositions and chances. *Synthese*, 34:423–55, 1977.

[5] D. Makinson. On the status of the postulate of recovery in the logic of theory change. *Journal of Philosophical Logic*, 16:383–394, 1987.

[6] Willard Quine. Two dogmas of empiricism. *Philosophical Review*, 60:20–43, 1951.

[7] Hans Rott. Two dogmas of belief revision. *Journal of Philosophy*, 97(9):503–22, 2000.
[8] Hans Rott and Sven Ove Hansson. Beyond recovery? a reply to tennant. *Erkenntnis*, 49:387–392, 1998.
[9] Oliver Schulte. Minimal belief change and the pareto principle. *Synthese*, 118:329–361, 1999.
[10] Neil Tennant. Changing the theory of theory change: Reply to my critics. *The British Journal for the Philosophy of Science*, 48:569–586, 1997.

Higher-Order Probability Theory and Defeasible Reasoning

CHARLES G. MORGAN

1 Introduction

In ordinary reasoning, we often draw conclusions about specific individuals based on generalizations about what is "usually" or "typically" the case. The following example is one of the most usually cited:

(I.1)
P1: Typically birds can fly.
P2: Tweety is a bird.
C1: Tweety can fly.

Such inferences are not deemed to be certain, of course. They are classic examples of inductive inferences. We are prepared to discover additional information that indicates that the specific individual is not typical, and to revise our conclusion accordingly. The following is a good example of how we might revise I.1 in light of additional information:

(I.2)
P1: Typically birds can fly.
P2: Tweety is a bird.
P3: Tweety is a penguin.
P4: No penguins can fly.
C2: Tweety cannot fly.

In this example, when we obtain the additional information P3 and P4, it is obvious that we should revise our conclusion to the opposite of our previous conclusion.

Such inferences are sometimes said to be nonmonotonic. By analogy with deductive consequence relations, it *appears* that we are dealing with an inductive consequence relation $\Gamma \vdash_I A$. It seems that the set of inductive consequences of a premise set is *not* a monotonically non-decreasing function of the premise set. To be more precise, we may define the inductive consequences of a premise set Λ by $ICN(\Lambda) = \{X : \Lambda \vdash_I X\}$. Technically, to say that the reasoning is nonmonotonic, is to say that in general we may have $\Delta \subseteq \Sigma$ but *not* have $ICN(\Delta) \subseteq ICN(\Sigma)$.

But I have elsewhere demonstrated the impossibility of a rational nonmonotonic consequence relation; see [1]. There is no doubt that we do *reason* inductively; however, it is logically impossible to base such reasoning on some weird inductive consequence relation and still adhere to cannons of rationality dictated by relative frequency considerations. Our problem then is how to give a formal account of this sort of inductive reasoning. Such an account is important, but not just from a theoretical point of view. Hopefully an analysis of such reasoning will point the way to techniques that can be implemented by computer, marking one more step toward artificial intelligence.

2 Basic defeasible logic

One illuminating approach to the sort or reasoning we have illustrated is defeasible logic; see [2] for a good survey. In defeasible logic, claims about what is typically or usually the case are treated as rules of inference. The sentence:

> If X then evidently, normally, typically, presumably Y.

is represented as a defeasible conditional $X \Rightarrow Y$. Note that we may very well adopt the rule $X \Rightarrow Y$ but *not* adopt the rule $(X \wedge Z) \Rightarrow Y$.

We must emphasize that it is best to think of defeasible conditionals as inference rules. Given $X \Rightarrow Y$ and X, we may *provisionally* infer Y. If we have independent reasons to doubt Y, the inference is *defeated*. Thus in the Tweety example, given that birds typically fly and that Tweety is a bird, we may provisionally infer that Tweety flies. But, given that Tweety is a bird, typically birds fly, Tweety is a penguin, and no penguins fly, we may infer that Tweety does not fly. The provisional inference that Tweety flies is defeated by the definite conclusion that Tweety does not fly, which we infer from the information that Tweety is a penguin and no penguins fly.

Thus the nonmonotonic conditional "$\Rightarrow$" is to be contrasted with the monotonic conditional "$\rightarrow$". Claims about what is always the case (as opposed to what is typically the case) are represented by the monotonic conditional. The sentence:

> If X then it is always the case that Y.

is represented as a monotonic conditional $X \rightarrow Y$. As with nonmonotonic conditionals, monotonic conditionals are to be viewed as inference rules. But monotonic conditionals are *not* defeasible. Note that if we are committed to $X \rightarrow Y$, then we are also committed to $(X \wedge Z) \rightarrow Y$.

Basic defeasible logic employs one other sort of conditional, the undercutting defeater, symbolized by "$\rightsquigarrow$". The undercutting defeater is not strong enough by itself to allow us to draw a conclusion. Rather, it identifies special circumstances in which one should not draw the conclusion. A good example is the claim "Injured birds might not be able to fly". Sometimes injured birds can fly, and sometimes they can not. It depends on the type and extent of the injury. We use the claim "Injured birds might not be able to fly" as an undercutting defeater for the nonmonotonic conditional "Typically birds are capable of flight". Knowing that Tweety is an injured bird leaves us in doubt as to whether or not Tweety can fly. We cannot infer that Tweety can fly, nor can we infer that Tweety cannot fly. The sentence:

If X then it might be the case that Y.

is represented as an undercutting defeater $X \rightsquigarrow Y$.

Formally the syntax of defeasible logic is based on a set of literals; a literal is an atomic proposition or the negation of an atomic proposition. A positive literal is an unnegated atomic sentence, while a negative literal is a negated atomic sentence. An atomic sentence and its negation are said to be complements. For notational simplicity, if p is a literal, then we take $\sim p$ to be the complement of p. Rules have sets of literals as antecedents and single literals as consequents. So the following would all be examples of acceptable rules:

$$\{p, \sim q\} \rightarrow r \quad \{p, \sim q\} \Rightarrow r \quad \{p, \sim q\} \rightsquigarrow r$$

A defeasible conditional with empty antecedent, $\varnothing \Rightarrow r$, represents a provisional assumption that r, held until contrary information is obtained.

In its simplest form, a defeasible theory is a pair $\langle K, R \rangle$ where K is a set of literals and R is a set of rules. The set K represents the background information, and R is the set of rules, consisting of monotonic conditionals, nonmonotonic conditionals, and undercutting defeaters. Because the language is so simple, it is possible to spell out elementary conditions under which a literal p is a monotonic consequence of a theory, written (K, R, p^+), and when a literal p is not a monotonic consequence of a theory, written (K, R, p^-). The details are just what intuitions would suggest and are not of importance here.

Defeasible conditionals do not allow one to draw conclusions that are certain. Instead of being certain, such conclusions are merely "evidently" true. Defeasible logic uses the monadic operator "E" to indicate such conclusions. For the simplest case, the monadic consequences of a theory are evidently the case:

If (K, R, p^+), then (K, R, Ep^+).

And if $\sim p$ is a monadic consequence of a theory while p is not, then we can say that evidently p is not a consequence:

If $(K, R, \sim p^+)$ and (K, R, p^-), then (K, R, Ep^-).

The intuitions behind more complex cases are easy to spell out, although the specification of the details can be tricky. Intuitively, we have (K, R, Ep^+) if both (1) we have a rule in K, either monotonic or nonmonotonic, with consequent p, and (K, R, Eq^+) holds for all of the antecedents q of the rule, and (2) for every rule in R with $\sim p$ as a consequence, there is some q in the antecedent of the rule such that (K, R, Eq^-) holds. In other words, "Evidently p" holds if there is some rule with consequent p, each of whose antecedents is evidently the case, but there is no rule whose consequent is $\sim p$, all of whose antecedents are evidently the case. Problems arise when the set R contains conflicting rules, but the details are not of importance in this brief exposition.

For illustration, we return to reasoning about Tweety. Recasting I.1, we have:

$$(\text{II.1}) \quad \begin{array}{c} b \Rightarrow f \\ b \\ \hline Ef \end{array}$$

Recasting II.1, we have:

$$(\text{II.2}) \quad \begin{array}{c} b \Rightarrow f \\ p \to b \\ p \to \sim f \\ p \\ \hline \sim f \end{array}$$

In II.2, the inference to Ef is defeated because we have the monotonic conclusion $\sim f$.

For just one more example, consider the often cited case of Nixon. Nixon was both a Republican and a Quaker. Quakers are typically pacifists, while Republicans typically are not. On the basis of this information alone, we should not draw any conclusion about whether or not Nixon was a pacifist.

$$(\text{II.3}) \quad \begin{array}{c} q \\ r \\ q \Rightarrow p \\ r \Rightarrow \sim p \\ \hline (\text{no conclusion about } p) \end{array}$$

One important point to note is that those who study defeasible logic generally take the defeasible conditional to be transitive, in the sense that if one has $X \Rightarrow Y$ and $Y \Rightarrow Z$, then from X one is entitled to provisionally infer Z. Given that students in my advanced logic class are typically in their fourth year, and given that fourth year students typically graduate in June, then from the fact that Joe is in my advanced logic class, I may provisionally infer that Joe will graduate in June. Again, the conclusion is only provisional and may be defeated by additional information.

3 Probability and defeasible reasoning

It is very tempting to interpret sentences about what is typically or usually the case in terms of relative frequency or probability. The claim that birds typically fly may reasonably be interpreted to mean that most birds are capable of flight. And claims of the form "Most X are Y" may reasonably be interpreted to be saying that the probability that something is a Y, given that it is an X, is "high". So it is natural to raise the question of whether or not the defeasible conditional can be interpreted in terms of high conditional probability. Is it reasonable to take "$X \Rightarrow Y$" to be roughly equivalent to "$P(Y, X)$ is high"?

There is a big problem with such an interpretation: the conditional of high conditional probability is not transitive. That is, we may have $P(Y, X)$ is high, $P(Z, Y)$ is high, *but* $P(Z, X)$ is low. For one example, consider the following:

(III.1)
        All albino crows are crows. P (crow, albino crow) is high.
        Most crows are black. P(black, crow) is high.
But: No albino crows are black. P(black, albino crow) $=0$.

For another, consider the following playing card example:

(III.2)
        All red kings are red cards. P (red, red king) is high.
        Most red cards are non-face cards. P (non-face, red) is high.
But: No red kings are non-face cards. P (non-face, red king)$=0$.

So, the following inference seems to be all right.

(III.3)
$$\frac{P(Y,X) \text{ is high}}{Y} \quad X$$

But the following inference seems to be problematic.

(III.4) $$\begin{array}{l} P(Y,X) \text{ is high} \\ P(Z,Y) \text{ is high} \\ \hline X \\ \hline Z \end{array}$$

The fact that the defeasible conditional is considered to be transitive, but the conditional of high conditional probability is *not* transitive is sometimes cited as evidence that we cannot interpret defeasible conditionals as high conditional probabilities. However, I want to suggest that this conclusion is much too hasty.

Let us revisit the transitivity of the defeasible conditional, and consider the following example:

(III.5)
Residents of district D typically have not finished grade 12.
Those who have not finished grade 12 typically have incomes lower than the national median income.
Sally is a resident of district D.
Sally's income is lower than the national median income.

Of course our conclusion is not certain, but subject to revision in light of additional information. For example, if we were to discover that Sally is the local doctor, then we would reject the line of reasoning in III.5. In short, defeasible logicians accept the following *pattern* of reasoning:

(III.6) $$\begin{array}{l} X \Rightarrow Y \\ Y \Rightarrow Z \\ X \\ \hline \text{Evidently } Z \end{array}$$

But there is no claim that this pattern leads to a correct conclusion *in all cases*. That is, the pattern is still accepted as being generally legitimate, *even though counter-examples to the pattern are known to exist*. The insight to be gained from this observation is that: *Defeasible logic is inductive reasoning about reasoning.*

In order to flesh out this claim, we need to reflect on the nature of reasoning in general. Most educated people are at least dimly aware of some distinction between deduction and induction. The understanding that most people have is that deductive arguments convey certainty to conclusions, while the conclusions of inductive arguments are less than certain. But this understanding fails to account for fallacies as well as simple mistakes of reasoning. Trying to distinguish between induction and deduction in terms of structural characteristics of arguments can be highly problematic and circular.

In introductory logic classes, we often distinguish between inductive and deductive reasoning by saying that these phrases refer to different criteria of argument evaluation. The criteria for deductive reasoning accept only air-tight arguments; all arguments are put into only two categories, the valid (good, acceptable) and the invalid (bad, unacceptable). In contrast, the criteria for inductive reasoning rank arguments on a more or less continuous scale. The air-tight arguments are at the top, but there are many acceptable arguments that are less than air-tight. In fact, most arguments that we use in every day affairs are less than air-tight. Inductive criteria for argument evaluation attempt to measure the degree of strength conveyed to the conclusion by the premises. In my introductory classes, I frequently use Figure 1 as a way of illustrating these points.

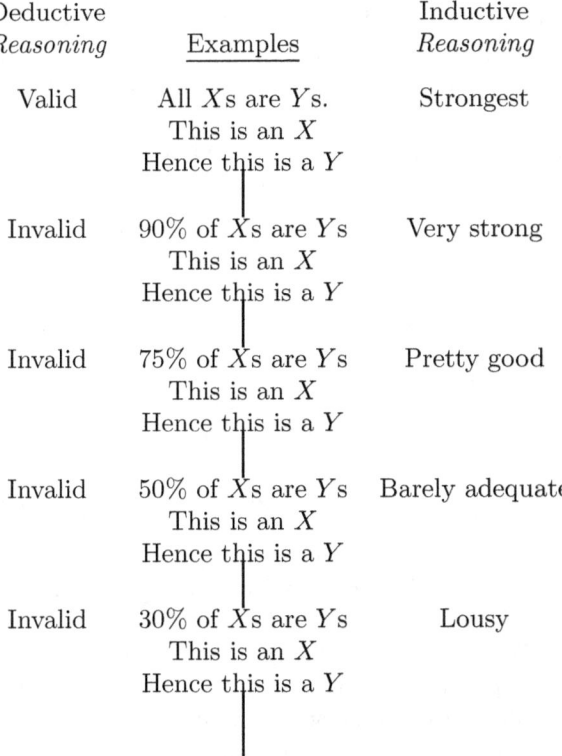

Figure 1. Inductive vs. deductive criteria for argument evaluation

A very important fact about natural languages is that they serve as their own meta-languages. Thus we use English (or French or German or ...) to talk about and reason about aspects of the language itself. We often reason *deductively* about reasoning. We reason *deductively* about *deductive* reasoning, for example when proving soundness and completeness theorems about standard logics. We also reason *deductively* about *inductive* reasoning, for example when deriving theorems about the probability calculus. On the other hand, we reason *inductively* about many aspects of our environment and our interaction with it. Do we ever reason *inductively* about reasoning? Of course we do. For example, as a logician or mathematician, I frequently reason from similarities in the structures of two proposed theorems to the conclusion that the proof of one might well be similar to the proof of the other.

So, I suggest that defeasible logic might usefully be treated as inductive reasoning about reasoning. This suggestion neatly accounts for the fact that defeasible logic treats the defeasible conditional as transitive, in spite of known counter-examples to the pattern.

Let us now return to the case of high conditional probability. From the examples cited previously (III.1 and III.2), we know that the conditional of high conditional probability is not transitive. What this fact means is that the following pattern is not *deductively valid*:

(III.7) $\dfrac{\begin{array}{l} P(Y,X) \text{ is high} \\ P(Z,Y) \text{ is high} \\ X \end{array}}{\text{Evidently } Z}$

But what about its *inductive* strength? That is, using "P2" for second-order probability, we would like to know whether or not the following holds:

(III.8) $P2(Z, \{X, P(Y,X) \text{ is high}, P(Z,Y) \text{ is high}\})$ is high.

Note that we are not even asking if it is possible to *deductively* derive III.8 from some principles of higher-order probability theory. We want to know if there are good *inductive* grounds for III.8.

As a simple test, refer to the Venn diagram in Figure 2. How hard is it to find numbers $n_1, \ldots, n_8$, such that III.7 fails? The interested reader should try to find such numbers in the abstract, without referring to III.1 or III.2 as guides. For one simple solution, the following will work:

(III.9)
n_1 : do not care $n_5 : 0$
$n_2 : 0$ $n_6 : 0$
$n_3 :> 0$ $n_7 :> n_3 + n_4$
$n_4 :> 0$ n_8 : do not care

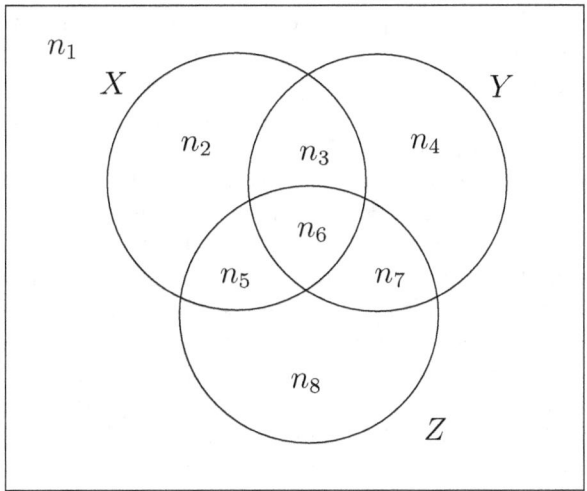

Figure 2.

In this case:

$P(Y, X) = \frac{n_3}{n_3} = 1$

$P(Z, Y) = \frac{n_7}{(n_3 + n_4 + n_7)} > 1/2$

$P(Z, X) = \frac{0}{n_7} = 0$

By making n_7 very large relative to $n_3 + n_4$, $P(Z, Y)$ can be made as large as we like, though always less than 1. So we have $P(Y, X)$ and $P(Z, Y)$ both high, but no matter which X you select, it will not be a Z.

When asking about III.8, at least part of what we are asking concerns how hard it is to find solutions of the sort given in III.9. One way of answering this question immediately suggests itself. We could just randomly assign integers to the areas in Figure 2, and check to see the proportion of cases in which $P(Y, X)$ and $P(Z, Y)$ are both high, but $P(Z, X)$ is low. After a short deviation into a few matters concerning the formal language, we will return to this approach.

4 The logic of categorical propositions

We begin this section with a brief comment on "categorical". Here we do not mean "categorical" in the sense of high powered category theory. Rather, we mean "categorical" in the simple sense of the familiar elementary Aristotelean logic of categories, or classes. Most discussions of examples in defeasible logic and in probability theory involve sentences that are more complicated than classical propositional logic, but that are little more complicated than classical Aristotelean logic. In order to be more precise, in this section I will outline a technique I have developed and been teaching in my elementary logic classes for many years. It uses a simple tabular method to extend the usual Venn diagram techniques but without all their limitations of Venn diagrams, and it allows for sentences more complex than those usually dealt with by Aristotelean logic. We will use the tabular representation as a means to investigate second-order probability.

Basically, our language of categorical propositions is a subset of that of the monadic predicate calculus, with a stock of monadic predicates, boolean sentence operators, individual variables and constants, along with universal and existential quantification. For the sake of definiteness, we specify the following:

Atomic monadic predicates: $P_1, P_2, ...$

Boolean operators: $\wedge, \vee, \supset, \equiv, \sim$

Individual variables: $x_1, x_2, ...$

Individual constants: $c_1, c_2, ...$

Universal quantifier: $(\forall X)$

Existential quantifier: $(\exists X)$

By a "general predicate", we mean any atomic predicate or boolean combination of atomic predicates. For simplicity, we use the term "predicate" instead of " general predicate".

For notational ease, we will avoid subscripts where possible, and we adopt the following conventions for categorical logic: we use upper case letters for predicates; we use the letters x, y, and z for variables; and we use other lower case letters for constants. We will also sometimes use upper case letters for categorical propositions, rather than for predicates. However, when discussing defeasible logic, we will continue to use our previous notation: when writing expressions of the form "$A \rightarrow p$", "$A \Rightarrow p$", or "$A \rightsquigarrow p$" we use "A" for a set of literals and "p" for an aribitrary literal. We will rely on context to sort out notation.

Permissible well formed formulas (WFFs) of our language are of two types: (1) any general predicate applied to a constant is a WFF; and (2) any single quantifier with respect to a variable, applied to a general predicate is a WFF. The following are examples of WFFs of type (1):

$$Bt \quad (\sim Pc \wedge (Lc \wedge Wc)) \quad ((Qn \supset Pn) \wedge (Rn \supset \sim Pn))$$

The following are examples of WFFs of type (2):

$$(\forall x)(Px \supset Bx) \quad (\exists x)(Bx \wedge \sim Fx)$$

We use the phrase "categorical propositions" to refer collectively to WFFs of type (1) and type (2).

Because our language is relatively simple, there are a number of notational simplifications which we can adopt. Since quantifiers never overlap, we can simply drop variables altogether. Further, the English locutions dealt with by standard Aristotelean logic occur so frequently that we find it convenient to adopt the special notation in Table 1.

Table 1. Special notatation

English expression	Usual notation	Special notation
Everything is B.	$(\forall x)Bx$	$a(B)$
There are Ps.	$(\exists x)Px$	$s(B)$
All Ps are Bs.	$(\forall x)(Px \supset Bx)$	$a(P, B)$
No Ps are Bs.	$(\forall x)(Px \supset \sim Bx)$	$a(P, \sim B)$
Some Ps are Bs.	$(\exists x)(Px \wedge Bx)$	$s(P, B)$
Some Ps are not Bs.	$(\exists x)(Px \wedge \sim Bx)$	$s(P, \sim B)$

Note that in this special notation, the "," corresponds to the English verb "to be" and thus sometimes represents "$\supset$" (when in a universal), and sometimes represents "$\wedge$" (when in an existential). But proper notation can always be unambiguously reintroduced.

Our final notational convenience is also of practical importance for the methods we will treat here. Essentially we will do away with individual constants altogether and replace them by predicates. For each constant, say "t" for Tweety, we introduce a new monadic predicate, say "T". Any WFF which consists of a general predicate applied to the constant, say "Bt", is replaced by two quantified expressions: (1) a universally quantified conditional, whose antecedent is the predicate replacing the constant, and whose consequent is the predicate of the original expression, say $(\forall x)(Tx \supset Bx)$ or $a(T, B)$; and (2) an existential expression asserting the existence of an item with the predicate replacing the constant, $(\exists x)Tx$ or $s(T)$ in our example. Thus we are making an existential assumption that whatever we name must exist. We could leave out the existential assumption, but we do not view it as extraordinary, since it is also made in standard first-order logic. Fictional entities require special treatment in the logic of categorical propositions, just as in first-order logic; the details are not relevant here.

We can now specify a simple tabular decision procedure for determining whether or nor an arbitrary finite set of categorical propositions is satisfiable in the sense of standard model theory for first-order logic. There are many other problems our tabular techniques can be used to solve (given an argument, is it valid; given a set of premises and a desired conclusion, what additional premise is required to produce the conclusion; etc.). However the satisfiability problem will serve to illustrate important aspects of the technique.

So our basic problem is this: given an arbitrary finite set S of categorical propositions, we need to determine whether or not the set is satisfiable. The general solution requires the construction of a "categorical table", which is like a generalized Venn diagram but without the geometric limitations, somewhat like a truth table. We assume that the set of categorical propositions has had all constants replaced by predicates in the way previously indicated. Thus our given set S of categorical propositions will consist of a set (possibly empty) of universal claims and a set (possibly empty) of existential claims:

$$S = \{a(A_1), \ldots, a(A_m), \ldots, s(B_1), \ldots, s(B_n)\}$$

Further, by using standard transformations, there is no loss in generality in assuming that the A_i and the B_i are in disjunctive normal form, each being a disjunctive sequence of sub-expressions, each sub-expression being a conjunction of atomic predicates and negations of atomic predicates.

We begin by setting up a categorical table, similar to a truth table, to represent the set S. This task is accomplished by the following steps.

1. We first list the distinct atomic predicates at the top, left of the table.

2. Then for k predicates, we make 2^k rows.

3. We then distribute "+" and "−" beneath the predicates in all 2^k possible ways, similar to distributing "T" and "F" on a standard truth table. Each row in the table represents those items which have the properties with a "+" on that row but do not have the properties with a "−" on that row.

4. To the right of the list of predicates, we add one column headed by "u" and additional columns headed by "e_i", one for each of the existential formulas in S. The information in all of the universal formulas will be represented in the one "u" column, but each existential formula will have its own column.

5. Each universal formula selects a number of rows on the table, corresponding to the conjunctive expressions in its disjunctive normal form. For example, the conjunction "$P \wedge B \wedge \sim F$" selects those rows with a plus beneath P and B but a minus beneath F. Note that as a special case, a flatly contradictory conjunction "$D \wedge \sim D \wedge E$" selects *no* rows. Each universal formula "$a(C_1 \vee \ldots \vee C_k)$" is making the claim that "Everything must be in the class of things that are C_1 or ... or C_k." In other words, it is making the claim that there is nothing outside these selected classes. So for each universal formula, we put a 0 in the "u" column in each of the rows *not* selected by that formula.

6. Once all of the 0s for all of the universal formulas have been entered in the "u" column, we move them across to each of the "e_i" columns. The 0s indicate rows where nothing is allowed to exist.

7. Each existential formula selects a number of rows on the table, corresponding to the conjunctive expressions in its disjunctive normal form, just as with the universal expressions. The existential expression is saying that there must be something on at least one of these rows. So for each existential expression $s(B_i)$, we put an X in the "e_i" column on each row selected by $s(B_i)$ that does not already have a 0 on it.

Once the table is constructed, the solution to the satisfiability problem is at hand. The set of formulas is satisfiable if the u-column is not all 0s and *each* e-column has at least one X in it. The set is *not* satisfiable if either the u-column is all 0s or there is at least one e-column that has no X in it. (Note, if we are dealing with free logic and allow an empty universe, then we can dispense with the requirement that the u-column not be all 0s.)

THEOREM 1. *If a set of categorical propositions S is satisfiable in the sense of first-order logic then on its categorical table the u-column is not all 0s and each e-column contains at least one X.*

Proof. We begin with the supposition that the set S is satisfiable in the sense of first-order logic. Then there is some first-order model $< D, V >$ in which every member of S is true. We first show that there must be at least one u-column without a 0. The domain D must contain at least one object, d. For each universal formula $a(A_i)$, there must be at least one conjunction

$C_{d(i)}$ in its disjunctive normal form such that d satisfies $C_{d(i)}$, that is such that $d \in V(C_{d(i)})$. Thus there is at least one conjunct from each universal proposition such that d satisfies the conjunctive predicate $C_{d(1)} \wedge \ldots \wedge C_{d(m)}$. Thus the conjunctive predicate cannot be contradictory, so there must be at least one row on the table selected by this conjunctive predicate. Thus there is at least one row on the table selected by all the universal propositions, so the u-column cannot be empty. Next we show that every e-column must have at least one X in it. Consider an arbitrary existential formula $s(B_i)$ in S. Since the model satisfies this formula, there must be an object d in D such that d satisfies the general predicate B_i. So there must be at least one conjunction $E_{d(i)}$ in the disjunctive normal form of B_i such that d satisfies $E_{d(i)}$. By the same argument given above, d must also satisfy some conjunctive predicate $C_{d(1)} \wedge \ldots \wedge C_{d(m)}$ from the universal propositions. Thus d satisfies the larger conjunctive predicate $C_{d(1)} \wedge \ldots \wedge C_{d(m)} \wedge E_{d(i)}$, so the larger conjunctive predicate cannot be contradictory. Thus there is at least one row on the table selected by all the universals and by $s(B_i)$. Hence there will be at least one row in the e_i-column on which there is an X. ∎

THEOREM 2. *If on the categorical table for a set S of categorical propositions, the u-column is not all 0s and every e-column contains at least one X, then the set of propositions is satisfiable in the sense of first-order logic.*

Proof. Let S be an arbitrary set of categorical propositions on whose categorical table: the u-column is not all $0s$, and every e-column contains at least one X. On the one hand, suppose there are no e-columns. Then the domain of the required model may consist of only one object d with d assigned the properties specified by one of the rows that is not 0 in the u-column, i.e., for each atomic predicate P, $d \in V(P)$ iff there is a "+" in the P-column on that row. Because the row is selected by all the universal propositions, any object with the properties indicated by the row will satisfy at least one of the conjuncts in the disjunctive normal form of each of the universal propositions. Since the domain contains only one object, all of the universal propositions are satisfied. On the other hand, suppose there are e-columns. Then for the domain of the required model, we take D to be the set of objects d_i, one for each of the existential propositions e_i. For each object d_i, we assign it the properties dictated by one of the rows in the e_i-column on which there is an X; that is, for each atomic predicate P if there is a "+" in the P-column on the chosen row for e_i, then we set $d_i \in V(P)$. Since this row is selected by the proposition $s(B_i)$, d_i will satisfy at least one of the conjuncts in the disjunctive normal form of $s(B_i)$, and hence $s(B_i)$ will be satisfied in the model. Further, since every row with an X in it is a row on which there is no 0 in the u-column, by the same argument used above, every d_i will satisfy at least one of the conjuncts from the disjunctive normal form of each of the universal propositions. Hence all the the universal propositions will be satisfied. ∎

As an aid to understanding, we will illustrate the technique with a simple example. Suppose we want to know whether or not the following set of propositions is satisfiable.

(IV.1)

Proposition	Formula	Type
No non-Earthlings are Martians.	$a(\sim E, \sim M)$	u
All Martians are Venusians.	$a(M, V)$	u
No non-Martians are Venusians.	$a(\sim M, \sim V)$	u
Some Earthlings are not Venusians.	$s(E, \sim V)$	$e1$
Venusians Exist.	$s(V)$	$e2$

We construct the categorical table given as Table 2.

Table 2. Categorical table for (IV.1)

row	E	M	V	u	$e1$	$e2$
1	+	+	+			x
2	+	+	-	0	0	0
3	+	-	+	0	0	0
4	+	-	-		x	
5	-	+	+	0	0	0
6	-	+	-	0	0	0
7	-	-	+	0	0	0
8	-	-	-			

There are three atomic predicates E, M, and V, giving us eight rows. There are three universal propositions, and all are represented in the single u-column. There are two existential propositions, represented by the two columns marked $e1$ and $e2$. First we represent the universal propositions on the table. The sentence "All Martians are Venusians" has the form "$a(M,V)$", which in more standard notation is just "$(\forall x)(Mx \supset Vx)$". The disjunctive normal form is "$(\forall x)(\sim Mx \lor Vx)$". The rows selected by this formula are those without M (i.e., rows $3, 4, 7$, and 8), and those with V (i.e., rows $1, 3, 5$, and 7). Hence the formula requires that all rows with M but without V be marked with 0; so rows 2 and 6 get a 0 in the u-column (rows 2 and 6 are the two rows *not* selected by the formula). Similarly, "No non-Earthlings are Martians" requires that all rows without E but with

M be marked with 0; so rows 5 and 6 get a 0 in the u-column. Finally for the universal propositions, "No non-Martians are Venusians" requires that rows without M but with V receive a 0; so rows 3 and 7 get a 0 in the u-column. Once finished with the universal propositions, we move the 0s in rows 2, 3, 5, 6, and 7 across to the e-columns. Now we deal with the existential propositions. The sentence "Some Earthlings are not Venusians" selects rows 2 and 4. There is a 0 on row 2, but row 4 is clear; so we put an X on row 4 in the $e1$ column. Finally, the sentence "Venusians exist" selects rows 1, 3, 5, and 7. Rows 3, 5, and 7 all contain a 0, so we put an X on row 1 in the $e2$ column. That completes the table. We note that (i) not all rows in the u-column contain a 0, and (ii) each e-column contains at least one X. Hence the set of categorical propositions is satisfiable.

Of course our example was very simple and could have been treated on a standard three circle Venn diagram. But we chose this simple example to illustrate the technique. Our techniques could handle problems not susceptible to standard Venn diagram techniques. Categorical tables may be used for problems with an arbitrary finite number of atomic predicates. Categorical tables can easily handle quite complicated propositions, such as: "Anything that is either a non-flying Martian or a swimming Plutonian is a non-smoking green Earthling and either a red Venusian or a Mercurian."

5 Categorical tables, second-order probability and defeasible logic

We observe that the rows on a categorical table are like Carnapian state descriptions. We can use categorical tables to express statistical information by putting numbers on the rows. It is then easy to determine probabilities from the statistical information on the table. As an example, consider Table 3. Given the numbers on the table, it is easy to determine the following probabilities.

$$P(F, P) = (0 + 0)/(0 + 100 + 0 + 0) = 0$$
$$P(P, \sim B) = (0 + 0)/(0 + 500 + 0 + 100000) = 0$$
$$P(B, P) = (0 + 100)/(0 + 100 + 0 + 0) = 1$$
$$P(B \wedge F, P \vee \sim P) = (0 + 1000)/(0 + 1000 + 100 + 20 + 0 + 500 + 0 + 100000) = .0098$$

However, there is a problem representing information about individuals (as opposed to information about classes) on a categorical table, or on a Venn diagram for that matter. In our representation, we are replacing individual constants by monadic predicates. Consider Table 4, on which we are representing "Tweety" as a predicate. If Tweety is only one thing, then

Table 3. Statistical example

row	Bird	Flyer	Penguin	Number
1	+	+	+	0
2	+	+	-	1000
3	+	-	+	100
4	+	-	-	20
5	-	+	+	0
6	-	+	-	500
7	-	-	+	0
8	-	-	-	100,000

Table 4. "Tweety" as a predicate

row	Bipedal	Penguin	Tweety	Number
1	+	+	+	?
2	+	+	-	
3	+	-	+	?
4	+	-	-	
5	-	+	+	?
6	-	+	-	
7	-	-	+	?
8	-	-	-	

exactly one of the rows 1, 3, 5, or 7 will have a "1" on it, and all the others must have a 0. It seems we cannot put any number higher than 1 on any of the rows 1, 2, 5, and 7; and, for example, if we put a 1 on row 1, then we must put a 0 on rows 3, 5, and 7. But this restriction seems to lead to some counterintuitive results. For example, the probability that something is a penguin, given that it is Tweety must be either 0 or 1. Further, the probability that Tweety is a penguin, given that Tweety is bipedal also must be either 0 or 1. Similarly, any probability claim in which the evidence contains conjunctive information about any individual will always be either 0 or 1. This result seems to be very counterintuitive.

The simple solution to this problem is to treat each individual as a "quantum mechanical smear". We may think of each object in the universe as a collection of some number $(10, 100, 1000, \ldots)$ of "potential instances", only one of which is actually realized in the real world. This technique will allow us to make sense of and to represent non-extreme (i.e., not 0 and not 1)

Table 5. Numerical conditions for various quantifiers

English phrase	Special notation	Numerical requirement
All X are Y	$a(x,y)$	$X \wedge \sim Y = 0$
Some X are Y	$s(X,Y)$	$X \wedge Y \neq 0$
Usually X are Y	$u(X,Y)$	$(X \wedge Y)/X > pc$
Evidently Y	$e(Y)$ $u(X \vee \sim X, Y)$	$Y > pc$
There is a significant chance that X are Y	$c(X,Y)$ not $u(X, \sim Y)$	$(X \wedge Y)/X \geq (1 - pc)$
There are significantly more X than Y	$m(X,Y)$ $u(X \vee Y, X \wedge \sim Y)$	$(X \wedge \sim Y)/(X \vee Y) > pc$

probabilistic claims about individuals.

Numbers on the rows of categorical tables may be used to represent a wide variety of statistical quantifiers, in addition to the usual existential and universal quantifiers. Typically, the statistical quantifiers make implicit reference to some probability cut-off; the value could be $0.5, 0.6, \ldots, 1 - \epsilon$. This value represents some sort of rational "line in the sand." If a probability value of a proposition is greater than the cut-off, then we are prepared to accept the proposition. Of course this naive picture is too simplistic. Our willingness to accept a proposition is often a function of various utilities as well as the probability value. For the present we will just use "pc" to stand for the chosen probability cut-off value. Table 5 lists some typical quantifiers and the numerical conditions required. The letters X and Y may be any general predicates. In the column listing the numerical requirements, we use formulas to refer to the sum of the numbers on the rows of the table selected by the expression. So the numerical requirement for "Usually X are Y" is given as "$(X \wedge Y)/X > pc$", which should be interpreted to mean that the quotient obtained by dividing the sum of the numbers on the rows corresponding to $X \wedge Y$ by the sum of the numbers on the rows corresponding to X, this quotient must be greater than the probability cut-off pc.

Let us now return to defeasible logic. Perhaps not surprisingly, it turns out that there are significant parallels between the three conditionals of defeasible logic and quantified expressions of numerically extended categorical logic. Before looking at these parallels, we need to make a few brief comments on generality and on notation.

The language of elementary defeasible logic is propositional, and thus more restricted than that of categorical logic. Typically the antecedent of a defeasible conditional is taken to be a set of literals, while the consequent is taken to be a single literal. When discussing examples, it is typical to use "$b \Rightarrow f$" to stand for "Birds are typically capable of flight" and "b" to stand for "Tweety is a bird". That is, the propositional language of defeasible logic normally fails to distinguish between monadic predicates, like "is a bird", and attributions to individuals, like "Tweety is a bird". The language of categorical logic allows us to keep such distinctions very clear.

In categorical logic, we will interpret the conditionals of defeasible logic as specially quantified expressions. We allow both the antecedent and the consequent to be any general predicate. Thus the defeasible conditionals of numerically extended categorical logic are rather more general than what is usually treated in standard defeasible logic.

In the material that follows, we will continue to use capital letters to refer to general predicates in categorical logic. However, we will occasionally need notation to refer to arbitrary WFFs of categorical logic. For simplicity, we will also sometimes use capital letters for this purpose, but the context should make everything clear.

The first conditional of defeasible logic is the standard monotonic conditional "$A \to p$"; in this form "p" is a literal, while A is a set of literals understood conjunctively. Monotonic conditionals state what is *always* the case. In numerically extended categorical logic, we may think of this conditional as "$X \to Y$", representing "Xs are always Ys." We allow X and Y to be any general predicates. In our special notation, we would represent this claim as the quantified expression "$a(X,Y)$".

The second conditional of defeasible logic is the nonmonotonic conditional "$A \Rightarrow p$" stating what is *typically* or usually the case. In numerically extended categorical logic, we may think of this conditional as "$X \Rightarrow Y$", representing "Xs are usually Ys." We allow X and Y to be any general predicates. In our special notation, we would represent this claim as the quantified expression "$u(X,Y)$".

The third conditional of defeasible logic is the undercutting defeater "$A \leadsto p$" stating what *might* be the case. In numerically extended categorical logic, we may think of this conditional as "$X \leadsto Y$", representing "There is a significant chance that an X is also a Y." We allow X and Y to be any general predicates. In our special notation, we would represent this claim as the quantified expression "$c(X,Y)$".

Recall that basic defeasible logic also employs the monadic sentence operator "E", for "evidently". So in basic defeasible logic, the formula "Ep" is to be understood as saying "Evidently p", which means that p is believed to hold, but that belief may be revised in light of future information. In terms of the conditionals, "Ep" is sometimes used for "$\varnothing \Rightarrow p$", where $\varnothing$ is the empty set of literals. In a similar way for defeasible categorical logic, we may take "EY" to mean "$X \vee \sim X \Rightarrow Y$", or just $u(Y)$.

Thus all of the three conditionals of defeasible logic and the special monadic operator "evidently" have a natural correlate in numerically extended categorical logic. We may think of that portion of numerically extended categorical logic which employs these conditionals as defeasible categorical logic. We now turn our attention to inferences in defeasible logic.

At this point we are in a position to make a useful observation concerning modifiers of conclusions and iterated quantifiers. Once again we will use the Tweety example (I.1) to illustrate the point. Let us recast (I.1) in terms of our notation for categorical logic, replacing the constant by a predicate.

$$\text{(IV.1)} \quad \frac{\begin{array}{l} u(B,F) \\ a(T,B) \wedge s(T) \end{array}}{a(T,F) \wedge s(T)} \quad \begin{array}{l} \text{Typically birds can fly.} \\ \text{Tweety is a bird.} \\ \text{Tweety can fly.} \end{array}$$

Most people feel uncomfortable just stating the bald conclusion "Tweety can fly" on the basis of the given premises. Rather, they want to say something like "*Probably* Tweety can fly". Is the modifier "probably" a part of the conclusion or merely a meta-theoretical sign, like "therefore"? In defeasible logic, one would not be allowed to draw the bald conclusion, but rather something like "Evidently Tweety can fly." The modifier appears to be part of the conclusion.

How are we to treat the sentence "Evidently Tweety can fly"? One obvious suggestion would be to replace "Tweety can fly" by our standard translation "$a(T,F) \wedge s(T)$" and then append the "evidently" modifier to the whole thing. However, our suggested translations in Table 5 do not indicate how to handle iterated probabilistic and classical quantifiers. And indeed as we have outlined categorical logic, iterated quantifiers are not permitted.

In order to be true to the inference patterns of defeasible logic, we would suggest that when evidently is appended to the front of a universal quantifier, the universal "all" is replaced by "usually". However, the sentence "Evidently Tweety exists" should not be taken to mean that most items in the universe are Tweety items. Instead, I would suggest that it is reasonable to interpret this claim as meaning that the quantum mechanical smear that is Tweety is not empty. In other words, we should take "Evidently Tweety exists" to mean just "The Tweety class is not empty", or $s(T)$. So, the correct representation of our Tweety example should be:

$$\text{(IV.2)} \quad \frac{\begin{array}{l} u(B,F) \\ a(T,B) \wedge s(T) \end{array}}{u(T,F) \wedge s(T)} \quad \begin{array}{l} \text{Typically birds can fly.} \\ \text{Tweety is a bird.} \\ \text{Evidently Tweety can fly.} \end{array}$$

We must now consider how inferences are to be drawn in the context of defeasible categorical logic. Recall that in standard defeasible logic, a defeasible theory is an ordered pair $<K, R>$, where K is a finite set of literals representing the background knowledge and R is a finite set of rules, consisting of conditionals of the various three types. For defeasible categorical logic, in a parallel fashion we take a defeasible theory to be an ordered pair $<K, R>$, where K is a finite set of *any* WFFs from standard categorical logic, and R is a finite set of rules, consisting of formulas of the sort $a(X,Y)$, $u(X,Y)$, and $c(X,Y)$. Thus a theory in defeasible categorical logic may be much more general than is permitted in standard defeasible logic.

For the monotonic core in standard defeasible logic, we determine those literals p that definitely follow from the theory, written (K, R, p^+), and those literals p that definitely do not follow from the theory, written (K, R, p^-). Thus for the monotonic core of a categorical defeasible theory, we need to be able to determine the monotonic consequences and non-consequences of the theory. We need to be able to determine those WFFs C from standard categorical logic which definitely follow from the theory, (K, R, C^+), and those which definitely do not follow from the theory, (K, R, C^-). For the purpose of determining the monotonic core, we may ignore any distinction between K and R. For any particular WFF C, we may use categorical tables to determine whether (K, R, C^+) or (K, R, C^-). All we need to do is to check the categorical table for $K \cup R \cup \{\sim C\}$ for satisfiability. If it is not satisfiable, then (K, R, C^+); if it is satisfiable, then (K, R, C^-). Further, given the nature of the basic language for categorical logic, if we have only a finite number of monadic predicates, then there will be only a finite number of logically distinct categorical WFFs. So, for a finite set of monadic predicates, it will be possible to completely enumerate the monotonic core of a defeasible categorical theory.

There is another way to think of the monotonic consequences of a defeasible categorical theory. Recalling our previous insight that defeasible logic is essentially just inductive reasoning about reasoning, we may think of the monotonic consequences of a defeasible categorical theory in terms of second-order probability. A standard categorical table is just a model universe. A categorical table with numbers attached to the rows is a model universe with definite statistical characteristics. Intuitively a theory (K, R) may be thought of as picking out a number of categorical tables or model universes, roughly those in which all of the claims made in K and R hold on the table. (We will make this naive intuitive picture more precise below). Quantified formulas (such as $a(X,Y), s(X,Y), c(X,Y)$, and $u(X,Y)$ for examples), make first-order probability claims ($P(Y,X) = 1, P(Y,X) >$

$0, P(Y, X) \geq 1 - pc$, and $P(Y, X) > pc$, respectively). To say that C is a monotonic consequence of the defeasible categorical theory (K, R) is to say that it holds in all the models satisfying $K \cup R$. If second-order probability $P2$ corresponds to relative frequency over the models, then we have the following:

(V.3) (K, R, C^+) if and only if $P2(C, K \cup R) = 1$
(V.4) (K, R, C^-) if and only if $P2(C, K \cup R) < 1$

If C is a monotonic consequence of (K, R), then C will hold in every model of (K, R). If C is not a monotonic consequence of (K, R), then there will have to be at least one model of (K, R) in which C fails.

For defeasible logic, not only do we determine those formulas which are valid consequences and those which are not valid consequences, we also determine those formulas which are merely "evident". Using our probability cut-off pc as the criterion for high probability, we have:

(V.5) $(K, R, e(C)^+)$ if and only if $P2(C, K \cup R) > pc$

(V.6) $(K, R, e(C)^-)$ if and only if $P2(C, K \cup R) \leq pc$

We do not here propose a calculus of second-order probability theory. Recall that we are treating defeasible reasoning as inductive reasoning about reasoning. Thus we propose to use Monte Carlo techniques to investigate the principles of defeasible logic. We propose to sample the space of first-order probability distributions to extrapolate to the second-order probabilities. That is, to determine second-order probability, we must sample the space of models, where a model is just a categorical table with numerical values assigned to the rows. We must now specify some of the details of how such a sampling is to be done.

6   The Statistics of Defeasible Reasoning

In general, we are trying to determine the value of $P2(X, K \cup R)$. The set K contains unquantified categorical sentences, generally about a single individual, such as:

> Tweety is a bird.
> Tweety is a penguin.
> If Tweety is in Antarctica, then Tweety is cold.

The set R contains quantified categorical sentences, such as:

All penguins are birds.
No penguins can fly.
Usually birds can fly.

The formula X is usually an unquantified sentence about a single individual, such as:

Tweety can fly.

Quantified expressions contain all-or-none restrictions on our models; for a given model, they either hold or they do not. This statement is true not only of standard universal and existential formulas; it is also true of statistical quantifiers such as "usually", "evidently", "there are significantly more", and "there is a significant chance that". If we are replacing all individuals by constants, then even K will contain only all-or-none restrictions, and we can simply collapse K and R. However, since we wish to be perfectly general we consider the case in which K contains non-quantified formulas.

Suppose K contains only non-quantified formulas, while R contains all and only the quantified formulas, and suppose we wish to sample probability distributions to determine the second-order probability: $P2(A, K \cup R)$. Obviously we can begin sampling first-order distributions by randomly assigning numbers to the rows on the categorical table. We throw away those tables in which any of the statements in R do not hold, keeping only those tables which satisfy all the members of R. If we were calculating a first-order probability for a given table, we would simply restrict our attention to the rows on the table on which the members of K hold, and we would calculate the proportion of the K rows which are also A rows. That is, for each R-table, we would calculate $\#(A \wedge K)/\#(K)$. But taking the mean of this value over the R-tables as the second-order probability will not satisfy the constraints of probability theory. In particular, the standard product rule for conjunctions will not hold.

In order to ensure that the usual product rule for probabilities is satisfied for the second-order case, we make the following standard definition:

(VI.1) $\quad P2(X, \{Y\} \cup R) = P2(X \wedge Y, R)/P2(Y, R)$ if
$\qquad P2(Y, R) \neq 0$
$\qquad = 1$ otherwise

So for the general case, calculating $P2(X, K \cup R)$ for $K \neq \varnothing$ is reduced to determining values $P2(Y, R)$, where Y can be some conjunction of quantified and unquantified categorical propositions. In this way, the second-order conjunction principle will be satisfied.

To determine $P2(Y, R)$, we generate a sample of R-tables, i.e., tables in which the restrictions in R hold. For each R-table, we then determine the first-order probability of Y. If Y is a quantified formula, the value will be 0 or 1. If it is a non-quantified formula, the value may be between 0 and 1. If it is a conjunction of quantified and non-quantified formulas, the value will be 0 if any of the quantified formulas fail; otherwise, the value will be the first-order probability of the conjunction of the non-quantified formulas in Y. Then for the second-order probability, we take the mean of the Y values over the sample of R-tables.

So for a given set of monadic predicates, to sample the space of models we need to assign numbers to the rows of the categorical table in a random way. Obviously, we will be limited to finite assignments to the rows. How large should we permit the numbers to be? In the abstract, we have no way of answering that question. In general, we simply set some maximum number n of items per row. Each row is then randomly assigned from 0 to n items. Thus for m rows, there would be a total of $(n+1)^m$ models. Obviously, as n and m grow, it quickly becomes impossible to look at all models, and we must extrapolate from a small sample. This raises the question of how good an estimate we can get from such sampling.

For 2 classes (4 rows), and for $n = 50$, we can look at *all* models in a reasonable amount of time. By experiment we found that for a variety of K, R, and X, the value of $P2(X, K \cup R)$ from the sample is within $\pm 1\%$ of the actual value as long as the sample size of models satisfying R is about 500 or more. In another series of experiments, we found that for 3 and 4 classes (8 and 16 rows) and for $n = 100$, the values of $P2(X, K \cup R)$ for a variety of K, R, and X, were within $\pm 1\%$ of each other as the sample size of R models varied from 1000 up to 500,000. These results gave us some confidence in the robustness of our approach. In this preliminary study, we did not do rigorous statistical tests with a determination of confidence intervals, etc.

7 Experimental results

We ran a series of experiments to check a number of defeasible inference patterns. Basically we sampled the space of first-order probability distributions to estimate the second-order probabilities of the form:

(VII.1) $P2$(conclusion, given background assumptions)

Generally, we allowed rows to contain any number of items from 0 to 100. We generated from $500,000$ to $2,000,000$ random tables, depending on the case, and discarded those in which the background assumptions were not satisfied. The number of cases in which the background assumptions were actually satisfied was generally well in excess of 1000. We then computed the second-order probability as indicated previously. (We have noted on the tables below when a probability was calculated based on a sample of less than 500.) Each experiment was carried out with three different values of the probability cut-off: 0.5, 0.6, and 0.7. With higher values of the cut-off parameter, it became more time consuming to generate models satisfying the background assumptions. In some cases the generated sample contained no instances of the background assumptions. In these cases, we entered "?" in the cells in the table reporting the results.

Before looking at the results of the experiments, we need to address the following question: How high does the second-order probability have to be in order for an inference pattern to be deemed to be acceptable? One answer is that the second-order probability should be as high as the value of the probability cut-off. Suppose we could assure ourselves that when the premises have a probability above a certain value, then the conclusion would also have a probability above that value. Under these circumstances, iterative arguments based on intermediate conclusions (e.g., arguments involving chains of conditionals) would preserve the given probability floor. Essentially this is the position taken by (V.5) and (V.6). While appealing on the grounds of consistency of criteria, this answer does not seem to me to be clearly correct. The probability cut-off is a cut-off for the first-order probabilities. It is not clear why it should apply to higher-order probabilities. In this context, we are not in a position to talk about the probability of the premises of the argument and how that affects the probability of the conclusion. So the analysis based on a chain of reasoning preserving the floor probability seems to be inapplicable, on second thought. Another proposal for how high the second-order probability must be is that the second-order probability should only be required to be greater than 0.5. Under these circumstances, given true premises the inference is more likely to lead to a true conclusion than to a false conclusion. And without utilities as a guide to the danger of false positives and false negatives, perhaps all we can expect of good inductive inference patterns is that they be right more often than not. I am inclined toward this second answer and will adopt it in the following discussion, though I do not feel strongly.

Our first series of experiments concerned the transitivity of the defeasible conditional. The results are recorded in Table 6.

The reader will recall the fact that the conditional of high conditional probability is not transitive, while the defeasible conditional is generally regarded as transitive in spite of known counter-examples. It was this observation which motivated us to consider second-order probability in the first place. Is the following an acceptable inference?

Table 6. Transitivity of conditional

	Inference		prob. cut-off: pc		
	Given	Concl.	.5	.6	.7
1	∅	$u(X,Z)$	.496	.175	.036
2	$u(X,Z)$	$u(X,Z)$	.502	.174	.036
3	$u(Y,Z)$	$u(X,Z)$	.664	.411	.189
4	$u(X,Y), u(Y,Z)$	$u(X,Z)$	.669	.453	$.410_{311}$
5	$u(Z,W)$	$u(X,W)$	.664	.411	.189
6	$u(X,Y)$	$u(X,W)$	.502	.174	.036
7	$u(X,Y), u(Y,Z)$	$u(X,W)$	.501	.177	.038
8	$u(X,Y), u(Y,Z), u(Z,W)$	$u(X,W)$	.656	.398	$.333_{(3)}$

(VII.2) $\dfrac{\text{Usually } X\text{s are } Y\text{s.}}{\text{Usually } Y\text{s are } Z\text{s.}}$
$\overline{\text{Usually } X\text{s are } Z\text{s.}}$

This is a chain of two defeasible conditionals. The results of the appropriate experiment are given in Table 6, particularly row 4. If the cut-off value is taken to be 0.5, then the inference is acceptable, having a second-order probability of 0.669. For higher values of the cut-off parameter, the inference is unacceptable. (The small figures in the 0.7 column for rows 4 and 8 indicate the small number of first-order distributions in the sample, and hence the unreliability of the second-order probability value.) Row 8 of Table 6 gives the value for a chain of three defeasible conditionals.

(VII.3) Usually Xs are Ys.
Usually Ys are Zs.
Usually Zs are Ws.
Usually Zs are Ws.

Again, the inference is acceptable for a cut-off value of 0.5, but not for higher cut-off values.

We also investigated a number of other positive inference chains, and the results are given in Table 7.

Row 1 is a chain of one monotonic conditional and one defeasible conditional, with the conclusion being a defeasible conditional.

(VII.4) All Xs are Ys.
Usually Ys are Zs.
Usually Xs are Zs.

Table 7. Positive inference chains

	Inference		prob. cut-off: pc		
	Given	Concl.	.5	.6	.7
1	$a(X,Y), u(Y,Z)$	$u(X,Z)$	.746	.715	.712
2	$a(X,Y), u(Y,Z)$	$a(X,Z)$	.0002 X at .1: .009 X at .01: .246	.0003	.0008
3	$a(X,Y), u(W,Z)$	$u(X,Z)$	.6325	.459	.297
4	$a(X,Y), u(Y,W), u(W,Z)$	$u(X,Z)$	.6332 X at .1: .487 X at .01: .314	.503	.525
5	$a(X,Y), u(Y,W), u(W,Z)$	$a(X,Z)$	.0002 X at .1: .009 X at .01: .244	.0003	?
6	$u(X,Y), X$	$u(Y)$	.750	.352	.090
7	$u(X,Y), X$	Y	.585	.660	.746
8	$u(X,Y), u(X)$	$u(Y)$	.751	.491	.383
9	$u(X,Y), u(X)$	Y	.550	.601	.686
10	$u(X,Y), u(Y,Z), u(X)$	$u(Z)$	.743	.383	?
11	$u(X,Y), u(Y,Z), u(X)$	$u(Y) \wedge u(Z)$	.599	.182	?
12	$u(X,Y), u(Y,Z), u(X)$	Z	.542	.584	?
13	$u(X,Y), u(Y,Z), X$	Z	.543	.590	$.670_{(341)}$
14	$u(X,Y), u(Y,Z), u(Z,W), u(X)$	$u(W)$	.743	$.370_{(92)}$	?
15	$u(X,Y), u(Y,Z), u(Z,W), u(X)$	W	.541	$.583_{(92)}$	?
16	$u(X,Y), u(Y,Z), u(Z,W), X$	W	.540	.572	$.641_{(3)}$

Consider the following inference: All snakes are reptiles; reptiles are usually oviparous; hence, snakes are usually oviparous. Or, alternatively, consider the following example: All Tweety instances are bird instances; typically birds can fly; hence, typically Tweety instances can fly. This latter example is the categorical version (without the existential assumption) of the standard example: Tweety is a bird and usually birds can fly, so evidently Tweety can fly. This inference was acceptable for all values of the cut-off parameter. Similarly, row 4 gives the results for a chain of one universal and two defeasible conditionals with a defeasible conditional as conclusion. Again, the argument is acceptable for all three values of the cut-off parameter, though it is much stronger for 0.5 than for the others.

As we discussed previously, it is important to treat "Evidently Tweety can fly" as "Typically instances of Tweety are capable of flight", rather than as "All instances of Tweety are capable of flight". The results for the Tweety argument with this latter conclusion are reported on row 2 of Table

7, and they indicate that the universal conclusion has a *very* low probability. Part of the problem may have been the relative size of the classes involved. For example, in the real world, we know there are *many* more bird instances than Tweety instances. As a partial test, we set the maximum number of X items at .1 and at .01 the maximum value allowed for the other classes. At a probability cut-off of .5, we found that the probability of the universal conclusion rose from .0002 to .009 and .246 for maximum X at .1 and .01, respectively, of the normal maximum value; see line 2 of Table 7. The smaller the maximum number of Xs relative to the maximum number of Z values, the more likely it will be that all Xs are Zs. However, with the increase in the probability of the universal conclusion, the same change produced a marked decrease in the probability of conclusions from longer chains of argument, even if the conclusion was not a universal; compare rows 4 and 5. Obviously there needs to be more investigation concerning the relative sizes of classes.

Next we examined the difference between stating a conclusion with the modifier "evidently" and without. Recall that in defeasible logic, "$\varnothing \Rightarrow A$" is equivalent to "Evidently A". Thus in our notation, "Evidently A" is just $u(A)$. On rows 6 and 7 of Table 7, both inferences begin with the two premises that "Usually Xs are Ys", and "This is an X". On row 6 the conclusion is "Evidently this is a Y", while on row 7 the conclusion is just "This is a Y". Similarly, on rows 8 and 9 both inferences begin with the two premises "Usually Xs are Ys", and "Evidently this is an X". On row 8 the conclusion is "Evidently this is a Y", while on row 9 the conclusion is just "This is a Y". For an inference chain with two conditionals, compare rows 10 and 11. For a three conditional inference, compare rows 14 and 15.

Recall that the second-order probability of Y, given the background, is the mean of the probabilities of Y in the models of the sample in which the background is satisfied. So a high value of the second-order probability of Y tells us that in a number of models, the first-order probability of Y was pretty high; however, it does not tell us anything about the proportion of models in which this was the case. But the second-order probability of "Evidently Y" tells us the proportion of models in which the first-order probability of Y was above the cut-off value. A simple example will help to clarify the difference. Suppose our sample found only three model universes in which the background was satisfied. In the first and the second models, suppose the probability of Y is .28, while in the third model, the probability of Y is 1. Then the second-order probability of Y over these models is $1.56/3 = .52$. However, for any value of cut-off parameter at .5 or better, the second-order probability of Y would be only $\frac{1}{3}$, since Y has a probability above the cut-off in only 1 of the 3 models. If we are in the first model or in the second model, we would say it is unwise to bet on Y; only in the third model would it be wise to bet on Y. So, if our conclusion is "Evidently Y" with a probability of only $\frac{1}{3}$, we are saying that in most universes it would *not* be reasonable to bet on Y. To summarize, a high second-order probability of "Y" tells us that in some models, Y has a high first-order probability; on the other hand, a high second-order probability of "Evidently Y" tells us that Y has a high first-order probability in a large proportion (as determined by the cut-off value) of models.

In all of the chains, although the second-order probability of Y got higher with increasing cut-off parameter, the second-order probabilty of "Evidently Y" decreased with increasing cut-off parameter. All these results indicate that as our cut-off increases, the mean first-order probability of Y gets higher, but the number of models in which an inference to Y is reasonable actually decreases. Somewhat surprisingly, given the premises, the conclusion "Evidently Y" is reasonable only for a cut-off value of .5. Thus if the standard inference rules of defeasible logic are to be preserved, it seems we should take the probability cut-off to be 0.5.

We are also in a position to make some comments concerning the role of "evidently" claims in the premise position. For a single defeasible conditional, compare (i) row 6 with row 8 and (ii) row 7 with row 9; for two conditionals, compare rows 12 and 13. For three conditionals, compare rows 15 and 16. For each pair, the conclusion is the same, but the premises differ by the fact that one uses "This is an X" while the other uses "Evidently this is an X". Within each pair, the second-order probabilities of the conclusion differ very little, especially for the cut-off parameter of .5. So using "Evidently this is an X" as a premise rather than the more definite "This is an X" seems to make little difference to the strength of the argument.

We also did a simplistic check of the naive picture of the way in which arguments may be chained together. Consider the following argument:

(VII.5)
P1: Typically Xs are Ys.
P2: Typically Ys are Zs.
P3: Evidently this item is an X.
─────────────────────────────
C: Evidently this item is a Z.

The way in which this is done in defeasible logic is that we first draw the intermediate conclusion "Evidently this item is a Y" from $P1$ and $P3$; we then use this intermediate conclusion along with $P2$ to arrive at C. So in order to get to C, we actually have to get both the intermediate conclusion and C. On row 7 of Table 7, we calculate the probability of the conjunctive conclusion on the basis of $P1 - 3$. The probability of the conjunctive conclusion is still well within the acceptance range for the cut-off parameter 0.5. Row 8 gives the value of the intermediate conclusion, and row 10 gives the value of the desired conclusion. The conjunctive conclusion is only slightly lower than either conjunct.

We conducted a number of experiments involving negative inference chains. These roughly correspond to the classical pattern of modus tollens. The results are given in Table 8.

Table 8. Negative inference chains

	Inference		prob. cut-off: pc		
	Given	Concl.	.5	.6	.7
1	$u(X,Y)$	$u(\sim X, \sim Y)$	.666	.536	.493
2	$u(X,Y)$	$u(\sim X, \sim Y)$	.498	.173	.003
3	$u(X,Y), u(\sim Y)$	$u(\sim X)$	.498	$.324_{(111)}$	?
4	$u(X,Y), u(\sim Y)$	$\sim X$	.501	$.571_{(111)}$	.?
5	$u(X,Y), \sim Y$	$u(\sim X)$	.499	.130	.020
6	$u(X,Y), \sim Y$	$\sim X$	.547	.610	.697
7	$u(X,Y), a(Z, \sim Y))$	$u(Z, \sim X)$	.796	.790	.787
8	$u(X,Y), u(Y,Z), u(\sim Z)$	$u(\sim X)$	.489	$.091_{(11)}$	.?
9	$u(X,Y), u(Y,Z), u(\sim Z)$	$\sim X$	.498	$.491_{(11)}$	?
10	$u(X,Y), u(Y,Z), \sim Z$	$\sim X$	.500	.523	$.595_{(341)}$
11	$u(W,X), u(X,Y), a(Z, \sim Y)$	$u(Z, \sim W)$	.532	.487	$.481_{(27)}$

Row 1 of Table 8 is the standard contrapositive inference, only using a defeasible conditional: from "Xs are typically Ys" conclude "non-Ys are typically non-Xs." The inference is fairly strong at a cut-off of 0.5, but decreases with increasing cut-off parameter. As a check, we also tried the standard fallacy of denying the antecedent: from "Xs are typically Ys" conclude "non-Xs are typically non-Ys". The fallacious inference was rejected by all cut-off values. A typical example of a defeasible modus tollens argument is the following:

(VII.6)
P1: $u(X,Y)$
P2: $u(\sim Y)$
C: $u(\sim X)$

In English the argument would read: "Typically Xs are Ys, and evidently this is not a Y, so evidently it is not an X." As shown on row 3, the argument was rejected for all values of the cut-off parameter. On rows 4, 5, and 6, we looked at the various alternatives for replacing "evidently" in $P2$ and C. Even with premise $P2$ strengthened (row 5), the argument is rejected. It is only when the conclusion is strengthened (rows 4 and 6) that the argument appears to have any value. This surprising result is because the second-order probability of $\sim X$ is just the mean of the first-order probabilities. Thus all it is really telling us is that is a few cases, $\sim X$ is very likely. However, rows 3 and 4 tell us that the conclusion does not have high probability in very many models. Rows 8, 9, and 10 show exactly parallel results for modus tollens style arguments involving two defeasible conditionals. The only negative inference chains with show much promise are those in which one of the conditionals is a monotonic conditional. For example the argument "Typically birds can fly, but Tweety can't fly, so evidently Tweety is not a bird" would be symbolized (without the existential assumption) as follows:

$$\text{(VII.7)} \quad \begin{array}{ll} \text{P1:} & u(X, Y) \\ \text{P2:} & a(Z, \sim Y) \\ \hline \text{C:} & u(Z, \sim X) \end{array}$$

Row 7 gives the outcome of our numerical experiment, which makes this argument seem rather good. This result is rather surprising, since the probability of the conclusion is even higher than would be the probability of just the contrapositive of $P1$ (see row 1 on the table). The problem is that our simulation process has introduced some statistical anomalies. Consider a categorical table (or a Venn diagram) for just two classes, say A and B. If we make the claim that "All As are Bs", then we are setting to empty that row corresponding to the A-non-Bs. That is, one of the 4 rows is empty. There remains only one A-row but two2 B-rows. So if the remaining rows receive on average the same number of items, the probability of A will be only $\frac{1}{3}$, while the probability of B will be $\frac{2}{3}$! Our experiments confirm this line of analysis; see rows 5 and 6 of Table 11. Hence in $P2$, we are automatically restricting the size of the Z class relative to the size of the other classes. Since Z will be small, generally speaking, it will be more likely that most of the members of Z will fall into the $\sim X$ class. So the apparently positive results on rows 7 and 11 are spurious.

We now turn our attention to arguments in which there is evidence which undercuts an inference which would normally be drawn from a defeasible conditional. The results of a few experiments are recorded in Table 9.

For the first example, we considered cases of the Nixon sort discussed above: Nixon was a Quaker, and most Quakers were pacifists; but Nixon was also a Republican, and most Republicans were not pacifists. So from this conflicting information, no conclusion should follow. Row 1 of Table 9 is basically the Nixon example, and indeed, no conclusion follows. On row 2, we have replaced the two premises "Evidently X" and "Evidently Y"

Table 9. Defeater inferences

	Inference		prob. cut-off: pc		
	Given	Concl.	.5	.6	.7
1	$u(X,Y), u(Y,\sim Z), u(X), u(Y)$	Z	.499	$.508_{(11)}$	?
2	$u(X,Y), u(Y,\sim Z), u(X \wedge Y)$	Z	$.496_{(18)}$	?	?
3	$u(X,Z), u(Y,\sim Z), u(X \vee Y)$	Z	.500	.499	.504
4	$u(X,Y), X$	Y	.585	.660	.746
5	$u(X,Y), u(Y,Z), X$	Z	.543	.590	$.670_{(341)}$
6	$u(X,Y), u(Y,Z), c(X \sim Z), X$	Z	.437	.520	$.606_{(200)}$
7	$u(X,Y), u(Y,Z), c(X, \sim Z), X$	Y	.585	.658	$.744_{(200)}$

with one premise "Evidently X and Y", and still no conclusion follows. On row 3 we replaced the two premises "Evidently X" and "Evidently Y" with the weaker single premise "Evidently X or Y", but again, no conclusion follows. So our probabilistic version of the defeasible conditional seems to respond as desired to undercutting information.

Our next concern was with the conditional known in defeasible logic as the undercutting defeater. Recall that in our probabilistic interpretation, "$X \rightsquigarrow Y$" is interpreted to mean that there is a significant chance that an X will also be a Y, i.e., that it is false that Xs are usually not Ys. Consider the following argument based on a chain of two defeasible conditionals:

(VII.8)
$$\begin{array}{ll} \text{P1:} & u(X,Y) \\ \text{P2:} & u(Y,Z) \\ \text{P3:} & X \\ \hline \text{C:} & Z \end{array}$$

As we would expect from previous discussions, this argument is acceptable; experimental results are given on row 5. But now, we want to see what happens if we add a premise containing the undercutting defeater: $X \rightsquigarrow\sim Z$. That is, we want to add the premise that Xs might not be Zs: $c(X, \sim Z)$. This additional premise should block the inference to Z, but not interfere with the inference to Y. On row 6, the numerical experiment confirms the fact that the inference to Z is disallowed, at least for a cut-off parameter of 0.5. While on row 7, it is apparent that the inference to Y is left unaffected; compare row 7 with row 4.

All of these results seem quite promising, but there are some problems lurking in the background. We now turn our attention to some statistical anomalies introduced by our current sampling techniques and how they may affect our results. In the context of our discussion of Table 7, above, we have already mentioned the problem arising from the relative sizes of classes. When modeling a real life situation, the number of items in a class designating an individual should obviously be considerably smaller than the number of items in a class designating a group of individuals. But placing restrictions on class sizes may alter second-order probabilities dramatically, as shown on rows 2, 4, and 5 of Table 7.

In the context of Table 8, we have also discussed anomalies that may arise from using universals as premises. These results are more clear in Table 10.

Table 10. Defeater inferences

	Inference		prob. cut-off: pc		
	Given	Concl.	.5	.6	.7
1	$u(X,Y)$	Z	.500	.500	.501
2	$u(X,Y)$	X	.500	.485	.460
3	$u(X,Y)$	Y	.543	.578	.614
4	$a(X,Y)$	Z	.500	.500	.500
5	$a(X,Y)$	X	.333	.333	.333
6	$a(X,Y)$	Y	.667	.667	.667
7	$u(X,Y), u(Y,Z)$	X	.500	.481	.438
8	$u(X,Y), u(Y,Z)$	Y	.543	.569	.584
9	$u(X,Y), u(Y,Z)$	Z	.543	.586	.641
10	$a(X,Y), a(Y,Z)$	X	.250	.250	.250
11	$a(X,Y), a(Y,Z)$	Y	.500	.500	.500
12	$a(X,Y), a(Y,Z)$	Z	.750	.750	.750

If I claim as a premise that "All Xs are Ys", then I am ruling out $\frac{1}{4}$ of the rows on the categorical table, namely those rows that are X but non-Y. With only $\frac{3}{4}$ of the rows remaining, $\frac{1}{3}$ of the remainder allow for Xs, while $\frac{2}{3}$ of the remainder allow for Ys; see rows 4, 5, and 6 of Table 10. For a class, say Z, not mentioned in the universal claim, the probability is unaffected; row 4. But for X (row 5) the probability drops to $\frac{1}{3}$, while for Y (row 6) the probability rises to $\frac{2}{3}$. However, the claim "Usually Xs are Ys" does not lead to such a strong statistical anomaly as does the universal claim. Claiming that "Usually Xs are Ys" is most often satisfied by cases in which the Y class is larger than the X class but the tendency is by no means true of all models. The sentence "Usually Xs are Ys" may hold even when all Ys are Xs but some Xs are not Ys. Thus there will be only a slightly elevated probability of Y. See rows 2 and 3 of Table 10. As expected, the probability of a class not mentioned in the defeasible claim will be unaffected; see row 1.

When we string together a number of conditionals, the problems become compounded. On rows 7, 8, and 9 of Table 10, we looked at a chain of two defeasible conditionals. The probability of the first class in the chain, row 7, changed very little, as would have been expected from row 2. But the probabilities of the middle and terminal classes in the chain, rows 8 and 9, were both elevated. The situation is much more dramatic when we chain together universal claims. On rows 10, 11, and 12 we examine a chain of two universal conditionals. The first class in the chain, row 10, has a probability of only $\frac{1}{4}$, while the probability of the last class in the chain, row 12, has risen to $\frac{3}{4}$.

These statistical anomalies may well bias the results of our numerical experiments. For good examples, refer again to Table 6 where we examined the transitivity of the defeasible conditional. Note that with no background information, the probability of $u(X, Z)$ is about $\frac{1}{2}$, as we would naively expect; see row 1. And, given $u(X, Y)$, the probability of $u(X, Z)$ is still only about $\frac{1}{2}$; see row 2. But, given $u(Y, Z)$, the probability of $u(X, Z)$ jumps to almost $\frac{2}{3}$. In retrospect, it is not difficult to understand why. When we impose $u(A, C)$, we impose no significant restrictions on the size of the antecedent class A; but we do impose a tendency for the consequent class C to be large relative to the antecedent. There will be more models in which $u(A, C)$ holds if the class of C is very large relative to the class of A. So, when we finally get to the conditional chain on row 4, most of the seeming dramatic increase in the conclusion is due to only the one premise. Adding the other premise has little effect; compare rows 3 and 4. And when looking at a chain of three conditionals, the probability of the conclusion based on only one of the premises, row 5, is actually generally *higher* than when given all three of the premises, row 8.

8 Conclusions and suggestions for further research

Using categorical logic and second-order probability certainly does seem to produce a rational defeasible reasoning system. Further, our system closely models the inference patterns advocated by the proponents of defeasible logic. However, our system seems to be more flexible; at the very least, our approach allows for the easy introduction of a great many semi-quantified operators. Our system also has the advantage of not requiring the formulation of obscure, complex inference rules. The simple Monte Carlo technique allows a quick check of almost any argument pattern. Further, the technique is highly computationally tractable, and even lends itself well to applications in large data bases.

However, we have alluded to the problems associated with various statistical anomalies which arise in our approach. Some research is required to

Table 11. Reprsentation of quantifers using orderings

English phrase	Speical notation	Numerical requirement
All X are Y	$a(X,Y)$	$X \wedge \sim Y = 0$
Some X are Y	$s(X,Y)$	$0 < X \wedge Y$
Usually X are Y	$u(X,Y)$	$X \wedge \sim Y < X \wedge Y$
Evidently Y	$e(Y)$ $u(X \vee \sim X, Y)$	$\sim Y < Y$
There is a significant chance that X are Y	$c(X,Y)$ not $u(X, \sim Y)$	$X \wedge \sim Y \leq X \wedge Y$
There are signficantly more X than Y	$m(X,Y)$ $u(X \vee Y, X \wedge \sim Y)$	$Y < X \wedge \sim Y$

determine whether or not there are computationally simple ways to avoid these problems associated with a numerical simulation.

There can be little doubt that the use of numerical simulations in these cases is highly artificial. So one suggestion for coping with the anomalies is to emphasize orderings rather than actual numbers. That is, rather than assigning actual numbers to classes, perhaps we should just consider well-orderings on the classes.

At several points in our discussion above, we have encountered situations which suggest that using a probability cut-off of 0.5 would give the most reasonable results. If we adopt this suggestion, then the representation of our various quantifiers in terms of orderings becomes quite easy. See Table 11.

Thus if we had a technique for the random generation of well-orderings on the classes, we could still employ the Monte Carlo approach and second-order probability to implement a defeasible reasoning system. But the problem of randomly generating well-orders is highly non-trivial.

Let us consider a simple example. Suppose we have only one atomic proposition, say p. The categorical table would have only two rows on it, one for p and one for $\sim p$. The Boolean lattice of propositions would then have only 4 elements. See Figure 3.

Any proposed well-orderings of the propositions that violates the lattice ordering should be considered illegitimate. Thus in this example, there are only six distinct orderings:

(a) $p \vee \sim p \quad > \quad p \quad > \quad \sim p \quad > \quad p \wedge \sim p$

(b) $p \vee \sim p \quad > \quad \sim p \quad > \quad p \quad > \quad p \wedge \sim p$

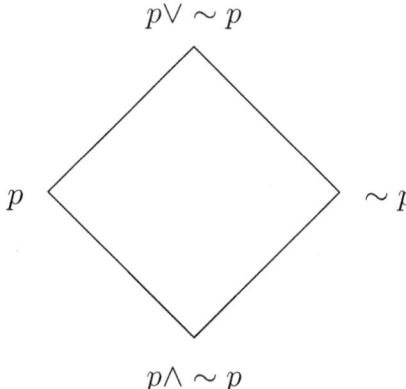

Figure 3. Lattice for one proposition

Table 12. Orderings generated by assignments to rows

Maximum row value	allowed row values	orderings generated
1	0,1	$c-1, d-1, e-1, f-1$
2	0,1,2	$a-1, b-1, c-2, d-2, e-2, f-1$
3	0,1,2,3	$a-3, b-3, c-3, d-3, e-3, f-1$
4	0,1,2,3,4	$a-6, b-6, c-4, d-4, e-4, f-1$

(c) $p \lor \sim p \; > \; p \; = \; \sim p \; > \; p \land \sim p$

(d) $p \lor \sim p \; = \; p \; > \; \sim p \; = \; p \land \sim p$

(e) $p \lor \sim p \; = \; \sim p \; > \; \sim p \; = \; p \land \sim p$

(f) $p \lor \sim p \; = \; p \; = \; \sim p \; = \; p \land \sim p$

Note that while these orderings can be generated by assigning numbers to the rows on the categorical table (i.e., to the state descriptions), such a technique introduces redundancies in the orders generated. For example, in Table 12 we have indicated allowed numbers for the rows, along with the type and number of orderings induced by all combinations of assigning the numbers to the rows.

So in order to avoid introducing anomalies by prejudicial redundancies, we must adopt some technique other than simply assigning random values to state descriptions.

One possible suggestion for generating compatible orders on the lattice elements is to generate orders on the state descriptions. But the problem with this suggestion is that the order of the state descriptions does not uniquely determine the order of all lattice elements. To see that this is so, we consider the lattice of two propositions. See Figure 4.

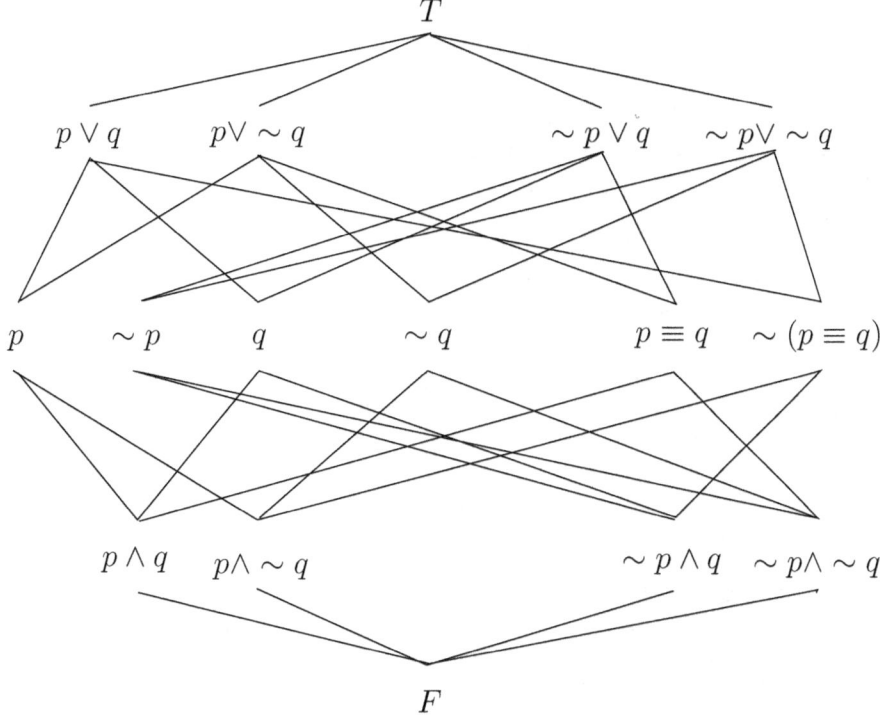

Figure 4. Lattice for two proposition

Our problem then is to generate well-orderings of the lattice elements that do not violate the lattice ordering. Consider the simple categorical table for two propositions, Table 13.

The values on row 3 should be considered alternatives. All of the value assignments will yield the same ordering on the state descriptions:

$$\sim p \,\wedge\sim q \;<\; p \,\wedge\sim q \;<\; p\wedge q \;<\; \sim p\wedge q$$

But if we use the value of 6 for row 3, we will have $\sim p \wedge q < p$. If we use the value of 7 for row 3, we will have $\sim p \wedge q = p$. And if we use the value of

Table 13. Some orderings for the lattice of two propositions

row	p	q	value
1	+	+	4
2	+	-	3
3	-	+	6,7,8
4	-	-	1

8 for row 3, we will have $\sim p \wedge q > p$. So imposing an ordering on the state descriptions does not impose a unique ordering on the lattice elements.

In summary, assigning random numbers to state descriptions does impose an ordering on the lattice elements, but it introduces unequal redundancies in the orderings. On the other hand, assigning an order on the state descriptions does not uniquely determine an ordering on the lattice elements.

There are a number of open problems with respect to the ordering question. First of all, it would be useful to have a formula for the number of distinct orderings of the elements of a lattice of n atomic propositions, the orderings to preserve the lattice ordering. But more importantly, we need to know how can we randomly generate such orderings without introducing bias into the sample. Once we can generate the orderings, we will then be in a position to see what effect using orderings will have on our categorical defeasible reasoning system.

BIBLIOGRAPHY

[1] Morgan, C. G. "The Nature of Nonmonotonic Reasoning", *Minds and Machines*, vol. 10 (2000), pp. 321-360.
[2] Nute, D. Defeasible Logic. In D. Gabbay and C. Hogger, editors, *Handbook of Logic for Artificial Intelligence and Logic Programming*, volume III. Oxford University Press, Oxford (1994).

Real Logic is Nonmonotonic

HENRY E. KYBURG, JR.

1 Introduction

In a number of recent papers [Morgan, 2000; Morgan, 1998; Morgan, 1991], Charles Morgan has defended the thesis that nonmnonotonic logic is impossible. That's a dramatic way of putting it, but what he has forcefully brought to our attention is the question of whether or not there is a *logic* that corresponds to ordinary reasoning. Morgan concludes that there is not, but that ordinary reasoning can be represented by a structure of presuppositions, together with classical monotonic logic. We shall argue here that in real life, what concerns us most is nonmonotonic logic; that neither presuppositions nor probabilities can stand in for the inductive relation that should be captured by nonmonotonic logic.

The plan of the paper is the following. First we shall examine the question of what logic is for – what should we ask of a logic? Are we using it to assist us in modelling the world? Or are we trying to model human reasoning? Or does it concern argument? Or all three?

Second, we should examine (briefly) Morgan's arguments. If they are sound, of course, we should fold our tents and steal away, rather than barking up a nonexistent tree at an impossible squirrel.

Third, we must look more closely at probability as a possible nonmonotonic representation of rationality. There are a number of confusions about probability and monotonicity.

Fourth, let us specify precisely what we want in the way of a nonmonotonic logic, and suggest one approach to nonmonotonic logic that avoids Morgan's strictures.

Finally, we will examine the way our conclusions fit in with Morgan's proposal in defense of monotonic logic.

2 Logic

Few people would say that logic is about the laws of thought. If they did, there would still be an ambiguity: descriptive laws or normative laws? But many people would say of logic that it concerns *reasoning*. Of course the idea is that logic is not psychology, but that it somehow captures the human talent for rational inference. According to Morgan, [Morgan, 2000, p. 324] "... our rational thought processes involve modeling and predicting aspects of our environment under conditions of uncertainty." It is not clear where "inference" fits into this story, but one of the things a logic does is to *sanction* some inferences and not others.

The test of a logic, from this point of view, is whether or not it by and large accords with common sense [Morgan, 2000, p. 327]:

> In order to be acceptable, a logic must sanction all (or at least most) of the arguments which our common sense tells us are rational.... [and] the logic must reject all (or at least almost all) of the arguments which our common sense tells us are not rational.

There is nothing wrong, of course, with having our goals for logic relativized to human abilities and intuitions. It would be senseless, for example, to demand of a logic that it only yield conclusions that are true, regardless of the premises employed. But it is still not quite clear what the relation between "mental" processes and "logic" is, or where the question of language enters.

These are difficult matters, and I am happy to leave them to one side. It seems to me that there is one context in which the role of logic is perfectly clear. That is the context of *argument*. It is not clear whether any sort of "language" is required for thought — on the basis of introspection, I rather think not — but it certainly is clear that language is required for argument. Perhaps by extension, certain kinds of mental processes can be construed as subject to logical sanctions, on the grounds that they are analogous to argument, and (at least) involve language.

2.1 Deductive Logic

What kind of a role does logic play in argument? Let us first consider classical logic as applied to deductive argument. In general, of course, an argument is designed by one agent to lead another agent to a certain belief. (Sometimes, in solitary ratiocination, the two agents are the same, but this is a bit perverse and we'll not dwell on it.) A formal argument consists of a sequence of formulas (typically, statements) each of which is one of a set of statements constituting premises, or is derivable from preceding statements in the sequence by one of the rules *sanctioned* by the logic, and which ends in the conclusion. Given that the first agent seeks to establish this conclusion as a belief of the second agent, there are some additional requirements that must be met. The second agent must agree to each of the premises, and the two agents must agree on logic that serves to sanction the moves.

There are two properties we expect a logic of this sort to have. One is essential: it is soundness. We expect an argument from premises that are *true*, via moves sanctioned by the logic, to lead only to conclusions that are also true. The other is merely desirable: it is completeness. If some sentence is true whenever the premises are true, we'd like our logic to lead to it. But that seems less essential.

How is logic, thus conceived, used? No one would demand that every argument be presented in terms of an explicitly characterized language, and in full logical detail. In some logics, for example, the only move permitted is *modus ponens*; but any such logic will be very tedious, and indeed difficult to follow. What it does make sense to demand is that the argument allow a faithful translation into a language such that in that language, using that agreed-upon logic, the argument is valid: i.e. can be prepresented by a *proof*.

To establish this, however, is generally much easier than to present a proof. Consider the linguistic objects called proofs in the literature of mathematics. Except in rare cases, many abbreviations and shortcuts are perfectly acceptable to the second agent. The value of logic — in particular, the value of first order logic in mathematics — is that IF there is dispute about the validity of an argument, THEN there is a court of last resort: is there a faithful representation of the argument in first order logic that is valid?

We have said nothing about universality. We have supposed that the language admits of a semantics that allows us to talk of truth; we have supposed that the agreed upon logic is classical logic, and not intuitionistic logic or fuzzy logic or modal logic. We are taking everything at its simplest face value, and to that end we are leaving the question of the universality of classical logic to one side. We will encounter an illustration later of how the lust for universality can lead us astray.

Is a nonmonotonic logic possible? Let us take a monotonic logic to be a logic such that an addition to the premises does not reduce the acceptability of the conclusion. In classical deductive logic, this can be expressed very simply: If the set of premises A is included in the set of premises B, then anything you can deduce from A can also be deduced from B.

$$A \subseteq B \supset (\forall \alpha)(A \vdash \alpha \supset B \vdash \alpha).$$

2.2 Inductive Logic

As induction is ordinarily construed, it is clearly nonmonotonic. A conclusion that is warranted at one time may come to be rejected at a later time, in the light of new and better evidence, and then, in the light of yet more evidence, we may go back to our original conclusion. This may happen in two ways. One way, described by Morgan [Morgan, 2000], is that the agent (or reasoner, or thinker) step by step takes more factors into account. The conclusion reached may flip back and forth as the evidence he takes account of increases.

The other way in which it may happen is that the agent, at each point, takes into account all the evidence he has, but new evidence becomes available over time, and leads to the rejection of statements that were once acceptable, and perhaps with yet more evidence, to their reinstatement. Carnap and others who have sought to regiment inductive logic have typically endorsed a *principle of total evidence* that requires the agent to take account of all the evidence he has available. If we adopt a principle of total evidence, the former sort of reversal will not occur, except as a matter of miscalculation or logical mistake. This allows us to focus on the logical questions.

The reversibility of inductive conclusions also raises the question of whether there are logical questions other than those answered by standard first order logic. Morgan denies this, and we will consider his arguments later. At this point, what we'd like to ask is whether, if there *were* an inductive logic, what would it be?

First, it would not be a psychological model of the way people think inductively, any more than first order logic is a psychological model of the way people think deductively. By analogy with first order logic, we could think of it as a a framework within which we can discuss and come to agreement concerning inductive arguments. In the case of first order logic, we seek to come to agreement concerning *validity*. Is there something akin to validity that is our goal in the case of inductive arguments? Something like "partial validity"?

That there is, is suggested by the fact that people present *arguments* purporting to support inductive conclusions. It could be maintained (and is maintained by some: Halpern, Morgan, Burks, and many others [Fagin and Halpern, 1988; Halpern, 1993; Morgan, 1991; Burks, 1953; Burks, 1977; Burks, 1954-55; Morgan, 2000] that these arguments, like the typical arguments even of mathematics and logic, are enthymemes, and are simply "presupposing" the premises necessary to become explicit deductive arguments. But it could also be maintained that some arguments are both inductive (lead to conclusions whose content goes beyond that of their premises) and rational (that is, subject to determinate canons of rationality that have intuitive appeal and can be made explicit.)

Of course, everybody can cheat. Every argument with premises P and conclusion C that purports to be inductive can be represented as an enthymeme with the suppressed premise $P \to C$. And an implausible "presupposition" such as "If most A are B then *this* A is a B" can be hedged around with provisos: Provided *this* A isn't known *not* to be a B, and isn't a D or an E or...

That there is no generally accepted inductive logic, as first order logic is generally accepted, is only inductive evidence (!) in favor of the presupposition view. Charles Morgan [Morgan, 2000] has presented four arguments that purport to show that nonmonotonic logic is impossible; if his arguments are sound, that would settle the matter. Before we examine his arguments we must take a look at the role of probability in inductive logic.

3 Probability

Probability is problematic in connection with induction. One possibility is to incorporate a probability operator into the object language. We definitely need to do this, since we want to accommodate probabilistic theories, such as statistical mechanics, the theory of measurement error, quantum mechanics, etc., but it is not clear what such a probability has to offer us with regard to induction or logic. What is clear is that probability functions, as mathematical functions, are monotonic in a natural sense of the term: $A \subseteq B \to \mathcal{P}(A) \leq \mathcal{P}(B)$; if A is a smaller set of possibilities than B — a smaller set of worlds, a smaller part of sample space — then the probability of A must be less than (or equal to) that of B. For the same reasons, conditional probability functions are monotonic in the first position, but of course not monotonic in the second: conditioning on a more restricted set of possibilities may either raise or lower the conditional probability.

This does not bear directly on our questions about inference, however. For these purposes there are two things we can do: we can think of probability as a logical operator in the object language itself, or we can think of probability as a metalinguistic operator applying to *sentences* or sets of sentences or pairs of sets of sentences. For present purposes the latter is somewhat simpler.

Of course as a mathematical formalism, probability is inferentially monotonic: From probability premises we get probability conclusions; from a superset of those premises we get the same conclusions or a superset of them. This applies as well to the "probabilistic logic" of Nilsson [Nilsson, 1986] as to the probabilities of statistical mechanics.

In particular, this applies to probabilities that are construed as degrees of belief. It is more natural to construe these probabilities as applying to a domain of statements, but it is also possible to construe them as functions in the object language having as domain propositions or some such abstract entities. The most general premises involving such object language functions consist of constraints they are to satisfy. (Note that we need not suppose that the constraints are in the form of a single measure function on the sentences of a language.) Whatever inferences we make from these premises are monotonic: our conclusions don't change with the addition of new premises.

For example, suppose that the probability of the conditional $A \to B$ and the probability of A are given as premises. Then the conclusion that the probability of B lies between the sum of these probabilities minus 1, and the probability of the conditional is derivable. Add more premises, and this conclusion will continue to be derivable: the logic, even though it talks about probabilities, is monotonic. This holds whatever these probabilities are purported to be.

Thus suppose we have $P(A \wedge B) = .4$ and $P(A) = .7$. We may infer, in line with the probability calculus, that $P(B|A) = 4/7$. We may also infer that $P(B) \geq 0.4$. Let us add the premise A to our system. What is the value of $P(B)$? We still have $P(B) \geq 0.4$. We could consistently add $P(B) = 0.4$, though that would not satisfy the Bayesian updater. What we'd *like*, of course, is to have $P(B) = 4/7$. But given the premises we have, that is not obtainable. In order to obtain this conclusions, we would need $P(A) = 1.0$, which directly contradicts one of our initial premises.

We might make a connection between probability and truth by claiming that $P(A) = 1.0$ *follows from* A [1]; but that, of course, means that when we add A to our set of premises, we have contradicted our original set of premises, which included $P(A) = 0.7$: we have done nothing nonmonotonic.

The same analysis applies if we construe probability, more naturally in this context, as an operator in the metalanguage. (Of course we can still have probabilities in the object language within such theories as statistical mechanics.) The premises now consist of constraints on the probabilities of *statements*. According to the Bayesian ideal, we have a probability measure on the statments of our object language. Inductive logic may then be taken to consist essentially in Bayesian conditioning.

While we *might* say "the conditional of conditional probability clearly seems to be nonmonotonic" [Morgan, 2000, p. 338] because $\mathcal{P}(A|\Gamma \cup \Delta) < \mathcal{P}(A|\Gamma) < \mathcal{P}(A|\Gamma \cup \Sigma)$ is possible, this would have little to do with inference — adding Σ to the evidence might either raise or lower the probability of A.[2] Speaking very loosely, we might say that the probability of A given

---

[1] Of course this can't be right, or we wouldn't need probability. What it follows from, if anything, is *our knowledge that A* or our acceptance of A as a premise.

[2] Inference concerning probabilities is still monotonic; what is displayed here is the fact that conditional probability functions are not monotonic in their second arguments.

background Γ may either increase or decrease in the light of new information.

But as Keynes pointed out long ago [Keynes, 1952], when we learn E and take our ideal degree of belief in H to be $P(H|E)$ rather than $P(H)$, we haven't *changed* our probability function — we have simply taken a *different* probability as relevant. Our initial premises are unchanged and our reasoning is strictly monotonic. In the Bayesian case we have moved from $\mathcal{P}(A \wedge \Gamma)/\mathcal{P}(\Gamma)$ to $\mathcal{P}(A \wedge \Gamma \cup \Delta)/\mathcal{P}(\Gamma \cup \Delta)$, where $\mathcal{P}$ is the a priori probability function with which we started.

Might we construe this reasoning as nonmonotonic by suppressing the evidence position? By saying that we've gone from $\mathcal{P}_1$ to $\mathcal{P}_2$? But then the probability functions themselves are being taken as premises (appropriate to different bodies of evidence), and the premises are *different*, not augmented.

Of course probability construed in this way is not the only way of taking account of uncertainty in induction or nonmonotonic inference. For example, while $P(H|E)$ gives the probability (in some sense of "probability"!) of H given E, this may be not as good a guide to the desirability of the hypothesis H when our total evidence is E as the *difference* $P(H|E) - P(H)$. A number of writers have come up with more or less complicated formulas designed to capture this desirability, Popper and Carnap, among others [Popper, 1959; Carnap, 1950]. Several of these views are compared in formal detail in [Kyburg and Teng, 2001]; they are discussed rather more generally, in [Fetzer, 1981].

A rule of inference that allows us to accept a hypothesis that receives a high degree of desirability according to some measure can clearly be nonmonotonic. The question then hinges on the other horn: can we legitimately call it a "logic"? Morgan argues that we cannot.

4 Morgan's Proofs

Morgan's proofs are expressed in terms of *belief structures*. A belief structure is a relation **LE** from sets of sentences to sets of sentences, subject to three constraints [Morgan, 2000, pp. 328,329]:

Reflexivity: Γ **LE** Γ
Transitivity: If Γ **LE** Γ' and Γ' **LE** Γ'', then Γ **LE** Γ''
The subset principle: If $\Gamma \subset \Delta$, then Δ **LE** Γ.

The relation LE may be thought of as "no more well confirmed than" or "no more acceptable than". A logic **L** is to be thought of as "any arbitrary set of belief structures **L** = { **LE** $_1$, **LE** $_2$,...}" the idea being that a logic simply imposes constraints on the set of belief structures deemed *rational*.

In this light, while reflexivity seems unexceptionable, both transitivity and the subset principle seem just a little suspicious. To have some doubts about the subset principle imagine that Γ is a sensible, coherent, set of statements, for example, the ones that spring unbidden to your mind when you are given Linda the banker's life story, for example in [Tversky and Kahneman, 1982]. Now let Δ be the subset of that story that includes a few fragments from Linda's radical school years, and the statement that she is a banker, but that leaves out some of the connecting material that makes the story coherent. It is not hard to imagine that Δ is less well confirmed than its superset Γ. Note that we are not doing probability theory on a small number of statements; we're allowing a reasonable amount of background knowledge. We'd want a higher return from a bet on both A and B than from a bet on A alone. And we are dealing with large numbers of related statements. Of course our intuitions might be wrong; but the question is whether the subset principle conforms to our intuitions.

A similar story throws doubt on transitivity. If your intuitions are at all captured by the story of Linda the banker, you should be able to imagine trimming Γ by a few sentences to get a set Γ' that is surely no less supported than Γ, Γ **LE** Γ', but which still stands in the same relation to Δ that Γ does.

There are two standard properties of logics that are desiderata of any logic: soundness and completeness. Ordinarily these properties are stated in semantic terms: a logic is *argument sound* if any conclusion it sanctions is true in every model in which the premises are true; it is *argument complete* if it sanctions any conclusion that is true in every model in which the premises are true. Since Morgan is characterizing logics in terms of belief structures, he states these properties somewhat differently [Morgan, 2000, p. 330] ("$\vdash_b$" represents the provability relation for the logic **L**.):

Soundness: If $\Gamma \vdash_b A$, then Γ **LE** $\{A\}$ for all (most) rational belief structures **LE** $\in$ **L**.
Completeness: If Γ **LE** $\{A\}$ for all (most) rational belief functions **LE** $\in$ **L**, then $\Gamma \vdash_b A$.

The fact that these conditions are stated in terms of belief structures, rather than in terms of models, reflects the fact that the standard on which Morgan is willing to depend is that of intuition: "we certainly want to AVOID making a system that will sometimes, in logically unpredictable cases, draw conclusion that most would regard as irrational" [Morgan, 2000, p.330] and "we want to AVOID making a system that will sometimes, in logically unpredictable cases, FAIL to draw conclusions that most would deem to be rational." [Morgan, 2000, p.330]

Leaving to one side the lovely rhetorical flourish ("in logically unpredictable cases") the idea seems to be that we should adopt a psychological or sociological standard for inference. If *most* people would infer the conclusion C from the premises P, then we want our logic to reflect that fact (completeness), and if most people would deny that it was rational to infer C from P, we want our logic to reflect that sociological fact, too.

In the minds of many, this would be a rather frail standard for logic. Nevertheless, there can be a case made for relativizing logic, in some degree, to human capacities. This might lead, in terms of belief structures, to the populist standard proposed by Morgan. If even such a standard were to preclude a nonmonotonic logic, there can't be much point in pursuing the nonmonotonic will-o-the-wisp.

Take careful note of the parenthetical "(most)" in both the statement of completeness and the statement of soundness. This is crucial, since no one would suppose that an inductive or nonmonotonic logic was always right. Even if $\Gamma \vdash_b A$, there may be *some* belief structures **LE** such that public logical opinion would reject Γ **LE** $\{A\}$.

Are these two principles plausible? Completeness seems to be asking a lot. If even number theory is incomplete, should we expect inductive logic to be complete? Even "most" seems to be asking a lot. To ask for soundness is, curiously, asking for very little: as defined, it is a *very* pale reflection of the semantic conception of soundness. In terms of belief structures what corresponds to semantic soundness is that if A is derivable from premises $\{P_1, \ldots, P_n\}$, then for every set of additional statements $\{Q_1, \ldots, Q_k\}$, $\{P_1, \ldots P_n, Q_1, \ldots, Q_k\}$ **LE** $\{A\}$. If soundness is expressed so weakly, how can we get to monotonicity? The argument depends crucially on transitivity and on the subset principle, applied to belief structures.

Let us now look at Morgan's **Theorem 1**.

> **Theorem 1**: Let **L** be an arbitrary set of belief structures which are reflexive, transitive, and satisfy the subset principle. Further suppose that logical entailment $\vdash_b$ is sound and complete with respect to the set **L**. Then logical entailment is monotonic: that is, if $\Gamma \vdash_b A$, then $\Gamma \cup \Delta \vdash_b A$.

The pattern of the proof is this: From the derivability of A, we obtain, by soundness, Γ **LE** $\{A\}$ for *most* belief structures **LE**. The subset principle requires that $\Gamma \cup \Delta$ **LE** Γ for *all* belief structures. Transivity is assumed to hold for *all* belief structures, and this yields the relation $\Gamma \cup \Delta$ **LE** $\{A\}$ for *most* belief structures, which allows us to gallop home on the basis of completeness.

Earlier we cast some doubts on both the subset principle and on transitivity. They don't *always* seem to work. Suppose we weaken them to holding for *most* belief structures. What happens to the proof? In the first step, soundness tells you what holds for most belief structures, say X. Now the subset principle only tells you what holds for *most* of those structures — Y, representing some relatively large fraction of X. Transitivity holds for most triples of belief structures, giving you a set of belief structures Z that represents a relatively large fraction of the triples of belief structures $\langle b_1, b_2, b_3 \rangle$ such that b_1 is in X, b_2 is in Y, and b_3 contains $\Gamma \cup \Delta$ **LE** $\{A\}$. But obviously we have no reason to think that Z, the set of belief structures containing $\Gamma \cup \Delta$ **LE** $\{A\}$ represents *most* belief structures: most of most of most need not be most!

Let us look at a specific example. Suppose that P_1 is the sentence asserting that 99% of R's are T's (R to suggest "reference" and T to suggest "target"). It seems reasonable to say that $\{P_1, R(a)\}$ **LE** $\{T(a)\}$. By the subset principle, of course $\{P_1, R(a), \neg T(a)\}$ **LE** $\{P_1, R(a)\}$. And so by transitivity, $\{P_1, R(a), \neg T(a)\}$ **LE** $\{T(a)\}$. This is patently wrong: it should hold for no logic.

Morgan's other theorems make use of conditionals, and need not detain us, except for his second theorem, which offers an interesting insight with regard to "universality". The second theorem is presented in terms of "belief units", which take the form of conditional belief functions, of which Carnap's c-functions are an example. Another example given by Morgan is Carnap's comparative relation **mc**, $\mathbf{mc}(h, e, h', e')$, which asserts that h is supported by e at least as much as h' is supported by e' [Carnap, 1950]. Carnap suggests that this relation should hold just in case, for all regular c-functions, $c(h, e) \geq c(h', e')$. Morgan's theorem shows that this relation is monotonic, in the sense that if $\mathbf{mc}(h, e, h', e')$ then $\mathbf{mc}(h, e \wedge d, h', e' \wedge d)$, which certainly seems surprising. But the requirement that the inequality hold for *all* regular c-functions is a strong requirement. Carnap, in fact, himself shows [Carnap, 1950, p.436] that $\mathbf{mc}(h, e, h', e')$ holds only if neither e nor e' is L-false, and either $\vdash e \supset h$ or $\vdash e' \supset \neg h'$ or $\vdash e' \wedge h' \supset e \wedge h$ and $\vdash e \supset (h \vee e')$ — a rather strong requirement. It is not so surprising that this relation is monotonic.

But of course at the time Carnap was more interested in quantitative degrees of confirmation than in the comparative notion. Thus what was true of *all* regular c-functions was not of as much interest as what was true of the "right" c-function. We have no reason to think that $c_{true}(h, e) \geq c_{true}(h', e')$ only if $c_{true}(h, e \wedge d) \geq c_{true}(h', e' \wedge d)$.

The moral is that we can be led astray by our thirst for universality.

5 Proof that Nonmonotonic Logic is Possible

The soundness of first order logic tells you that it cannot go beyond what its premises require: Any conclusion we derive from premises in first order logic holds in *every* model — every world — in which the premises hold. The only constraints on the future to which monotonic logic can lead us by argument are constraints that are already embodied in the premises.

Since it is constraints on the world that concern us (in the form of predictions and anticipations), and since first order logic can only make us aware of constraints that are already implicit in our background knowledge, it cannot lead us to new constraints. In fact, since only soundness is needed for this result, we have the following lemma:

LEMMA 1. *If a logic is sound, it cannot lead by valid inference to conclusions that go beyond the contents of our background knowledge.*

What we need is a way of *adding to* our background knowledge. We need a logic that is *unsound*, if that's possible. We need rational inductive procedures, or real rules of inference. David Israel puts it this way: "Real rules of inference are precisely rules of belief fixation; deductive rules of transformation are precisely not." [Israel, 1980, p.100]

Like Morgan, Israel believes that *logic* ("the logic we have, know, and ... love" [Israel, 1980, p. 101]) is monotonic. But if we think of logic as concerned with *argument* rather than *reasoning*, there is no a priori reason that "rules for the fixation of belief" — or at least some of them, in some contexts — cannot be formalized, and that the formalization cannot be regarded as a logic, in the sense that it can serve as a standard of rational or reasonable argument. James Fetzer, in [Fetzer, 1993], draws a detailed analogy between valid and sound deductive arguments, on the one hand, and proper and correct inductive arguments on the other.

The most straightforward way to refute a claim about the non-existence of a certain kind of structure is surely to exhibit an instance of such a structure. We cannot present a nonmonotonic system in detail. On the other hand, we can give some idea of the *kind* of system we have in mind. It will be enlightening to see just how it conflicts with Morgan's impossibility proof, and how it is related to what he offers as a substitute for nonmonotonic logic.

Take Γ as background knowledge, and S as a statement that is rendered inductively plausible — but not entailed — by that background knowledge. Let $m(\Gamma, S)$ be the set of ordinary first order models in which the statements of Γ are true, and to which our attention is directed by our consideration of the statement S. In induction we have no guarantees, but perhaps we are content to run a risk smaller than ϵ of being wrong. If that is so, then (barring a few complications) we might want to accept S; let's write this rule: $\text{Accept}(S,\Gamma,\epsilon)$ if and only if S is true in a fraction of at least $1-\epsilon$ of the models in $m(\Gamma,S)$, where ϵ is determined by context.

What is it to "$\text{Accept}(S,\Gamma,\epsilon)$"? One natural response is to say, "Add S to Γ." But this way lies monotonicity: Once S is added to Γ it becomes true in all the models of the (revised) Γ. If S is true in all the revised models of Γ' of Γ it is certainly true in all the models of $\Gamma' \cup \Delta$. However strongly we are led toward $\neg S$, we can never accept it, since the proportion of $m(\Gamma \cup \{S\}, \neg S)$ in which $\neg S$ is true is always 0. Thus although we can accept sentences that are not first order consequences of Γ, we can never get rid of them: we will always have $\text{Accept}(\Gamma \cup \Delta, S, \epsilon)$ if we have $\text{Accept}(\Gamma, S, \epsilon)$ and construe acceptance in this way.

Perhaps this is just what Morgan's theorems are telling us!

But here's another way to construe acceptance. The idea is just the commonsensical one that one ought to believe what is highly probable, relative to the evidence one has. Distinguish between *evidential* certainties (statements accepted as evidence) and *practical* certainties (statements accepted as a basis for action). It is when the body of evidential certainties supports S that S becomes accepted into the set of practical certainties. Let us represent the set of evidential certainties by Γ_e and the set of practical certainties by Γ_p.

We may reasonably suppose that what is acceptable as evidence is also practically acceptable: $\Gamma_e \subseteq \Gamma_p$. In Morgan's system, Γ_p **LE** Γ_e, in view of the subset principle. But we have no reason to think that Γ_p **LE** $\Gamma_e \cup \Delta$, i.e., that augmenting the evidence will leave Γ_p unchanged. For example, if we have $\text{Accept}(\Gamma_e, S, \epsilon_p)$, then $S \in \Gamma_p$; but while we have $\text{Accept}(\Gamma_e \cup \{\neg S\}, \neg S, \epsilon_p)$, we do not have have $\text{Accept}(\Gamma_e \cup \{\neg S\}, S, \epsilon_p)$ because the relevant set of models has changed.

Our evidence may, of course, change less drastically. For example, S might have the form $a \in T$, and Γ_e might include the knowledge that $a \in R_1$ and that practically all members of R_1 are members of T. But then we may get more evidence; Γ'_e may include the knowledge $a \in R_1 \cap R_2$, and that it isn't the case that practically all members of $R_1 \cap R_2$ are members of T. So S simply fails to appear in Γ_p.

At least some of the right behavior seems to be captured by this approach, though there are a number of problems. What is clear here, though, is that whether it be called "logic" or not, this scheme for the fixation of belief is both nonmonotonic and non-absurd. It is not caught by Morgan's more or less plausible constraints, since it is not representable by a single relation **LE** defined for pairs of sets of sentences that satisfies Morgan's conditions.

Although this vague suggestion has earned its keep merely by being a counterexample to Morgan's proofs, there are several questions that have to be mentioned. There is the question of how, given S and Γ_e we find the set of models in which the frequency of the truth of S is to be counted. There is the question of whether any such approach is committed to flat-out foundationalism, Γ_e being construed as the set of incorrigible evidence statements, or whether there is some non-circular way of treating *uncertain evidence*. There is the related question of the treatment of perceptual judgments. There is the collection of problems raised by the lottery paradox [Fetzer, 1981]. And finally — we shall devote a section to this — there is the question of the relation between this view and the view (Morgan's, but also that of many others) that we can explain uncertain inference by talk of presuppositions.[3] We will devote the next section to the comparison of the approach to real inference through presuppostions, and the approach to real inference through nonmonotonic acceptance. It is precisely here that the very important issues raised by Morgan's arguments lie.

The question of how we find the right set of models in which to calculate the proportion in which S is true is a complicated one. Tentative answers have been offered in [Kyburg, 1994], [Kyburg, 1997], and [Kyburg and Teng, 2001]. This is not the place to attempt to articulate and justify those answers.

With regard to the question of "foundationalism" it should be clear that we are not committed to any set of statements that is immune from correction. Whatever level of confidence (tolerance for error) characterizes a set of statements, we can construe that level as *practical certainty* and seek evidence of a higher level of confidence relative to which each of those statements is *acceptable*.

Can we do this without circularity? There is certainly no mathematical reason why not. Given a set of statements characterized by any level of confidence, we are obliged only to find a set of statements characterized by a higher level of confidence, relative to which that first set is acceptable. In principle there is no reason why we can't do this, however high the level of confidence from which we start.

How about perception? Many writers in AI suppose that there is an incorrigible level of perception whose deliverances we cannot but take at face value. This is clearly a mistake: we could not make the distinction between perception and reality — which we do, on sound grounds — unless perception and reality could conflict. In point of fact, it is these conflicts that introduce us to the notion of perception in the first place. Were we

---

[3]There is a long history of "presupposition" treatments of induction. Perhaps the most articulate proponent of this view is Arthur Burks [Burks, 1977; Burks, 1953], but we should also mention David Harrah [Harrah, 1956; Harrah, 1961].

unable to distinguish between the stick that *appears* bent and the stick that *is* bent, we would have had no need to invent perception.

Again, the details of how to treat this phenomenon in the correct epistemic way are complicated, and lie beyond our present concerns. Nevertheless the general idea is this: it turns out that we can simplify our body of knowledge if we suppose that *some* of our perceptual judgments are wrong. Given that some small fraction are wrong, it is still the case that an arbitrary such judgment is *credible* in the sense that it should be *accepted*: the chance of error is less than ϵ.

Although there are these serious questions to deal with, none of them seem sufficient to undermine the *possibility* of a nonmonotonic logic of the kind sketched. Whether such an approach offers advantages over the apparently simpler approach provided by presuppositions is the topic of the next section.

6 Presupposition vs Acceptance

Nobody seems to argue against the possibility of, or even the necessity for, nonmonotonic *reasoning*. "Logic is a tool to help us understand the process of reasoning..." [Morgan, 2000, p. 348] The way in which Morgan proposes to use logic to help us understand *nonmonotonic reasoning* is the following: "...we associate with each set Γ [of formulas] some set of 'presupposed' models PM(Γ)" where PM(Γ) $\subseteq M(\Gamma)$; "...when reasoning inductively about the consequences of Γ, we select some 'presupposed' set of models ...in which Γ holds; we do not consider all possible models of Γ. If all of these presupposed models of Γ turn out to be models of A, then we say that A is an inductive consequence of Γ. ...if $\Gamma \|\!\!\!\vdash_D A$, then $\Gamma \|\!\!\!\vdash_I A$, but not the reverse, just as desired. Further, there is no reason to expect that PM($\Gamma \cup \Delta$) $\subseteq$ PM(Γ), so monotonicity would not follow in general." [Morgan, 2000, p.349–350]

"When I reason inductively, I just draw standard deductive consequences from my mental models. When I get new information, I update or change my mental models, and inductive consequences of the new information are just deductive consequences of the updated models." [Morgan, 2000, pp, 350–351].

"But just how models are actually updated by human beings is a matter of empirical fact, not a question of logic. ...the effort spent trying to develop some nonmonotonic logic is totally wasted; that effort should be redirected to potentially more fruitful areas, such as how humans update their presupposed models or shift from one to the other." [Morgan, 2000, p. 351]

This is a strong recommendation indeed, and that is why I have quoted it at length. It also seems to conflict with an earlier statement: "Whatever else it may be, logic is not psychology." [Morgan, 2000, p.329]

From our point of view, which focuses on argument rather than on reasoning, we may translate the requirement in terms of "mental" models into a requirement concerning the statements that are taken as premises to convert an inductive or nonmonotonic argument into deductive form. Construed in this way, there have been other supporters of presuppositions or assumptions as throwing light on nonmonotonic argument. Perhaps the most vigorous defender of a presupposition theory of induction was Arthur Burks [Burks, 1977; Burks, 1953; Burks, 1954-55], but here have been others, including Harrah [Harrah, 1961; Harrah, 1956], and, in computer science, Ray Reiter and Johan de Kleer [Reiter and de Kleer, 1987; de Kleer, 1986].

Now of course, just as we might be interested in the empirical psychological question of how people "reason" (whatever psychological process that may be), so we may be interested in the empirical sociological question (a little more clear cut) of how people *argue*.

But whatever else logic may be, it is no more sociology than it is psychology. It is surely not an empirical science at all. If we think of logic as concerned with reason, it is concerned with *right reason*. If is concerned with argument, it is concerned with *good arguments*. That is to say, whether inductive or deductive, logic contains an ineliminable *prescriptive* element. Simply to suppose that a conclusion is logically warranted if it is validly deducible from *some* set of premises (if it is true in each of *some* set of models), is surely too easy. Given the appropriate presuppositions about angels and pinheads, there is no doubt a justified conclusion concerning the number of angels that can dance on the head of a pin.

Morgan recognizes that some people are interested in the prescriptive questions that attend the process of reasoning, but dismisses detailed consideration of these questions ("... it is not our goal here to answer such questions." [Morgan, 2000, p. 351]) Yet without some consideration of when premises are acceptable, it is not clear what we gain from the reconstruction of nonmonotonic reasoning or argument in terms of deductive argument.

Furthermore, if our concern is with updating or changing "presuppositions" or "assumptions", and our stance toward logic is that it is to be normative, we need to be concerned with the *reasonableness* of the assumptions. It is true, as we suggested earlier, that establishing the reasonableness of the assumptions can be regarded as a different argument from the one that makes use of those assumptions to establish a conclusion. This need not be circular. The point is that these assumptions need not hold in *all* the models "presupposed" by the argument under consideration. It suffices, surely, that they hold in "almost all" of those models. But if that is the case, it is not clear what role the "presupposed" models (or the premises that pick them out) are playing!

Let us put this more formally. Let Γ be Susan's total background knowledge at a certain time. Taking Γ as her *evidence*, Susan reasonably concludes A. I take that to mean that there is a good argument (not necessarily deductive) leading from Γ to A. Susan then comes to accept some more sentences, Δ. Now she no longer accepts A, because there is no good argument leading from $\Gamma \cup \Delta$ to A.

Here is a reconstruction in terms of presuppositions:

We associate the set $PM(\Gamma)$ of "presupposed models" with Γ. This set of models is the set of models of some set X of sentences of our language.[4] A is true in every model of $PM(\Gamma)$, and there is therefore a (very!) good argument leading from $X \cup \Gamma$ to A — namely a deductive argument.

When Susan's evidence has been expanded by Δ, the situation is changed: $PM(\Gamma \cup \Delta)$ is simply a *different* set of presupposed models, associated, say, with the set of sentences Y. But A does not deductively follow from $Y \cup \Gamma \cup \Delta$. There is no good (i.e. deductive) argument from $Y \cup \Gamma \cup \Delta$ to A. There are sentences in $X \cup \Gamma$ that are *not* in $Y \cup \Gamma \cup \Delta$, that are necessary for the construction of the original deductive argument.

Prima facie all we can easily say about X is that it is a set of sentences that entails the members of Γ. Quite clearly, since there is a deduction from $X \cup \Gamma$ to A, but none from Γ to A, it actually adds content to Γ. But what justifies this added content? Presumably another "presupposition". It is perfectly all right that we require another presupposition – after all, we are asking for a different argument. But note that we still have the same premises Γ. Thus the set of presupposed models, $PM(\Gamma)$, if it is a function of Γ, as Morgan suggests, can only be justified circularly: We justify A by means of a deductive argument from $X \cup \Gamma$; but the only justification of the sentences of X is that they can be deduced from the premises $X \cup \Gamma$. Alternatively, we can take the "presupposed models" to be a function both of the premises Γ and the target sentence A to be deduced, so that we could call on the sentences $Z \cup \Gamma$ to justify the set of sentences X deductively, where Z is the union of the sentences presupposed by the arguments leading from Γ to each sentence in X. This is not circular (since at each stage we are calling upon a different set of sentences) but it sure is counterintuitive.

Let's try the nonmonotonic approach. Let us drop the demand that there

---

[4]Of course we can devise tricky cases where the resources of our language are not adequate to pick out $PM(\Gamma)$; I assume Morgan's thesis is not intended to depend on such trickery.

be a deductive argument leading from Γ and some other sentences to A, and suppose that there is a genuine inductive argument leading to A. Since this argument is inductive, it is of course not sound: A is not true in every model of Γ.

Although what follows is inspired by the idea of probabilistic acceptance, it is by no means restricted to this approach. It could make use of any of the approaches to inductive logic that employ the idea of acceptance or rejection: approaches through corroboration, or through statistical testing, or through the attempt to maximize epistemic content, or any of a number of other approaches.

To dress this situation up semantically, we would say that that there is a set of models that is a function of both Γ and the conclusion A; this set of models is a *superset* of Γ. If A is false in a fraction no larger than ϵ of them, then we (Susan) will justifiably accept A in her corpus of practical certainties Γ_ϵ.

An important point of comparison is that the sentences picking out the set of models relevant to A, given background Γ are *weaker* than Γ rather than stronger than Γ.[5] Note that, as Morgan shows, we cannot add A to Γ; we must consider a separate set of formulas, those justified inductively by the premises Γ.

In the second situation, when Susan has learned Δ, $\Gamma \cup \Delta$ represents Susan's total knowledge. The set of models picked out by the pair, $\Gamma \cup \Delta$ and A, is again a superset of the models of $\Gamma \cup \Delta$ — rather than adding content, we are bracketing content. In this set of models, however, the frequency with which A is false is *greater than* ϵ, so that A is no longer acceptable "at the ϵ level."

We need no evidence that is not in Γ to justify Susan's acceptance of A (at the ϵ level), and there's an end of the matter. Similarly, we need no evidence that is not in $\Gamma \cup \Delta$ to justify Susan's inability to accept A when her body of evidence has been expanded. Of course, in at least some cases we can ask for Susan's grounds for believing a given statement in Γ. That's a different question, and must be answered by citing a different collection of evidence, relative to which, for example, the error associated with the suspect sentence in X is $\epsilon/2$. There is patently no circularity here, though some philosophers might worry about the possibility of an infinite regress. That problem, if it is a problem, lies outside of our concerns here, which have to do with the possibility and desirability of nonmonotonic logic.

---

[5]This is the idea developed in [Kyburg and Teng, 2001]. In fact to make it work generally we may need to consider a finite set of sets of models picked out by the data, and to require that the maximum error in *any* of those sets of models be less than ϵ.

7 Conclusion

Morgan shows that nonmonotonic reasoning must violate soundness. If we want to go beyond our evidence, in a reasoned and rational way, that is just what we require: the violation of soundness. Exactly what we want is a nonmonotonic or inductive argument. That is what "real logic" comes to: deduction leaves us right where we started.

What is clear from Morgan's arguments is that no system of nonmonotonic logic that represents some form of closure on a set of sentences will work. This closure is built into the consideration of rational belief structures. The evidence and the conclusion must belong to the same set of belief structures. In order to avoid this, we must have a separate stash for the nonmonotonically concluded sentences. We must allow for models of our premises that are not models of our conclusion.

If we do this, then far from requiring *added* added information in order to obtain inductive conclusions, we obtain inductive conclusions by looking at a *superset* of the models of the premises. It is this trick that allows us to achieve what we want to achieve as scientific reasoners: a set of conclusions that goes beyond the premises with which we start.

With a certain amount of handwaving, we can illustrate this in the probabilistic framework of [Kyburg and Teng, 2001]. Consider a large set of objects, G's, and a property H that some of them have. Our body of knowledge Γ is limited to the following statements:

- There are a great many G's.

- S is a set of n G's.

- In S, there are m H's.

If this is all we know, then it seems to make sense to infer that approximately m/n — say $m/n \pm \delta$ of the G's are H, where δ is determined as a function of n.

It is quite clear that the premises do not entail that conclusion. You should have no trouble at all constructing a model in which the premises are true and the conclusion false. If this is some sort of inference, it is clearly unsound.

We take n to be large enough so that it is true, and indeed logically true, that all but a fraction ϵ of subsets of the set of G's are *representative*: contain a fraction of H's that differs by less than δ from the fraction of H's among the G's in general.[6]

---

[6]No assumptions are needed: we have said nothing about sampling, selecting, or anything like that. This is a purely set theoretical fact.

How do we get this conclusion? There are models of our three premises in which every possible relative frequency of H among G's is represented. Among models in which the proportion of G's that are H lies far from m/n the proportion of representative sets is low; among models in which the the frequency of H among G's is within a distance δ of m/n, the frequency of representative sets is 1.0. All we can say a priori is that the proportion of models of our three premises in which the conclusion is true lies betwen 0.0 and 1.0.

On the other hand, if we ignore the third premise, we can be sure that at least $1 - \epsilon$ of samples are representative, regardless of the true frequency of H among G's. It is the extra knowledge of the proportion of H's in S that renders the frequency of representativeness indeterminate.

Thus, if we are willing to tolerate a chance of error as large as ϵ, we are free to conclude nonmonotonically that S is representative. Note that we are *not* free to add this to our premises. But we can add it to our stock of nonmonotonic conclusions. Another thing we can add to our stock of nonmonotonic conclusions is the third premise. But Lo! the combination of the third premise with the nonmonotonic conclusion that S is representative yields just the conclusion we wanted.[7]

How would this inference be handled in the deductive framework? Presumably one would "presuppose" that S was representative. We'd get the conclusion we want all right. And we could *deductively* infer a number of other conclusions: for example, that the probability of obtaining a random sample of G's of size $1000n$ in which the frequency of H is less than $m/n - 1/3$ and more than $m/n + 1/3$ is preposterously low.

But now suppose Γ changes; suppose we get some new evidence. Well, our presupposition is a function of Γ (and perhaps also of the conclusion we seek), so it can change; this is what captures the nonmonotonicity of presupposition reasoning. But note that the Γ of which the new presupposition is a function includes the material from the previous Γ. This has the following peculiar result. Let X capture the presuppositions corresponding to the first evidential state. We supposed that this would deductively imply our desired conclusion, which would, in consequence, be added to Γ. But it also deductively implies itself, so that it, too, would be added to Γ. Let the expanded Γ be $\Gamma \cup \Gamma'$. We now observe some more G's — say, n', of which m' are H. Let the sentence:

- S' is a set of n' G's, disjoint from S, of which m' are H.

be added to this $\Gamma \cup \Gamma'$.

---

[7] A detailed analysis of just such an inference is provided in [Kyburg and Teng, 2001]. Note that no prior distribution on models of the various sorts is needed.

What is the new set of presupposed models? It must be a set of models that is included in the models of $\Gamma \cup \Gamma' \cup \{$"$S'$ is a set of n' G's, disjoint from S, of which m' are H"$\}$. It is quite true that we will have a new presupposition, and be able to make new inferences. But can we get rid of the old presuppposition, or the results of the old inference? It is clear already from Morgan's opening story about Sarah that old results (including old presuppositions) can only be deleted if they are marked or kept separate from the statements comprising Γ, so that *when new evidence comes in it is combined only with the old evidence*, and not with the old evidence plus what we inferred from it. There is obviously a lot more to be said about how the presupposition theory suggested by Morgan will work, but it is already doubtful that soundness of inference, bought at the price of presuppositions, is worth the price.

We certainly want more than we can get by deduction from our evidence. To adhere to deductive logic in scientific inference is not only a bore, but self defeating; as Morgan says, we want to be able to anticipate the future, and deduction does not allow that. So *real inference*, the inference we need for the conduct of life, must be nonmonotonic. The question is whether the *logic* of this inference (these arguments) can be best represented as a *sound* logic based on presuppositions that go beyond the evidence we have, or as an *unsound* logic that is genuinely nonmonotonic, i.e., supports nonmonotonic acceptance. The issue goes beyond probabilistic acceptance. Other ways of picking out sentences to accept or reject could be considered. I think it is clear that so far from being "impossible" a certain kind of nonmonotonic logic in which conclusions are kept distinct from the body of evidence is essential. Turning our backs on the possibility of rationalizing nonmonotonic acceptance is hardly the best way to improve the standards of nonmonotonic argument.

Acknowledgements

This work has been supported in part by the National Science Foundation.

BIBLIOGRAPHY

[Burks, 1953] Arthur W. Burks. The presupposition theory of induction. *Philosophy of Science*, 20:177–197, 1953.

[Burks, 1954-55] Arthur W. Burks. On the presuppositions of induction. *Review of Metaphysics*, 8:574–611, 1954-55.

[Burks, 1977] Arthur W. Burks. *Chance, Cause, Reason*. University of Chicago Press, Chicago, 1977.

[Carnap, 1950] Rudolf Carnap. *The Logical Foundations of Probabilty, second edition*. University of Chicago Press, Chicago, 1950.

[de Kleer, 1986] J. de Kleer. An assumption based atms. *A I Journal*, 28:127–162., 1986.

[Fagin and Halpern, 1988] Ronald Fagin and Joseph Y. Halpern. Belief, awareness and limited reasoning. *Artificial Intelligence*, 34:39–76., 1988.
[Fetzer, 1981] James H. Fetzer. *Scientific Knowledge*. Reidel, Dordrecht, 1981.
[Fetzer, 1993] James H. Fetzer. *Philosophy of Science*. Paragon House, New York, 1993.
[Halpern, 1993] Joseph Y. Halpern. Let many flowers bloom: A response to 'an inquiry into computer understanding,'. *Computational Intelligence*, 9:000–000, 1993.
[Harrah, 1956] David Harrah. Theses on presuppositions. *Review of Metaphysics*, 9:000–000, 1956.
[Harrah, 1961] David Harrah. A logic of questions and answers. *Philosohy of Science*, 28:40–46, 1961.
[Israel, 1980] David Israel. What's wrong with nonmonotonic logic? In *Proceedings of the First Annual National Conference on Artificial Intelligence*, pages 99–101, 1980.
[Keynes, 1952] John Maynard Keynes. *A Treatise on Probability*. Macmillan and Co., London, 1952.
[Kyburg and Teng, 2001] Henry E. Kyburg, Jr. and Choh Man Teng. *Uncertain Inference*. Cambridge University Press, New York, 2001.
[Kyburg, 1994] Henry E. Jr. Kyburg. Believing on the basis of evidence. *Computational Intelligence*, 10:3–20, 1994.
[Kyburg, 1997] Henry E. Kyburg, Jr. Combinatorial semantics: the semantics of frequent validity. *Computational Intelligence*, 13:215–257, 1997.
[Morgan, 1991] Charles G. Morgan. Logic, probability, and artificial intelligence. *Computational Intelligence*, 7:94–109., 1991.
[Morgan, 1998] Charles G. Morgan. Non-monotonic logic is impossible. *Canadian Artificial Intelligence Magazine*, 42:18–25, 1998.
[Morgan, 2000] Charles G. Morgan. The nature of nonmonotonic reasoning. *Minds and Machines*, 10:321–360, 2000.
[Nilsson, 1986] Nils Nilsson. Probabilistic logic. *Artificial Intelligence*, 28:71–88, 1986.
[Popper, 1959] Karl R. Popper. *The Logic of Scientific Discovery*. Hutchinson, London, 1959.
[Reiter and de Kleer, 1987] Raymond Reiter and Johan de Kleer. Foundations of assumption-based truth maintenance systems. In *AAAI-87*, volume Los Altos, pages 183–189. Morgan Kaufman, 1987.
[Tversky and Kahneman, 1982] Amos Tversky and Daniel Kahneman. Judgments of and by representativeness. In Daniel Kahneman, Paul Slovic, and Amos Tversky, editors, *Judgment under Uncertainty: Heuristics and Biases*, pages 84 – 98. Cambridge University Press, Cambridge, 1982.

Part III
Formal Metaphysics

Branching Histories Approach to Indeterminism and Free Will

NUEL BELNAP

ABSTRACT. An informal sketch is offered of some chief ideas of the (axiomatic) "branching histories" theory of objective possibility, free will and indeterminism. Reference is made to "branching time" and to "branching space-times," with emphasis on a theme that they share: Objective possibilities are in *Our World*, organized by the relation of causal order.

Recent work has suggested rigorous but simple notions of indeterminism and free will based on the idea of "branching histories."[1] It is of course not so obvious in advance at just which target we are aiming, although below we recall some contributions by baseball's Yogi Berra that help clarify our hopes. In the meantime, although it will hardly be surprising if you find yourself harboring definite reservations and uncertainties, I hope the meaning of our ideas will become moderately clear.

Philosophy has always contained separate scientific and humanistic pictures of humans in their world (Sellars's well-known scientific and manifest images), and many philosophical enterprises can be described as either focusing wholly within one while either ignoring or being contemptuous of the other, or as trying in some sense to reduce one to the other. The branching-histories enterprise can be seen as an effort to find ways in which the two images fit together, without diminution of either. Our particular strategy is to look for very general quasi-geometrical structures that underlie both.

---

[1] Many of these ideas related to agency were first developed by von Kutschera almost twenty years ago. Since about the same time Paul Bartha, Mitchell Green, John Horty, Michael Perloff, Matthew Weiner, Ming Xu and the author have intermittently worked at different aspects of the topic, often jointly. For book-length reports, see Horty, *Agency and deontic logic* (New York: Oxford, 2001) and Belnap and Perloff and Xu, *Facing the future: Agents and choices in our indeterminist world* (New York: Oxford, 2001). The latter, which contains numerous references, is cited below as "FF." More recently, there are a handful of articles by Belnap or T. Müller or T. Placek that (a) further explore "funny business" as described below, (b) advance a theory of causation that requires indeterminism, and (c) presents a theory of how objective probabilities (not just possibilities) might fit into our world.

In this sense our theory could be described as equally proto-scientific and proto-humanistic. The enterprise is not itself either scientific or humanistic, but it does try to provide some ways of thinking that are intended as useful for each in just the way that plain old Euclidean geometry helps us to know our way around some aspects of physics and some aspects of perception.

I am going to begin by describing some features of the general "branching histories" framework. Second, I shall try to give you some of the flavor of how the theory of branching histories applies to the humanistic concepts of action and agency and choice and free will, without itself being humanistic. Third, I shall say something about how branching histories help us to get a little clearer on how indeterminism ought to work in our scientific views—again, without itself being scientific.

1 Branching histories

The "branching histories" framework offers a theory of possibility, or, much better, *possibilities*.

1.1 Importance of objective possibility

Every philosophy must somehow or other take account of the category of possibilities, a foundation on which many of our most fundamental concepts rest. Here there is a great divide. For some applications one needs only *unreal* possibilities. Perhaps they are given in the mind, as imaginary or fancied alternatives to our actual situation. Or perhaps the possibilities are constructed in some clever way out of concepts or language or social structures such as conversations. For example, in making sense out of fiction or belief or justification or good reasoning, the alternatives one brings into play need only be plausible.

It is the same in science. For many purposes, scientific possibilities need to have only epistemic, which is to say, mental status, in someone's mind, or perhaps *social* status in a family of practices by scientists. For these limited, chiefly heuristic, purposes, the time-worn phrase, "consistency with the laws," has some utility as an account of possibility. This remains true even though, as is obvious, "the laws" are just slippery pieces of language, made by man. The point is that for heuristic and practical purposes, there is often no need for anything more.

But for certain concepts, one must insist on — in a phrase of Xu — "possibilities based in reality." To settle for some kind of "compatibilism" that would combine "scientific" or "objective" determinism with slippery subjective or linguistic notions of possibility is, we think, to lose one's grip. Let me list some obvious places in which one needs real (objective) possibilities.

1. There is no objective probability without objective possibility. It

is easy to neglect this. We teach students to race through the probability calculus without paying attention to what it means. And even though philosophers debate endlessly and fruitlessly about the meaning of probability, this much is plain: If you are unable to give an account of the possible and the impossible, you will never be able to give an account of the probable and the improbable. How could you? In technical terms, it is the real possibilities that provide the so-called probability space that must be found under any objective probability measure. If you do not have possibilities you do not have a probability space; and if you do not have a probability space you certainly cannot have a probability.

2. There is no action, no doing, no responsibility, no agency, without possibility. This is a principle theme, and I shall return to it later. There is neither justified hope nor justified fear, neither obligation nor license, neither justified pride nor regret, unless there be possibilities rooted not just in someone's mind, but in reality as well.

3. Perhaps of most significance, there is no causality without objective possibilities. This is a second principle theme, and again it is one to which I shall return, although very briefly and without the likelihood, in this brief compass, of much clarity. In the meantime, keep in mind that there are many causal concepts without the word cause. Here are just a few: influencing, interfering, intervening, and experimenting. None of these make real sense unless there are real possibilities.

Since Leibniz, however, much philosophy has either neglected to take real possibilities seriously, or, having taken up the challenge that they present, has declared them null and void. (I regret that because of my ignorance I am able to speak only of "western" philosophy.) Because many of us participate in the strict-deterministic attitudes engendered by this philosophical history, it is worth pausing a moment in order to ask why. After long preparation by theological meditation on the meanings of Omnipotence and Omniscience, presumably a fresh cause was the marvelous practical success of deterministic mathematical physics. Laplace says that his demon leaves no room for really alternative possibilities. To be consistent with this worldview, Hume says that causality is not objective at all, but instead a habit of mind. Kant, sharing his century's conviction in the absolute accuracy of the deterministic vision, says that there is no possibility beyond actuality, and indeed, that there is no actuality that goes beyond ironclad necessity. In Kant's effort to make sense out of strict determinism, possibility, actuality, and necessity are the same thing. With the spread of lockstep clocks and machines, and with so much genius philosophizing in behalf of strict determinism, it is hardly surprising that many philosophers fail to take seriously the idea of objective possibilities.

Without urging this explanation of why philosophy has tended largely (but certainly not entirely) to avoid the idea of real possibility, let us pass on to the central ideas of branching histories relevant to the problem of fitting objective possibilities together into a single world. There are some generic ideas about branching histories that come from the idea of possibility itself. And then there are two special cases. The special cases have been called, somewhat ponderously, "branching time" and "branching space-times"; but in this essay there is little need for these heavy words.

1.2 How objective possibilities fit together

Let us begin with the more general ideas of branching histories. They are as follows: (1) *Our World* and its possibilities, (2) events, (3) histories, (4) consistency, (5) branching, and (6) causality.

1. First and foremost, *Our World*. In contrast with the ideas of the metaphysical modal logician, David Lewis, possibility based in reality calls for only one world, yours and mine. Many things belong to *Our World*, certainly many more, as Hamlet teaches, than find themselves in anyone's dreams. Among the contents of *Our World* are possible events. In fact *Our World* is filled with possibilities. These are not, however, ghost creatures of mind or language, nor are they facts about other worlds. Possibilities for you and for me are real possibilities inside of *Our World*. Consider the possibility that in two or three minutes you stop reading and start singing. We should reject the advice of many philosophers that, to locate this possibility, we must investigate our own mental or linguistic creations. We must reject the advice of others that we turn our ontological attention to other worlds. The odd but reality-based prospect of you finding yourself singing is rather for us the worldly, here and now. Nor, for another example, do we need to look beyond this world for the possibility that some short time ago you could have refrained from starting to read these words. Real possibilities are neither inventions nor otherworldly. They are firmly located inside our very own world. This is what needs to be made intelligible. This is the topic of branching histories.

2. So *possible events* are part of *Our World*. The sticker is this. It can happen that two events are each individually possible, while at the same time they cannot happen together: Peter may turn left or he may turn right, so each is a real possibility. But it is impossible that he does both. This is a fundamental fact about how possibilities fit into *Our World*: Each of two events can happen, but it is not possible that both happen. It sounds to the naive ear as if we are saying that at most one of the two events can be part of *Our World*, but that is precisely wrong. What we need to overcome the difficulty is the concept of a "history."

3. A *history* is a collection of events that can indeed all live together with consistency. Past history is certainly like that. Since everything that did happen did happen, there is no doubt that the entire past fits together into a single, consistent story. There is, however, more to the idea of history than the past. Each history (in the sense at issue) stretches also into the future. A history goes all the way back and all the way forward. There is not only past history but future history.

Here we come both to the technical heart of the scheme in which we are working, and to a challenging problem in the philosophical analysis of temporal language. On the technical side, each history is seriously maximal. Each history contains every event that it can contain, subject to the consistency requirement. A possible event is excluded from a history if it is not consistent with some portion of that history; but that is the only limit. A history is as big as it can possibly be. (Of course there is a rigorous definition here.) That is why, on this conception, histories stretch into the remote future, long after the heat death of the sun.

On the analytical side, we must keep constantly in mind that serious attention to alternative possibilities implies that there is no unique "future history." Instead there are many alternative and inconsistent possibilities. In the language of logic, although the phrases "my left shoe" and "my world" have unique referents determined by the context of utterance in the sense of Kaplan, "my future history" does not — simply because an utterance event, like any other event, belongs to many histories each of which represents a distinct unfolding of possibilities. This is spelled out in tedious detail in chapter 6 of FF.

4. We can now say the following: Two or more possible events are *jointly consistent* exactly when they fit into a single history. The point is that we can say that not as if it were a new thing, an idle thought. Instead, because we have taken the trouble to be rigorous, we can say it confidently and use it as a sure guide when thinking about difficult matters such as action or indeterminism.

5. What, however, about branching? Here is the idea. Since there are many inconsistent groups of events, there must be many histories. There are the histories in which Peter goes left, each of which must be distinct from each history on which Peter goes right. The question now is, How do these histories fit together? On one all too common answer, each history is a "world" unto itself. According to this answer, histories stand independently, like a row of parallel lines that never, never meet. This answer, championed by David Lewis, is popular, but it must be rejected. It is not an accurate account of our world. Picture Peter facing the future, not having decided whether to turn left or to turn right. Here is the critical point.

His momentary indecision certainly belongs to only one world, our world, but with equal certainty it belongs to *more than a single history*. There is the continuation in which Peter goes left, and there is the continuation in which he goes right. As we say idiomatically, there are in this world of ours two things that Peter can do. Going left is a historical possibility and going right is also a historical possibility. Theory now extracts the following from this picture of Peter at the crossroads.

5a. The past portions of these two histories are identical. The independent worlds of Lewis's theory never overlap, whereas in contrast the two histories literally overlap. Each of the two histories literally contains Peter's indecision, and everything that led up to it. A mental or linguistic theory would make these pasts "similar" instead of straightforwardly identical. But that is wrong. We began by contemplating that there were for Peter two possibilities, left and right, just as I have two shoes, say L and R. And just as it is unhelpful to say that L's owner is only "similar" to R's owner, but not identical, so it is unhelpful to say that the indecision in the past of Peter's possible left turn is only "similar," but not identical, to the indecision lying in the past of Peter's possible right turn.

5b. The future portions of these histories are entirely separate. One contains the possible event of Peter's going left, but excludes the possibility of his going right. The other contains the (equally) possible event of Peter's going right, while excluding his going left. These portions are not merely dissimilar to each other "under some description," in the way, perhaps, that, for example, Quine's spy is descriptively dissimilar from Orcutt. They are straight-out, not to say radically, distinct.

5c. But although the future portions of these histories are and remain totally inscrutable each to each (no telescopes peering from the history-portion with the left turn into the history-portion with the right turn), nevertheless, they are connected in an important way: They share a common past. The possible event of Peter's going left has in its past Peter's painful indecision; and so does the possible event of Peter's going right. These two inconsistent events have the same past. That is how they fit together into our one and only world. English tenses get the matter exactly right: If we locate ourselves at the event constituting the possibility of a left turn, there and then we may truly say, "Yes, Peter turned left, and a right turn is not now a possibility for Peter, but it was true that he could have turned right.

5d. And that is what we mean by "branching histories." Histories and therefore events fit together to form a single world, *Our World*, and *Our World* looks, to an approximation, like a "tree." In the past all is consistent, and looking back from our present prospect, we see a single stem or trunk. As, however, we look towards the future — sometimes called the "open" future — there is a branching into many possibilities, each consistent in itself, but only some combinations of which go together to form a total history. (Let me interrupt to note that later on we shall need to modify the picture. That is the job of branching *space*-times.)

5e. This, then, is the branching-history account of how events that are individually possible but jointly impossible can constitute a single, unified world. The central point is that each pair of events, and especially inconsistent events, are mediately connected by means of a past out of which they arise. If a being were to stand off and look at the tree as a whole, it would see no loose or disconnected pieces. Every possible event, no matter how remote, is connected in some way or other to the here-now with which we begin.

6. Causal relation. The theory of branching histories also gives us a kind of principle of causality. It says — rigorously, with no kidding around — that, in a simple case, if you find yourself in one history instead of another, then you can always look back into the past for a crucial branch point at which the world offered a turn one way rather than another. What happens at that branch point serves as a truly originating or productive cause. We call this the "prior choice" principle. The prior choice principle says this: When we are looking for a token-level cause of some outcome, we may always look to the past. (The choice of "may" here over "must" is critical; see note 3.) This is a true and deeply important feature of *Our World* (we think), but watch out: We do not say that it holds for "epistemic" causes or "linguistic" causes or "scientific" causes, or any other man-made relation. To say that it did would be to make an unreliable generalization about the workings of an unreliable instrument, the human mind. Instead, the prior choice principle concerns only causes based in reality.

So much for the chief ideas of the theory of branching histories. When worked out, the theory is rigorous and indeed axiomatic. It is a theory about *Our World*, the only one we have. It tells us that there are events that stand in a causal order. It tells us that these events are organized into histories. It tells us that these histories branch, but only forward. It tells us that causal choice points can always be found in the past. Above all, it tells us that the causal order of our world permits alternative possibilities for the future, whereas, in the words of a poet, the past is fixed in stone.

One thing that I cannot make clear with this over-brief word picture of Peter at the crossroads is this: I am alluding to an absolutely rigorous theory, which, though omitted here, is given in detail in the works cited.

2 Agency, choice and unpretentious free will

Having given the chief ideas of branching histories themselves, how is this application applied to action and agency? And how does this application give a low key account of free will? The answers are related. They rest on four principles.

2.1 Four principles concerning agency

The first principle about agency in *Our World* is a logical principle about language. It is this: Whenever we can truly describe Peter as the agent in some affair, we can find a particular sentence X such that Peter sees to it that X. Example. For Peter to turn left is for Peter to see to it that he turns left.

This is a principle that only a logician could love. It nevertheless turns out to be enormously helpful in thinking about agency. We did not make it up. In fact, the principle that agency can always be described as a seeing-to-it-that is originally due to St. Anselm, who discovered it nearly nine hundred years ago. To my knowledge the principle was then absolutely and completely forgotten for over eight hundred of those nine hundred years (§1D of FF gives a kind of mini-history of the matter). If we live by Anselm's principle, we do not have to think about or worry about or ask unanswerable questions about peculiar ontological entities such as "Peter's turning left," or worse "Peter's turning left either slowly or not at all," or perhaps worst, "Peter's refraining from turning left." With what strange properties should we endow these postulated entities? Anselm's "sees to it that" formula directs us away from such unhelpful ontological inquiries. That is one way in which his principle keeps our metaphysics low key.

Anselm's "sees to it that" idea is simple. This very simplicity, however, gives a solid impetus to further progress by use of the following very general fact about language: New sentences can be built from old sentences. For example, refraining is a difficult concept in the philosophy of action. We can use the Anselm perspective to give a helpful analysis of refraining. Example. For Anselm to refrain (say) from accepting his church office from the tyrant, King William Rufus, is precisely for Anselm to see to it that Anselm does not see to it that Anselm accepts his episcopal office from William Rufus. That is of course a mouthful, or better, an earful. But after all, the situation is precisely one in which logic helps: It helps us, by providing us a logical notation (not here displayed) that is easy for the eye exactly when English gives us complicated and confusing sound-patterns that overburden the ear.

The second principle is this: There is no action, no agency, no doing without choice. Furthermore, and when spelled out this is part of the deep theory, the choice must come before any outcome that is settled by the choice. You cannot choose to modify the settled past. If we put these ideas together, we come to something like the following major analytical equivalence: To see to it that X is to make a prior choice that guarantees that X. Example. Peter has seen to it that he turned left if and only if Peter has made a prior choice that guarantees that he turns left. Probably it needs explicit mention that we are not saying that Peter's choice must precede his action of turning left; after all, our Anselm-based "sees to it that" theory says nothing at all about some "action" to be called "Peter's turning left." The second principle concerns only the conditions under which sentences are true. It says nothing at all about when actions exist — or whatever it is that actions do. This is yet another way in which our theory is low key.

The third principle works together with the others. It has not been urged as often in an axiomatic tone of voice, but seems to us just as obvious and just as critical: There is no choice without choices. That is, if the objective situation is such that Peter is truly described as having any real choice at all, then Peter must have open to him more than once choice. Peter cannot really and objectively choose to turn left unless he has another option available to him that does not guarantee his turning left.

How, you may ask, are Peter's objective options organized? Since they are objective, there must be a principle of organization that does not lie entirely in his mind, nor in language, nor even in logic. There must be a level at which we can say how his options are organized in terms of the purely objective theory of branching histories. In these terms, the outcome in which Peter turns left resides (not in a single history but) in a certain family of histories. No history in this family can (possibly) contain the outcome in which Peter turns right. In fact the correct picture to have is that Peter's choice constitutes a branch point. And that is exactly what is claimed by our theory of agency. (Certainly only very simple choice situations can be represented in terms of a single branch point. Our research strategy has been to try to clarify the simple case before attacking the more complex ones, some of which we also treat.)

The fourth principle involves an additional subtlety. The theory of agency when set against the theory of branching histories gives rise to a new principle, a principle that has not yet been studied with the care it deserves. The reason for this is that the principle cannot even be properly stated without a rigorous development of the idea of branching histories. Nevertheless, I can give you its flavor in a slogan: You cannot make tomorrow's choices today. You can plan and plan and plan, but if tomorrow is when you are given the choice whether or not to eat fish for breakfast, then as an objective matter, it is impossible for you to make that choice today. Sometimes we call this fourth principle "no choice before its time." Attention to this principle — first rigorously formulated by von Kutschera and (later but independently) by P. Kremer, only in the mid-eighties(!) — can only enrich moral philosophy and the philosophy of action.

To summarize: (1) Agency is well codified with "seeing to it that" sentences. (2) There is no agency without choice. (3) There is no choice without choices. And (4) there is no choice before its time.

2.2 Unpretentious free will.

With these four principles I can quickly come to our unpretentious account of free will. There are three key ways in which "seeing to it that" helps us to keep a claim to "free will" simple and straightforward.

In the first place, a serious claim to free will must always mention a particular agent. Our recommended "sees to it that" formula is ideal for this purpose, precisely because one cannot complete the formula without specific reference to an agent.

Second, any meaningful claim to free will must make specific reference to a possible outcome. Again, the "sees to it that" formula always requires a specific sentence. Example. The Bishop won the lottery. Question: Did the Bishop see to it that the Bishop won the lottery? Well, no, it was a matter of chance. No free will for that specific outcome. Change the example if you like. Perhaps the Bishop illegally "fixed" the lottery. Perhaps it is a matter of the Bishop buying a ticket. In any case, if you do change the example, please notice what you are doing. Free will does not float free of particular agent or particular outcome.

Last and of critical importance, our account of action and agency in the context of branching histories requires reference to a particular moment or locus of choice.

Let us gingerly approach an example with these three ways in mind. First, we are tempted to ask, Is there any free will, or is the world instead a place of blind adherence to natural law? When we frame the question in this tempting way, we are tempted to respond in its own immodest terms. We know that stars and machines are fixed in their trajectories, and so are tempted to answer that not only stars and machines, but each thing whatsoever, follows out its preordained path. Perhaps, having been tempted by the form of the question, we do not notice that this extremely universal theory is pretentious. We are better off if, to begin with, we ask a much more particular question. Ask instead if Peter has free will. Can Peter ever see to anything? That is much less immodest. It is a virtue of our "sees to it that" formula that it is never complete without the name of a definite agent, and therefore suggests the humbler question. The theory counsels that one be specific about the agent.

All right, so let us name the agent. Turning now to the second way in which "seeing to it that" helps, one should ask as follows: Is Peter, in particular, free, or is he instead a creature of external and impersonal forces? That question is also too general and will tempt you into immodesty. Be specific. The "sees to it that" formula will help you. Do you want to know whether Peter can see to it that he flies to the Moon on silken wings? No, he cannot. Or do you ask if Peter can see to it that wins the Irish Sweepstakes? No, he does not have available a choice that guarantees that outcome. Or do you rather wonder whether Peter can see to it that he turns left? Yes, he can. "Seeing to it that" forces us to be specific about the outcome. It makes a plain difference. For now, according to the major analytical equivalence quoted above, we are asking in a pedestrian fashion whether or not Peter has a choice in the matter of his turning left. And of course he does. You will have observed that nowhere do we offer positive arguments against immodest determinism. Instead, we turn to thinking about problems, too little considered, that have low-key indeterminism as a presupposition. Perhaps this is a mistake. In any event, that is the spirit in which we say "of course he does."

The third and last way in which "seeing to it that" helps depends on our having been specific about both the agent and the possible outcome. Can Peter see to it that he turns left? Or can he do so only if he is in the grip of an appropriate combination of character, desire and belief, a combination that is all by itself causally sufficient to bring about his turning left? Even that is immodest. The third way insists that we be specific about the moment. Suppose that at a certain moment Peter has available a choice that guarantees his turning left. Then certainly our theory says that *after* that moment he has used up his choice. His turning left is already guaranteed, and Peter cannot undo that choice. He cannot alter the settled past, he cannot make the same choice again. But also remember the principle of "no choice before its time." Our theory also asserts that no choice can be made before the moment at which it becomes available. (And I remind you that although that sounds like a barren tautology, it is instead a deep principle concerning how choices fit into *Our World*.) So there is for Peter and for his turning left a particular moment of choice. We may turn over the moments before and after to the fierce determinist. But at that very moment, neither sooner nor later, Peter has just a little free will in the matter of his turning left. Moments of choice come and go. *Carpe diem* is too crude. To choose, you must not only seize the day, but you must seize the very moment.

For summary, American philosophy has yielded none better than three famous baseball aphorisms often attributed to Yogi Berra. Here, first, is Berra's statement of the principle of no choice before its time: "It's not over 'til it's over." Second, Berra's phrasing of the causal principle and the uniqueness of the past: "When it's over, it's over." And last, Berra's own account of the practical attitude required of an agent making choices in our indeterminist world: "When you come to a fork in the road, take it."

The upshot is that at that very moment of choice, we claim for Peter a portion of unpretentious free will: At the moment of choice, Peter can make a choice guaranteeing that he turns left, and he can also make a choice that goes right. The theory is of course only the bones of a rich account of agency. It deploys in its axiomatics none of the ideas of "the free will debate" that go beyond those that can be expressed in terms of the causal order of *Our World*. These richer ideas are of course essential to a more full-bodied account. We only suggest that whatever additional flesh is supplied, it should be added to the underlying structure supplied by the branching-histories account of agency. The bones do not have to show, but if they are not there, the flesh will sag or even melt away. The suggestion to build an account of agency on top of the theory of branching-histories embodies what we sometimes think should be called "the new compatibilism."

3 Branching space-times and modestly local indeterminism

Finally I turn briefly to the problem of modestly *local* indeterminism as a pre-scientific idea. The fact is that histories do not really branch like a tree. Such a picture would work if there were an objective meaning for a simultaneity-slice that ran from one edge of the universe, so to speak, to the other. Such a simultaneity-slice would allow histories to split globally. But we know from Einstein that to think of such simultaneity-slices as objective is corrupt. We need another picture.

The new picture comes from the following observation. Individual histories are not really ordered like a line. Our modern reverence for classical mechanics and our related love of clock time deludes us. Not only fancy Einstein physics, but even our ordinary experience (when uncorrupted by uncritical adherence to Newton or mechanical addiction to clocks and watches) shows us that events are not strung out one after the other. Take the event of our being here now. Indeed some events lie in our future — or, better, keeping possibilities firmly in mind, we should say that some events lie in our future of possibilities. Others lie in our causal past. But there is a third category, always intuitive, and now scientifically respectable, since we have learned in this century to be suspicious of the idea of *action at a distance*. In this third category are events that neither lie ahead of us as possibilities, nor do they lie behind us as determinate facts. Instead, they have a space-like relation to us. Neither later nor earlier (nor frozen into simultaneity by a mythical world-spanning clock), they are "over there."

The jargon word for this structure of events is well known: It is called a space-time. So each history, each possible course of events, is a space-time. It needs zero training in mathematics to see that the theory of how such histories fit together into a single world will be more complicated than the theory that we pictured with a single tree. I mention only four key points underlying the theory of "branching space-times."[2]

Here is the first point. You will remember that histories are closely related to the ideas of possibility and consistency. A key idea here is that what allows two events to share a history, and therefore to be consistent, is that at least one event lies in their common future. As long as there is a standpoint in *Our World* from which one could truly say "both of these events have happened," even if the two events are not themselves arranged one after the other, one may be confident that the two events can live together in single history. Peter's (possible) going to the dentist in one village and Paul's (possible) staying home in another village are consistent just in case there is some (possible) standpoint at which someone could truly say, using the past tense, that both events came to pass. Let us also turn this around: If two events are *inconsistent*, then no event can have both of them in its past. For example, although Peter's choice to turn left or right is altogether local, and although we cannot picture *Our World* as a tree, nevertheless, there is no standpoint anywhere in *Our World* that has in its *past* both of the inconsistent events represented by Peter's having turned left and his having turned right. These inconsistent possibilities can and must lie ahead of the point at which he makes the choice, but they cannot both lie behind anything whatsoever.

The second point is this. There have to be choice points, definite local events at which two histories split into radically inconsistent portions. It is presumably not true and we must not assume that when splitting occurs, it occurs in some magical worldwide way. When Peter is given the choice to go left or right on a certain occasion, that occasion is confined in space as well as in time. His little bit of free will is local, not global. And the same might be true when the choice is only metaphorical, a matter of a random outcome of some natural event such as, perhaps, the decay of a radium atom in Paris. It might be that the decay is a strictly local matter, neither influencing nor influenced by contemporary happenings in, say, Beijing. Whenever there

---

[2]The theory of branching space-times is described in Belnap, "Branching space-time," *Synthese*, XCII, 3 (September 1992): 385–434. T. Placek offers an alternative version in *Is Nature Deterministic?* (Krakow: Jagiellonian University Press, 2000). Further contributions by Belnap, Müller, and Placek may be found in *Non-locality and Modality*, ed. Placek and Butterfield (Dordrecht: Kluwer Academic Publishers, 2002). For some of the more recent work, you may wish to consult http://www.pitt.edu/ belnap.

is indeterminism, whether of choice or of chance, a good theory must give meaning to the difficult idea that the indeterminism is local, not worldwide.

The third point is critical to understanding *Our World*. When I put the point in everyday language, it sounds so obvious that you will yawn, and yet as far as I know a thoroughly controlled statement has never been made apart from the present theory of branching space-times. The key postulate for locating choice points may be put informally in the following way: Whenever we find ourselves in one history instead of in another, we may always look to the past for a choice point responsible for the splitting. Example. Suppose that on a certain Friday in March a cat is sleeping on its mat in a certain living room in Chicago. Think of this as a particular concrete event, and let it be contingent. Take any history in which that event fails to occur, perhaps a history in which the cat spends the whole of the Friday high in a tree in Lincoln Park. The theory guarantees that if you look in the causal past of the given concrete cat-on-the-mat event (the one that we are supposing occurred), you will find a definite choice point at which things could have gone either in the direction of keeping the cat-on-the-mat event possible, or in the direction of keeping the cat-in-the-tree history possible. (The theory will not let you exchange "event" and "history" here; precision of statement is essential.) You do not need to look in the future, and you also do not need to look far away at events going on "over there." The point is that examination of the causal past of the cat-on-mat event suffices. (The theory does not presume to say if the choice was up to the cat, or up to some human, or perhaps a bit of natural randomness or some combination.)

The fourth and last point records a recognition of an important way in which the theory should not be strengthened. The following is a tempting principle that an unwary philosopher might easily be inclined to endorse: If two choice points are related in a "space-like" way, so that the second is "over there" with respect to the first, then their respective choices are entirely independent of each other.[3] Example. Aristotle tells us how two market-goers meet at the market, as an "accidental" result of their choices that morning, made separately in far-away villages. Their individual choices, we all suppose, are bound to be totally uncorrelated, that is, independent, and that is what the tempting principle says must be so.

The theory of branching histories, however, resists this temptation. And it does not do so *a priori*. It does so because *Our World* seems, as a matter

---

[3] In "EPR-like funny business" (ibid.) this principle is suitable generalized and shown to be provably equivalent to a principle whose temptation is equally to be resisted saying something like "every situation that is cause-like with respect to a certain outcome event lies in the past of that event."

of fact, to contain violations of the tempting principle. With reference once more to Einstein, modern physics seems to tell us that in fact it is possible for two utterly random choice points to be space-like related, with no hint of a line of causal connection between them, and nevertheless fail to be independent. I call this "funny business." Reichenbach has taught us that whenever we find the long arm of coincidence stretching across space, it is in our nature to look for a common cause. Funny business precisely happens when there is objective coincidence — which is to say, a failure of independence — across space, without a common cause. Since modern-day physics tells us that funny business happens, it is good that the theory of branching histories has room for funny business — and indeed has the virtue of permitting us to offer a stable (albeit conjectural) account as to the difference between (1) mere indeterminism without funny business and (2) indeterminism with funny business.

These necessarily too-brief points allude to a theory of branching histories that gives a satisfying account of how physical indeterminism can be local instead of global. It gives us an account of how choices and outcomes of natural random processes can affect only what lies in their causal future, touching neither their past nor the vast region of space-like related events. But it does so in such a way as to allow plenty of room for individually random processes to be, as the physicists say, "entangled." Or, in the phrase I just used, the theory of branching histories helps us to come to terms with funny business.

The result is that the theory of branching histories, in addition to helping us clarify ideas of action and agency, provides low key suggestions for articulating some of the strangest phenomena uncovered by contemporary physicists. It does this by avoiding careless or fuzzy or sloppy formulations. It does this by insisting on a careful and rigorous axiomatic account of what it is for indeterminism to be not immodestly global, but modestly local.

So much for branching histories. So much for the application to action, agency, and choice. So much for the application to physical indeterminism, and especially to funny business. In closing I should like to emphasize one critical feature of our point of view. It is this: For indeterminism and free will, we need to consider just one world. This world, *Our World*, is big and complicated enough to contain everything, both agents and atoms, both choices and chances, and of course much else. The objective causal order binds all together, without benefit of "laws" or other products of the imagination. And *Our World*, yours and mine, is especially rich in possibilities for our future.

www.ingramcontent.com/pod-product-compliance
Lightning Source LLC
Chambersburg PA
CBHW050852230426
43667CB00012B/2252